Harold Innis's Final Course

Lance Strate
General Editor

Vol. 14

W. T. Easterbrook

Harold Innis's Final Course

Edited with introduction by
Edward A. Comor

PETER LANG
New York - Berlin - Bruxelles - Chennai - Lausanne - Oxford

Library of Congress Cataloging-in-Publication Data

Names: Easterbrook, W. T. (William Thomas), 1907–1985, author | Comor, Edward A., editor, writer of introduction.
Title: Harold Innis's final course / [edited by] Edward A. Comor ; [lecture notes by William Thomas Easterbrook].
Description: New York : Peter Lang, [2025] | Series: Understanding media ecology, 2374-7676 ; volume 14 | Includes bibliographical references and index.
Identifiers: LCCN 2024031625 (print) | LCCN 2024031626 (ebook) | ISBN 9781636679600 (paperback) | ISBN 9781636679617 (ebook) | ISBN 9781636679624 (epub)
Subjects: LCSH: Innis, Harold A. (Harold Adams), 1894–1952. | Communication–Study and teaching (Higher)–Canada. | Mass media–Study and teaching (Higher)–Canada.
Classification: LCC P92.5.I56 E27 2025 (print) | LCC P92.5.I56 (ebook) | DDC 302.2071/2713541–dc23/eng/20240802
LC record available at https://lccn.loc.gov/2024031625
LC ebook record available at https://lccn.loc.gov/2024031626
DOI 10.3726/b22150

Bibliographic information published by the Deutsche Nationalbibliothek.
The German National Library lists this publication in the German National Bibliography; detailed bibliographic data is available on the Internet at http://dnb.d-nb.de.

Cover design by Peter Lang Group AG

ISSN 2374-7676 (print)
ISBN 9781636679600 (paperback)
ISBN 9781636679617 (ebook)
ISBN 9781636679624 (epub)
DOI 10.3726/b22150

© 2025 Peter Lang Group AG, Lausanne
Published by Peter Lang Publishing Inc., New York, USA
info@peterlang.com - www.peterlang.com

All rights reserved.
All parts of this publication are protected by copyright.
Any utilization outside the strict limits of the copyright law, without the permission of the publisher, is forbidden and liable to prosecution.
This applies in particular to reproductions, translations, microfilming, and storage and processing in electronic retrieval systems.

This publication has been peer reviewed.

Photograph of Harold Innis (circa 1950) courtesy of University of Toronto Archives.
Source: Federal Royal Commission on Transportation (1948–1950), University of Toronto Archives.

Contents

Acknowledgments ix
Introduction xi

Tom Easterbrook's Lecture Notes for *Innis 4b* 1
    September 23, 1952: *How best to get at the work of Harold Innis?* 1
    September 30, 1952: *Main subjects and readings* 7
    October 7, 1952: *Innis's interests and methodology* 11
    October 14, 1952: *Why so much fuss about communications?* 14
    October 21, 1952: *Receptivity to Innis* 25
    October 28, 1952: *Greece—Innis's ideal-type culture* 28
    November 18, 1952: *The value of studying antiquity* 31
    November 25, 1952: *Innis's transition to the subject of communications* 36
    December 2, 1952: *Capacities involving Roman and common law* 41
    January 6, 1953: *Ways of thinking and developments in law* 46
    January 20, 1953: *Conditions enabling the Byzantine empire* 52
    January 27, 1953: *Byzantium: history of an ideal-type empire* 56
    February 3, 1953: *Implications of media—Byzantium to the 20th century* 64
    February 10, 1953: *A brief comment on Innis's methodology* 78
    February 17, 1953: *The press, time, economics, and Innis's unfinished paper* 79

Appendix I Course documents   103
    Summer vacation reading list (no author, n.d.)   103
    Fourth-year reading list in Economic History (likely prepared by Harold Innis, 1950)   106
    Reading list for Economics 4b (likely prepared by Harold Innis, 1951)   107
    First essay topic (prepared by Harold Innis and Tom Easterbrook, 1952)   108
    Final examination questions (prepared by Harold Innis, 1951)   109
    Final examination questions (prepared by Tom Easterbrook, 1953)   110
Appendix II Innis's final paper: Harold Innis, "The Decline in the Efficiency of Instruments Essential in Equilibrium" from the *American Economic Review* Vol. 43 No. 1 (1953), 16–22   111
Appendix III Tom Easterbrook, "Harold Adams Innis 1894–1952" from the *American Economic Review* Vol. 43 No. 1 (1953), 8–12   119
Appendix IV Tom Easterbrook, "Innis and Economics" from *The Canadian Journal of Economics and Political Science* Vol. 19 No. 3 (1953), 291–303   125
Appendix V Tom Easterbrook Interview, 21 November 1972   139
Index   151

Acknowledgments

Thank you to Dr. Michael Easterbrook for permission to publish his father's notes. Thanks also to series editor Lance Strate, acquisitions editor Lizzie Howard, and production editor Naviya Palani. Their support in shepherding this project has been greatly appreciated. Debts of gratitude are owed to Hossein Nafchi for performing the onerous task of transcribing a first draft of Easterbrook's 1952–3 lecture notes, Maxwell Webb Comor for transcribing the interview with Easterbrook for this volume, as well as Tys Klumpenhouwer and Marnee Gamble at the University of Toronto archives for their professionalism and many kindnesses. A special thank you must be conveyed to Professor Vincent Manzerolle not only for providing me with insightful feedback on early drafts of the introduction but also for his many years of enthusiasm concerning my work on Innis. Finally, and above all, thank you to Larissa, Max, and Clarence for their immeasurable contributions. Together, they have helped me better appreciate the more meaningful things in life.

Introduction

From the Second World War until his death in 1952, Harold Innis initiated a radical transition, changing his focus from economic history to research that would become foundational for communication studies and media ecology.[1] In this effort he developed a methodology that very few understood.[2] There was, however, one person who grasped his project better than others: his colleague and former student, William Thomas (Tom) Easterbrook.

---

1 Neil Postman writes that "media ecology looks into the matter of how media [...] affect human perception, understanding, feelings, and value; and how our interaction with media facilitates or impedes our chances of survival." Postman, "The Reformed English Curriculum," in *High School 1980: The Shape of the Future in American Secondary Education*, ed. A.C. Eurich (New York, NY: Pitman, 1970), 161. Lance Strate adds that "Postman's definition could actually be reversed to reveal an important and too often unacknowledged aspect of what media ecology represents: *the study of environments as media.*" Strate, *Media Ecology, An Approach to Understanding the Human Condition* (New York, NY: Peter Lang, 2017), 7.
2 According to historian Rudolf Coper (who shared a library workspace with Innis in the 1940s), Innis's departmental colleagues "talked about him, rather condescendingly, but without animosity [...]." This was due, he thought, to Innis's "withdrawal, at least outwardly, from current events" and his immersion, instead, "in topics [...] that could not have been further from the concerns of the day." Quoted in Alexander John Watson, *Marginal Man: The Dark Vision of Harold Innis* (Toronto, ON: University of Toronto Press, 2006), 254.

Easterbrook had been the first PhD candidate Innis supervised. Nine years after Easterbrook received his doctorate (in 1938), Innis, who headed the Department of Political Economy at the University of Toronto, invited him to join the faculty. His appointment was prompted in part by Innis's desire to reduce his teaching responsibilities concerning Canadian economic history (one of Easterbrook's specialties) to focus more on his new fourth-year course. Initially offered in 1945 and officially listed as *Economics 4b*, the course soon came to be known simply as *Innis 4b*. According to the university's *Calendar*, it was "[a] discussion of the significance of major economic factors in Western Civilization with special reference to technology and its implications to knowledge." In the autumn of 1952—just days before the class was scheduled to begin another year—with Innis on his deathbed, Easterbrook agreed to teach it.

Innis had been diagnosed with prostate cancer in 1950 and by 1952 his health had declined dramatically. According to historian and friend Donald Creighton, by March, those who knew him were shocked by his appearance. "His tall figure," wrote Creighton, "was gaunt and bowed; his untidy hair was nearly white; his face was pale and drawn with pain and exhaustion."[3] That summer through until mid-September, Easterbrook visited Innis at his home almost weekly, initially to get feedback concerning a manuscript he was working on called "The Climate of Enterprise."[4] Soon, however, their conversations turned to other subjects, including the paper Innis was preparing for his inaugural presentation as president of the American Economic Association (AEA), gossip about university affairs, and Innis's reflections about his life and work. In an interview recorded twenty years later and transcribed for the first time for the present volume, Easterbrook described what he called an "extraordinary summer with Innis":

> [H]e was a man who the doctors had written off, his time was up, and yet I saw him week after week, right up to nearly the end. Never any acceptance [by Innis regarding his fate]—a flat rejection of all the medical evidence. It was extraordinary. It wasn't a matter of heroics—it was the fact that he was so enormously engrossed in his explorations that it was quite inconceivable that the end was near. And he was working intensively on a paper—he was president of the American Economic Association—to be read in December. [...] You can see a mind flatly rejecting reality as it stood

---

3 Donald Creighton, *Harold Adams Innis, Portrait of a Scholar* (Toronto, ON: University of Toronto Press, 1957), 144.

4 Easterbrook's manuscript is in file 10, box 015, Accession B1975-0039, University of Toronto Archives. It appears to be an elaboration of his previously published paper also titled "The Climate of Enterprise," *American Economic Review* 39, no. 3 (May 1949): 322–35.

because it was inconceivable. [...] [H]e was beginning to pull things together in a larger framework and he was cut off.[5]

During one of the class's first meetings, Easterbrook insisted that he was *not* taking over "Innis's course."[6] However, on a chilly overcast morning, barely two months into the semester and just days after his 58th birthday, Innis passed away. Years later, Easterbrook revealed that his assignment to teach the 80 undergraduates enrolled in *Innis 4b* presented him with "a staggering problem." It was well-known that Innis's lectures were hard to follow and that most found his course to be extremely difficult.[7] In Easterbrook's blunt words, Innis's students "didn't know what the hell he was talking about."[8] However, he also acknowledged that some found Innis's teaching to be inspirational. To explain this contradiction, Easterbrook attributed this minority response to the "aura" that surrounded "the great man." Unfortunately for Easterbrook, he had no way of recreating Innis's persona and, given that he was teaching Innis's year-long course (involving his reading list and assignments), Easterbrook was compelled to explain several works that he was not intimately familiar with, especially as he knew he had "to be far more specific

---

5   Easterbrook Interview, 1972. Cassette recording in box 003, Accession B1974-0001, University of Toronto Archives. An edited transcript of this interview is in Appendix V of this volume.
6   As they are published in the current volume and to avoid onerous footnotes, quotes from Easterbrook's lectures are not formally cited in this introduction.
7   Watson, *Marginal Man*, 126–7 and 239–40. According to former *Innis 4b* student Frank Genovese, one reason why Innis was not easy to follow "was that he mentioned a variety of things without taking the time to explain them and show their significance to the other matters he was talking about. [...] His students would have to scramble." Genovese, "The Lecture Notes on Communications of Harold Adams Innis," *Revue Européenne des Sciences Sociales* 30, no. 92 (1992): 238.
8   From tape recording of Tom Easterbrook Interview, 1978, Item 1, Accession B1978-0029, University of Toronto Archives. As Genovese explains, "Innis would arrive [to the lecture] [...] and start speaking more or less from an abominable collection of notes in a file folder. The notes themselves were in his execrable handwriting on fragile cheap yellow typewriter copy paper, as close a medium to papyrus as was then easily available." Genovese, 237. According to another former student, Innis "was not a notably lucid or forcible expositor of ideas. His rapid delivery and his tendency to place in juxtaposition statements whose connection was not readily apparent [...] had the effect of bewildering many students; they were puzzled as to what he meant." Alexander Brady, "Harold Adams Innis, 1894–1952," *The Canadian Journal of Economics and Political Science* 19, no. 1 (February 1953): 95. By referencing papyrus, Genovese was alluding to the purposeful impermanence of Innis's lectures. Innis (likely with tongue in cheek and in the context of his disdain for what he called the mechanization of knowledge) in 1948 told an audience at Oxford that "Lecturers should be encouraged to write books as a means of compelling them to give new lectures." Harold A. Innis, *The Bias of Communication* (Toronto, ON: University of Toronto Press, 1951), 195.

and clear" than Innis had ever been. As things turned out, *Innis 4b* in 1952 was not only Innis's final course, under Easterbrook it also became the first course *on* Innis ever taught. It is not surprising then that Easterbrook recalled 1952–3 to have been a "terribly involving, grueling year."[9] But by being thrown into the deep end, Easterbrook had little choice but to engage in what he called "a voyage of discovery," one in which he sought to fairly represent Innis's "search for a unifying thesis in the social sciences."[10]

As his lecture notes produced for the course and published for the first time in this book demonstrate, Easterbrook provided a nuanced and accessible overview of Innis's methodology and end-of-life concerns. But more than this, his lectures are unmatched due to at least three attributes: they are a detailed, contemporaneous, and intimate analysis of Innis's research and thinking.[11]

Easterbrook told students early in the semester that his primary focus would be "Innis's approach and methodology," but he would go well beyond this to address avenues of research that Innis had initiated or planned to pursue. Among these were his thoughts on the capacities and conditioning implications of law, language, nationalism, and other institutions. Another involved the universal dialectics informing Innis's later work, especially those related to values concerning order and freedom. In sum, Easterbrook's notes for *Innis 4b* are a remarkable precis of Innis's later research; one that includes concepts and concerns that have been widely referenced as pillars of communication studies and media ecology.

Innis's foundational role and representations of Innis in media ecology

According to Daniel Czitrom, for the "most radical and elaborate American media theory, one must look to the work of two Canadians, Harold Adams Innis and

---

9   Easterbrook Interview, 1978.
10 Easterbrook, "Remarks" (n.d.) in file 08, box 014, Accession B1979-0039, University of Toronto Archives. The fact that Easterbrook taught the course just three times may indicate how challenging it was, as does a remark he made about his decision to stop teaching it: "the range or scope of his [Innis's] research [...] led me to pull back to [...] more manageable areas of enquiry." Ibid. However, in an interview conducted in 1978, Easterbrook also said that his experience teaching *Innis 4b* furthered his interest in communications. Easterbrook Interview, 1978.
11 The lectures published in this volume are from Easterbrook's original notes held in file 10, box 014, Accession B1979-0039, University of Toronto Archives. Perhaps one reason why they appear to have been forgotten is that the file in which they are kept is vaguely titled, "Notes on Harold Adams Innis," and was found by this volume's editor among the Easterbrook (rather than the extensively searched Innis) fonds.

Marshall McLuhan."[12] James Carey went further arguing that it was Innis's work, not McLuhan's, "which is the great achievement in communications on this continent."[13] And more broadly, in the words of Robert Babe,

> Innis was likely the first to [relate] [...] shifts in media technologies to changes in the distribution of political and economic power [...]. He invented the term 'monopolies of knowledge' to represent not only concentration of media ownership and control, but also of the knowledges circulating in society as they affect people's perceptions and understandings. He coined the term 'information industries' to highlight the economic/industrial dimensions of cultural production. He related industrial processes generally, such as the quest for economies of scale and mass marketing, to the production and distribution of culture through such constructs as 'the mechanization of knowledge.' Moreover, Innis's analyses of the political-economic dimensions of media and changes in media technologies and patterns of media control were fully integrated to such cultural categories as conceptions of time, conceptions of space, education, literacy, the news and mass entertainment, and the mass production of culture.[14]

John Watson, in his unparalleled biography, *Marginal Man, the Dark Vision of Harold Innis*, states that Innis's work "represents the old testament of communications theory, which, when paired with Marshall McLuhan's new testament, forms the 'Toronto School' of communications."[15] This 'school'—which began in earnest just one year after Innis's death thanks to the efforts of McLuhan and Edmund Carpenter—played a significant role in what would become media ecology.[16] It was through the McLuhan-Carpenter partnership along with others (including Easterbrook) that a seminar series featuring Innis's work called "Changing Patterns of Language and Behavior and the New Media of Communication" was

---

12 Daniel J. Czitrom, *Media and the American Mind: From Morse to McLuhan* (Chapel Hill: University of North Carolina Press, 1982), 147.
13 James W. Carey, *Communication and Culture: Essays on Media and Society* (Boston, MA: Unwin Hyman, 1989), 109. Indeed, McLuhan conceded that his book, *Gutenberg Galaxy*, constituted "a footnote of explanation" to Innis's research, as it was Innis who first "hit upon the *process* of change as implicit in the *forms* of media technology." Marshall McLuhan, *The Gutenberg Galaxy: The Making of a Typographic Man* (Toronto, ON: University of Toronto Press, 1962), 65.
14 Robert E. Babe, *Cultural Studies and Political Economy, Toward a New Integration* (Lanham, MD: Lexington Books, 2009), 21.
15 Watson, *Marginal Man*, 3. Although many have resisted linking Innis and McLuhan directly as founders of a shared 'school' (for some due to their significant differences and, for others, given Innis's resistance to any such school), the mostly informal scholarly affiliations it represents were inspired by their pioneering work at the University of Toronto. In addition to Innis and McLuhan, it includes others who taught at that university, such as Eric Havelock and Edmund Carpenter. Others not at Toronto but associated with it include McLuhan's student, Walter Ong.
16 Strate, *Media Ecology*, 46.

initiated in late 1953.[17] Years later, Neil Postman, who coined the term media ecology, insisted that far from inventing it he had drawn on the work of others, including McLuhan, Carpenter, and Innis. Also, Postman, regarding his book *The Disappearance of Childhood*, stated that he took "as a guide the teachings of Harold Innis" as it was Innis who stressed that once a machine is built "it is quite capable not only of changing our habits but [...] our habits of mind [also]."[18] To give just one more quotation regarding Innis's influence, Paul Heyer (another Innis biographer) is unambiguous: "Within the tradition of media ecology, Innis' legacy [...] looms large in the pantheon of luminaries" associated with it.[19]

Given the role played by Innis in both communications studies and media ecology, and Easterbrook's position as Innis's closest intellectual confidant at the time of his death (as discussed below), a book on Easterbrook's comprehension of Innis is long overdue. Indeed, the lectures transcribed for this volume constitute more than Easterbrook's intimate introduction to Innis's thinking as they also clarify aspects of his contributions that have since been obscured or ignored. Before directly addressing these, some observations should be made as to how Innis's research has been interpreted, most particularly by students of media ecology.

Among the overarching questions pursued by scholars involved in media ecology are the following: "what drives human history?", "how are we to survive as a species?", and "how are we to retain our humanity?"[20] These were of great importance to Innis also. In a speech made at the end of the Second World War, for example, he told his audience that "western civilization has collapsed" and its "rehabilitation" constituted an urgent task.[21] In addressing this, he sought to understand what intellectual and cultural capacities were needed to go forward. "Stability

---

17 The funds for the seminar came from a grant McLuhan and Carpenter won from the Ford Foundation for their proposal that featured Innis's research. Two years earlier, in 1951, McLuhan had broached the idea (which Innis entertained as Head of the Department of Political Economy) of formally pursuing an interdisciplinary project uniting political economy and the humanities under the organizing theme "Communication Theory and practice." Money from the Ford grant also was used to publish *Explorations*, a journal based on the seminars. Easterbrook at one point became one of its co-editors. Philip Marchand, *Marshall McLuhan, The Medium and the Messenger* (Toronto, ON: Random House, 1989), 117–20; Marshall McLuhan, *Letters of Marshall McLuhan*, ed. Matie Molinaro, Corinne McLuhan, and William Toye (Toronto, ON: Oxford University Press, 1987), 223.
18 Neil Postman, *The Disappearance of Childhood* (New York, NY: Laurel, 1984), 23.
19 Paul Heyer, "Harold Innis' Legacy in the Media Ecology Tradition," in *Perspectives on Culture, Technology and Communication, The Media Ecology Tradition*, ed. Casey Man Kong Lum (Cresskill, NJ: Hampton Press, 2006), 144.
20 Strate, *Media Ecology*, 1.
21 Harold A. Innis, *Political Economy in the Modern State*, ed. Robert E. Babe and Edward A. Comor (Toronto, ON: University of Toronto Press, 2018), 73.

which characterized certain periods in earlier civilizations," he realized, "is not the obvious objective of this civilization. Each civilization has its own methods of suicide."[22] Among his other conclusions, Innis argued that people—especially fellow academics—need to understand their own circumstances by becoming actively engaged in self-reflective, philosophical thought. But given that most in the 20th century had little interest in this seemingly obsolete (if not elitist) pursuit, Innis became preoccupied with identifying the means through which the importance of this kind of intelligence might at least be recognized. His most cited concepts from these latter years—media bias and monopolies of knowledge—were developed and applied with this in mind.[23]

Classicist Eric Havelock recalls that Innis was never a popular writer in part due to his interest in "large ideas and major efforts of synthesis" that focused on "the possible interconnections between things rather than giving exclusive consideration to the things themselves."[24] As a contemporary and someone whose work Innis drew upon, like Easterbrook, Havelock's reading of Innis differs in some key respects relative to others, including McLuhan's. Havelock, for example, recognized that Innis situated his communications research in the context of his political economy—an approach in which economic and political structures condition one another and are interrelated with developments involving both culture and media (including technologies). Of course, for Innis, communications technologies and techniques were important in terms of their influence on intellectual capacities. But having said this, Havelock argues that technology was never *the* central factor for Innis. For one thing, Innis recognized (as did Easterbrook) that communications enabling genuine forms of understanding are achievable primarily through speech. Although language is a social activity profoundly influenced by the technologies and techniques used to record and disseminate, the material means of communication are not themselves determinative.[25] To quote Havelock, while these means affect "the nature of what is communicated, [for Innis] the content still remains the fruit of human thought."[26] For Havelock, "as one reads him,

---

22 Innis, *Bias of Communication*, 141.
23 As Postman later put it regarding a commonality among media ecologists, in some way each one is asking the kinds of questions that "have to do with the present and the future. Mostly the future." Postman, *High School 1980*, 161.
24 Eric A. Havelock, *Harold A. Innis, A Memoir* (Toronto, ON: The Harold Innis Foundation, 1982), 35.
25 Ibid., 30–2.
26 Ibid., 38.

one senses a note of humanism, a sense of values which, to be sure, he assumed could be compromised by technology, but which are not created by it."[27]

These features of Innis's approach—the importance of political economy, his dialectical treatment of technological developments and their implications, and his emphasis on language and humanist values—are recognized in the lectures published in this volume. Arguably, both Havelock and Easterbrook represent Innis more accurately than did Easterbrook's lifelong friend, Marshall McLuhan.[28] This is an important point, especially given the extraordinary challenges most face when reading Innis.[29] For media ecologists and others, one outcome has been a heavy reliance on secondary sources and arguably the most influential of these has been McLuhan's, beginning especially with his introduction to the republication of *The Bias of Communication* in 1964. Although McLuhan's attention gave Innis's communications work the prominence it never achieved while he was alive, his portrayal also shaped decades of readings that likely benefitted McLuhan more than they clarified Innis.[30]

In contrast to Havelock and Easterbrook, McLuhan argued: "Once Innis had ascertained the dominant technology of a culture he could be sure that this was

---

[27] Ibid. Havelock first encountered Innis while teaching at the University of Toronto in 1930 but the two did not develop a personal relationship. However, in the autumn of 1951, after Havelock moved to Harvard, Innis telephoned to invite him back to give seminar presentations early in the new year. Havelock accepted. During his visit it may be assumed that the two had several conversations concerning their mutual interests.

[28] During his undergraduate years at the University of Manitoba, Easterbrook became close friends with McLuhan and, in the summer of 1932, having worked their way across the Atlantic as crewmen on a cattle boat, toured England together. Upon graduating a year later, McLuhan was awarded the university's gold medal for attaining the highest standing in English and the silver in economics, while Easterbrook won the gold in economics and the silver in English. In late 1948, after both had secured faculty positions at Toronto, Easterbrook introduced McLuhan to Innis by inviting them to a meal. This meeting did not go well. According to Easterbrook, their personalities were not complementary. Watson, *Marginal Man*, 405.

[29] On this, a review of *Political Economy in the Modern State* that appeared in *The Economist* held no punches: "Incoherence [...] is Professor Innis' besetting sin [...]. He suffers from an extraordinary lack of organization. Facts and quotations are less marshalled than hurled pell-mell at the reader, who is never certain whether the juxtaposition of two statements is meant to imply a causal connection, an illustrative parallel, a whimsical contrast or the chance neighbourhood of two items in Professor [Innis's] card index. Coupled with a style even more atrocious than is normally to be expected of North American academics, this characteristic goes far to make his essays totally unreadable." In "Rambles Among the Social Sciences," *The Economist*, 5398 (February 8, 1947): 239. There are several explanations for Innis's prose style but one of note (and pursued below) is that it involved pedagogical reasons.

[30] William Buxton, "The Rise of McLuhanism, the loss of Innis-sense," *Canadian Journal of Communication* 37, no. 4 (December 2012): 577–93.

the cause and shaping force of the entire structure."[31] McLuhan went on to say (correctly) that Innis lauded the oral tradition as a means of counterbalancing mechanized (mostly printed) forms of biased knowledge. The spoken word, for Innis, facilitated many of the virtues that the written tradition restricted as, in most circumstances, human speech is a more engaging, flexible, and tentative means of communication. Orality thus constituted a (potentially) superior means of enabling people to pursue reflective and creative thought, especially through interpersonal discussion (Innis's model being the Socratic dialogue). But having said this, McLuhan was incorrect in assuming that orality in and of itself was Innis's ideal.

In several of the lectures prepared for *Innis 4b*, Easterbrook references that Innis embraced the cultural vibrancy of ancient Greece as a means of gaining perspective on the capacities of modern society. With it in mind, Innis thought that the oral tradition—represented by the humanities, art, philosophy, and other forms of intellectual engagement—constituted a primary means of counterbalancing the deleterious implications of print capitalism and mechanized knowledge. For Innis, the dominance of *either* the written or oral tradition undermined the conditions needed for order and freedom to exist in the state of balance or propitious tension that sustainable societies require. It was in this context that Innis understood Plato's critique of the manipulative implications of ecstatic poetry not to be a one-sided endorsement of writing over orality. According to Innis,

> Plato attempted to adapt the new medium of prose to an elaboration of the conversation of Socrates by the dialogue with its question and answer, freedom of arrangement and inclusiveness. A well-planned conversation was aimed at discovering truth and awakening the interest and sympathy of the reader. The dialogues were developed as a most effective instrument for preserving power of the spoken word on the written page and Plato's success was written in the inconclusiveness and immortality of his work. His style was regarded by Aristotle as half-way between poetry and prose. The power of the oral tradition persisted in his prose [...].[32]

Just as Plato pushed back against (but did not dismiss) orality, McLuhan's misrepresentation of Innis as its unreserved champion can be discerned by recalling that Innis himself criticized the disingenuous qualities of much discussion, especially its propagandistic and ignorant representations that circulated widely in the 1930s and, again, at the dawn of the Cold War. It was *balance*, not the dominance of one tradition over the other, that was most important. The "well-planned conversation" requiring both freedom and order was Innis's ideal, and this required the

---

31 Marshall McLuhan, "Introduction," in Harold A. Innis, *The Bias of Communication* (Toronto, ON: University of Toronto Press, 1964), xii.
32 Harold A. Innis, *Empire and Communications* (Oxford, UK: Clarendon Press, 1950), 68–9.

structuring of media (including organizations and institutions) in ways that might facilitate a more thoughtful and self-reflective polity.[33]

Easterbrook's analysis concerning Innis's quest for balance demonstrates that McLuhan failed to situate his work in these relatively nuanced terms. Indeed, formulations that McLuhan represented as those of Innis are more unidirectional and deterministic than what Innis ever said or believed. Unlike Innis, McLuhan idealized the auditory (which he related to tribal man, monastic capacities in the Middle Ages, and the modern electronic age) and contrasted the aural with sight and the objectifying and linear thinking he associated with printing and typographic man. Tribal man, he claimed, is nonalienated, imaginative, and open to a prospectively global cosmic consciousness, whereas literate man is alienated, controlling, and nationalistic. For Innis, despite his many shorthand associations and juxtapositions, such direct associations are not possible (more on this below).

Related to McLuhan's misrepresentation of Innis on orality, the concept bias often has been read and applied in sometimes oversimplified or inaccurate ways. The comparatively nondeterministic approach developed by Innis can be seen in his treatment of the Greeks. Like Havelock, Innis stressed that the beginning of the written tradition facilitated a brief period of unprecedented (and never duplicated) reflective thought. McLuhan resisted such associations. According to Innis, the brilliance of Greece emerged amid conditions and mediations involving writing *and* orality that reflected and facilitated an extraordinary state of intellectual vibrancy. But also, Innis (as Easterbrook elaborates) emphasized the political-economic dynamics in which this hothouse of creativity took place, including its wealth, political system, and other capacities involving some very particular spatial (i.e., geographic) and temporal (i.e., historical) conditions. Indeed, Innis developed bias from his earlier research using economic theories concerning fixed capital formations and capacity. The latter was a concept rooted in Innis's earlier studies concerning Canada's development involving the exploitation of its staples products (especially cod, furs, timber, wheat, metals, pulp and paper, and hydroelectricity) and it implied both the potentialities and limits of any given political-economic formation. Bias, more specifically, emerged from his work concerning *unused* capacity which, as Robert Babe and Edward Comor demonstrate, became "a sort of *éminence grise*" for Innis, "exerting influence or constituting a historical

---

33 Arguably, the influence Innis had on Postman's reading of Plato is apparent in the latter's strategic approach to education. For example, see Postman, "The Information Environment," *ETC: A Review of General Semantics* 36, no. 3 (1979): 234–45. Other similarities between Innis and Postman are outlined below.

dynamic that is, for the most part, unnoticed."[34] In referencing both capacity and bias, Innis emphasized causal relationships that connote tendencies and dialectical interactions rather than unidirectional determinants. Here it should be noted that despite McLuhan's influence, media ecology involves a range of perspectives, some of which resonate more with Innis's dialectics than McLuhan's tendency toward reductionism.[35]

McLuhan chastised Innis for being inconsistent in not recognizing the liberating effects of electronic communications and incorrectly assumed that Innis associated mechanized (unreflective) knowledge almost entirely with the industrialization of printing. As such, in McLuhan's mind, Innis's view that radio likely would extend this kind of thinking made little sense. Radio and other electronic media, argued McLuhan, were mediating the retribalization of humanity through the all-encompassing engagement of the aural (vs. the eye and sight). Innis, however, did not reductively associate a spatially biased world with sensual orientations mediated by dominant technologies. Instead, the time-annihilating implications of mechanized forms of knowledge (which Innis sometimes related to modern academic specializations generally and statistics, administration, and accounting, more specifically) involved and emerged from the collapsing capacity to engage in reflective thought. As Innis once put it, "[w]e have all the answers and none of the questions,"[36] and it was the dynamics and monopolistic conditions characterizing 20th-century capitalism and the powers exercised by the modern state that constituted the first (and itself complex) step to understanding the crisis, not just the biases associated with predominant media.[37]

34 Robert E. Babe and Edward A. Comor, "Introduction," in Harold A. Innis, *Political Economy in the Modern State*, ed. Robert E. Babe and Edward A. Comor (Toronto, ON: University of Toronto Press, 2018), LXXXIII.
35 In *Media Ecology*, Strate provides a nuanced overview of this range. See esp. 34–7.
36 Innis, *Political Economy in the Modern State*, 128.
37 As McLuhan wrote in his introduction for *The Bias of Communication*, Innis's treatment of radio is "an example of Innis failing to be true to his own method. After many historical demonstrations of the space-binding power of the eye and the time-binding power of the ear, Innis refrains from applying these structural principles" (p. xii). A fuller comprehension of Innis would have shown that biases are not reducible to the physical characteristics of a medium. While Innis was alive, for instance, radio had the capacity to engage people in what he considered to be a potentially thoughtful dialogue, especially in the form of listener call-in programs. Such possibilities were, however, undermined as commercial interests (and their spatial priorities, i.e., delivering listeners to advertisers) largely shaped its development. Radio's potentialities were undermined further as political interests turned to it as a means of delivering audiences to the voices of the powerful (on this Innis mentions several examples, from Franklin Roosevelt to Adolf Hitler). Innis also recognized that the accumulated spatial (and time-neglecting) biases of most Western societies influenced what radio broadcasters produced and what listeners anticipated hearing. In sum,

Another widely read interpreter of Innis was James Carey who, among other things, wrote the introduction to the 2004 edition of *Changing Concepts of Time* (Innis's most overtly critical book and one in which Easterbrook played a direct role in its posthumous publication).[38] Like McLuhan, Carey ignored or undertheorized Innis's dialectical materialism but, unlike McLuhan (who Carey argued was a media determinist), he interpreted Innis to be what he called a soft determinist. The importance of communications for Innis, suggested Carey, involved what McLuhan referred to as the extensions of man—that technologies "are attempts to extend man's physical capacity" as well as his/her "consciousness" and "perceptual capacities."[39] Innis according to Carey "sees communication technology principally affecting social organization and thought,"[40] but, like McLuhan, he failed to fully recognize the range of dynamics Innis associated with their development and use. An example of this is found in Carey's references to Innis on the historical implications of film and electronic media. Alongside their ascent, Carey argues that the spatial bias associated with printing was being reversed. According to Carey, "Space in the modern world progressively disappears as a differentiating factor" as how space is organized and conceptualized "becomes more continuous" and "regional variations in culture and social structure become ground down."[41] Carey, by concentrating on a particular medium, ignores or oversimplifies Innis's approach and analysis of, among other factors, core-periphery (political-economic) and center-margin (cultural) relations, historically contingent dynamics, and the implications of these on media developments and their applications.

To summarize, various forms of media determinism are found in the work of most theorists referencing Innis. For some, technologies are treated ahistorically as if *they* are inherently biased and affecting. For Innis, instead, the capacity of a given medium or media environment involves interactions taking place in the context of political-economic dynamics and structured relations. Furthermore, although Innis was most explicit about the implications of biases he associated with communications technologies, the mediating roles of organizations (such as schools, churches, governments, corporate entities, etc.) and institutions (educational, religious, economic, and others) also factored into his work. To illustrate this, in what

---

McLuhan abstracted components of Innis and then applied these in terms of his own sensory-focused probes, whereas Innis framed and tested his approach in the context of a complex of historical conditions, dynamics, and mediated relations.

38 James Carey, "Introduction," in Harold A. Innis, *Changing Concepts of Time* (Lanham, MD: Rowman & Littlefield, 2004), vii–xx.
39 James Carey, "Harold Innis and Marshall McLuhan," *The Antioch Review*, 27, no. 1 (Spring 1967): 7.
40 Ibid., 15.
41 Ibid., 30.

can be read as an overview of the rise and fall of monopolies of knowledge, Innis's paper "Minerva's Owl" (which Havelock recognized to be his "first seminal contribution to the history of communication"[42]) references a range of communications technologies that mediated history. These include clay, the stylus, papyrus, the brush, the pen, parchment, paper, the printing press, celluloid, and radio. But Innis also points to the implications of dozens of other technologies, organizations, and institutions. For example, the use of coinage after 700 B.C. provided for the flexible development of market systems while it also facilitated abstractions in human relationships. He writes that the horse and chariot enabled the unity of city-states through applications of force and raised awareness regarding Rome's corporal powers. The use of contracts reduced the costly need for public ceremony and clarified social obligations. The development of libraries and museums enabled or furthered the conservation and utilization of the past. The rise of monasticism provided the Roman Catholic Church with agents who reproduced its selections of written knowledge while also promoting faith and the Bible throughout Europe. The later rise of commerce involved institutions such as the price system that encouraged the extension of orderly exchange relations as well as individualism. Especially from the 19th century, advertising promoted selective aspects of existing reality while also stimulating new and more abstract realities.

In these and many other instances, Innis demonstrates that media (broadly defined) are developed, modified, and applied to influence or further particular capabilities and orientations. Typically, they are used to extend existing or emergent power capacities while also they may facilitate disruptions to status quo relations. Indeed, it may be less helpful to debate whether or not Innis was some kind of media or technological determinist than it is to acknowledge the importance of contextualizing such questions in light of his analysis of political economy and other factors.[43]

The first paragraph of the Preface for *The Bias of Communication* contains the most direct statement Innis made concerning determination. Here he writes that his book is an attempt to answer the philosophical question, "Why do we attend to the things to which we attend?" and that its chapters "emphasize the importance

---

42 Havelock, *Harold A. Innis*, 39. It was later published as the first chapter in *The Bias of Communication*.

43 For example, at least implicitly, Innis recognized the determinative significance of what some political economists call forces and relations of production dynamics and the influential role played by technologies, organizations, and institutions in their dialectical relationship. Easterbrook raised the question of Innis's determinism in his lectures, including when he told students about a review of *The Bias of Communication* by Karl Deutsch, published in *The Canadian Journal of Economics and Political Science* 18, no. 3 (August 1952): 388–90.

of communication in determining 'things to which we attend' and suggest also that changes in communication will follow changes in 'the things to which we attend.'"[44] Thus, while communication developments influence what people think about and how they think, it is important to underline that for Innis these follow "the things to which we attend" such as a society's predominant political-economic relations.[45]

Before leaving this section, Neil Postman's media ecology should be mentioned as it is, relatively speaking, an exemplary example of Innis's methodology being adopted and adapted. Like Innis, Postman treats organizations and institutions as media environments (obvious examples being schools and the educational system) and, along with technologies, assessed their cultural and intellectual implications historically and dialectically. A brief listing of additional similarities might begin with the fact that Innis and Postman pursued a cross-disciplinary approach; both were inspired by and frequently referenced the Greeks and the European Enlightenment as comparative ideals; both stressed the need to ask questions that specialists, relativists, and those subsumed by the cult of science refuse to conceptualize; and, related to all of these, both men embraced education and the humanities as primary means of seeking complex truths which may yield greater understanding. Unlike Postman, however, Innis chose to employ a cryptic presentation style in most of his communications writings, in part as a means of compelling reader engagement (as if he is involving them in a kind of Socratic dialogue).

---

44   Innis, *The Bias of Communication*, xliii.
45   This is the approach of a sophisticated (non-Marxist) dialectical materialist whose analysis emphasizes mutual or reciprocal relations but also relations that reference political-economic conditions. It is with this in mind that one of Innis's most widely cited passages can be read with some precision. In *Empire and Communications* he relates time and space biases to communications technologies as follows (emphases added): "The concepts of time and space *reflect* the significance of media to civilization. Media that *emphasize* time are those that are durable in character, such as parchment, clay, and stone [...]. Media that *emphasize* space are apt to be less durable and light in character, such as papyrus and paper. The latter are *suited* to wide areas in administration and trade [...]. Materials that emphasize time *favour* decentralization and hierarchical types of institutions, while those that *emphasize* space *favour* centralization and systems of government less hierarchical in character. Large-scale political organizations such as empires must be considered from the standpoint of two dimensions, those of space and time. Empires persist by overcoming the bias of media which overemphasizes either dimension. They have *tended* to flourish under conditions in which civilization *reflects* the influence of more than one medium, and in which the bias of one medium towards decentralization is offset by the bias of another medium towards centralization." Innis, *Empire and Communications*, 7. Here and elsewhere, in choosing words such as *reflect*, *emphasize*, *suited*, *favor*, and *tended*, instead of deterministic outcomes Innis stressed capacities afforded by different technologies in certain (dialectically related) political-economic circumstances and cultural contexts.

As mentioned above (and developed in the section below), the implications of 20th-century publishing—involving its commercial motivations, scale, and visual qualities—on the growing *in*capacity of readers to think reflectively and creatively was one of Innis's primary concerns. While Postman championed what he called the courage to publish clearly articulated arguments, Innis thought that most forms of accessible writing were contributing to the very mechanization of knowledge he associated with the decline of modern civilization.[46] As he wrote near the conclusion of "Minerva's Owl,"

> Enormous improvements in communication have made understanding more difficult. [...] Commercialism has required the creation of new monopolies in language and new difficulties in understanding. Even the class struggle, the struggle between language groups, has been made a monopoly of language. When the *Communist Manifesto* proclaimed, "Workers of the world unite, you have nothing to lose but your chains!" in those words it forged new chains.[47]

46 Innis (as did Postman decades later) referenced Plato on the apprehensions expressed by Socrates concerning writing and its implications for memory: through their use of "written characters" learners "will be hearers of many things and have learned nothing; they will appear to be omniscient and will generally know nothing; they will be tiresome company, having the show of wisdom without the reality." Innis goes on to relate this warning to modern applications involving the printing press and radio, stating that they also "have enormously increased the difficulties of thought." Innis, *Political Economy in the Modern* State, vii. In relation to this, Innis drew from the Promethean paradox of humanity's mastery over nature in that scientific and technological progress, essential as they are to civilizational advance, also imply the shackling of the intellect. He thought that a turning point for Western civilization was the invention of the printing press in the context of capitalist dynamics. With the ubiquity of the printed word from the late 19th century, mechanized thinking flourished as commercial and political applications of improving printing technologies mediated an unreflective inter-subjective mentality. This, from Innis's perspective, furthered the capacity to manage, administer, and control—to apply power on an unprecedented scale.

47 Innis, *The Bias of Communication*, 31. Another reason why Innis opted to write and lecture using a less than direct prose style involved his attempt to protect his then considerable status (and thus potential influence) while also producing scathing critiques, especially during the early years of the Cold War. Postman, by comparison, published in a post-Red Scare culture, did not have to be as concerned about his reputation (at least not vis-à-vis the status quo of a small country such as Canada), and was not directly bridled by forces threatening to shut down his academic department. In an address Innis made in 1947 to an audience of non-academics (an address he chose not to publish), he said the following: "The danger of shaking men out of the soporific results of mechanized knowledge is similar to that of attempting to arouse a drunken man or one who has taken an overdose of sleeping tablets. The necessary violent measures will be disliked. [...] I am reluctant to make speeches in public for various reasons [...]. The Department of Political Economy, if I may judge from personal experience, is under constant surveillance by a wide range of individuals. If in the course of an article I make a reference to a large government department or a large business organization, I will receive in an incredibly short time [...] a personal letter

As Lance Strate observes, "there is no media ecology except for media ecology as it is understood by a given individual, or group."[48] Assuming he is correct and given that the most referenced of media ecologists owe much to Innis's foundational studies, the recently discovered lecture notes by Tom Easterbrook for *Innis 4b* should be of much explanatory value. To further appreciate their potential, Easterbrook's unique relationship with and insights concerning Innis are elaborated in the next section.

Easterbrook's relationship with Innis

As Innis moved forward in his studies concerning communications and civilization, the number of colleagues who he might have called intellectual confidants dwindled. While, according to Easterbrook, he had several good friends, Innis lacked an intellectual circle.[49] "I don't think anybody on an intellectual basis ever achieved full communication with Innis," said Easterbrook, especially as he was developing his methodology using new techniques.[50] Innis, he continued, was "exploring, he was on the trail punching his way through the thickets in a new land."[51]

> [...] explaining that my remarks are liable to misinterpretation and inferring that the head of such an influential department in a large university should be very careful about the way in which his views are expressed. [...] For these reasons I am largely compelled to avoid making speeches [...] and to resort to the careful preparation of material to be made available in print. In most cases *this involves writing in such guarded fashion that no one can understand what is written* [...]" (emphases added). Harold A. Innis, *Staples, Markets, and Cultural Change*, ed. Daniel Drache (Montreal: McGill-Queen's University Press, 1995), 459, 463.

48 Strate, *Media Ecology*, 3.
49 Innis, said Easterbrook, "was an immensely social man with a very small group of close associates" who were his "cronies, on a social level." Interview, 1972. The shift in Innis's research baffled most partly because it seemed unrelated to his established areas of expertise. His son, Donald, later revealed that his father was depressed because this new work was ignored even by those he knew to have similar interests. John Nef, Chester Wright, and Frank Knight all acknowledged receiving mailed copies of what Innis sent them, but none responded. Watson, *Marginal Man*, 251. In early 1952, although Innis and McLuhan never developed a close relationship, Innis wrote to McLuhan conveying his gratitude (and perhaps relief) that in an earlier correspondence McLuhan expressed his thoughtful appreciation of *The Bias of Communication*: "I was immensely pleased to get your warm letter particularly as it is the first I have had which indicated that the reader had taken the trouble to understand what it is all about." Quoted in Cameron McEwen, "McLuhan on First Meeting Innis," n. 20, dated 10 May 2018, available at <https://mcluhansnewsciences.com/mcluhan/2018/05/mcluhan-on-first-meeting-innis/#fn-49167-20>.
50 For example, said Easterbrook, "when he read 'Minerva's Owl' [...] [in 1947], I don't think anyone had a clue." Easterbrook Interview, 1972.
51 Ibid.

Easterbrook's relationship with Innis began in 1933 after he entered Toronto's graduate program in economics.⁵² "I came down here [to Toronto] with no interest in history," but this changed soon after attending "a lecture or two by Innis [...]. [In these, I] watched a long lean guy loping in with his scattered notes [...] [who then] proceeded without any attention to his audience." As he continued,

> It became apparent that what he was doing was picking up his notes from a manuscript he was just working on, bringing it into class, and there you had it. But there was a curious feeling about the whole thing that he'd taken what seemed to be a very simple proposition and he began to develop a much larger theme of that [...]. Before you knew it, in spite of yourself, you're interested, and that took me then back to see what this guy was really talking about because he was obviously using a different way of looking at things. It wasn't the narrative style.⁵³

This introduction and their subsequent conversations led Easterbrook to conclude that "Innis had the most revealing mind I'd ever encountered."⁵⁴ With Innis's guidance, Easterbrook shifted his MA thesis work from a survey on the financing of farmers in Canada to, instead, a more historical analysis. He then pursued his PhD at Harvard but was unsatisfied with its faculty's limited interest in the historical approach inspired by Innis. Easterbrook returned to Toronto to finish it under Innis's supervision and completed his doctorate there in 1938.⁵⁵ After Innis appointed Easterbrook to the department of Political Economy nine years later, they worked together on several projects. One of these took place in 1949 when Easterbrook chaired an initiative organized by Innis called "the Values Discussion Group."⁵⁶ Easterbrook and Innis also co-authored a book chapter in

---

52   Easterbrook was born in 1907 and raised in Winnipeg. As had Innis from 1937 until his death, Easterbrook headed Toronto's Department of Political Economy from 1961 to 1970. He died in 1985.
53   Easterbrook Interview, 1972.
54   Easterbrook Interview, 1978.
55   His dissertation, which Easterbrook described as a detailed elaboration of his MA research, was published as *Farm Credit in Canada* (Toronto, ON: University of Toronto Press, 1938). Innis wrote the Forward. Subsequent research reflected his supervisor's influence as he pursued Innis's assertion that economic history had to address power relations, the role of the state, and what Easterbrook referred to as "sanctions"—"the social approval and authorization of particular institutions and economic actions." Ian Parker, "Editor's Introduction," in W.T. Easterbrook, *North American Patterns of Growth and Development: The Continental Context*, ed. Ian Parker (Toronto, ON: University of Toronto Press, 1990), xiii.
56   William J. Buxton, "The 'Values' discussion group at the University of Toronto, February-May 1949," in *Canadian Journal of Communication* 29, no. 2 (February 2004): 187–204. Innis had secured funds from the Rockefeller Foundation to hold nine meetings in Toronto (McLuhan was among its eleven participants). According to Buxton, "for the three figures who would eventually leave their mark on the emergent field of communications—namely Innis, McLuhan, and

1950.[57]

Easterbrook was one of very few colleagues who Innis invited to read and comment on his drafts. Likely, this reflected his recognition of Easterbrook's knowledge concerning both economics and communications. Significantly, the first piece he read for Innis was "Minerva's Owl" (the paper that most explicitly marked Innis's turn to communications). With its presentation in 1947, according to John Watson, there emerged "a division between, on the one side, the economic historian [...] and other established colleagues who did not follow Innis into the new field, and, on the other, younger scholars who learned the new vocabulary without understanding its significance."[58] Easterbrook was an exception. "He'd hand me manuscripts before publication," said Easterbrook, "and I'd make my marvellous notes and [would] find that the manuscript would come out intact and [thus] maybe I had nothing to say [...] On the other hand, I felt I sometimes did." But rather than Innis dismissing his feedback (unlikely given that he invited Easterbrook to read his work again and again), Easterbrook thought that something more subtle had taken place: "It was [as] if he sifted [...] [my comments] through [...] his mind and it came out very different from what you had thought."[59]

Easterbrook took notes during their meetings at Innis's home in the summer of 1952.[60] More than a record of topics discussed and Easterbrook's impressions of Innis's health, these provide some sense of the quality of their intellectual engagement.[61] Examples of this can be discerned in what Easterbrook wrote regarding

> Easterbrook—the series of discussions appears to have been of some consequence. For Innis, the meetings undoubtedly provided him with the opportunity to explore questions of values and economic life with a group of hand-picked colleagues; the issues examined were very much in line with his own ongoing investigations into how communications were implicated in the rise and fall of civilizations. [...] Easterbrook's subsequent trajectory [...] appeared to have been directly affected by the meetings" as he pursued research on the subject of "entrepreneurial values" and worked on a manuscript (the one that Innis helped him with in the summer of 1952) in which he said that Innis's study of communications was invaluable. Buxton, "The 'Values' Discussion Group," 198–9.

57 Harold A. Innis and W.T. Easterbrook, "Fundamental and Historic Elements," in *Canada*, ed. G.W. Brown (Berkeley: University of California Press, 1950), 155–64.
58 Watson, *Marginal Man*, 306–7. Innis asked only three colleagues—Easterbrook, R.H. Fleming, and Grant Robertson—to read the manuscript for *Empire and Communications* before it was submitted for publication. His son, Donald Innis, also read it. Ibid., 277.
59 Easterbrook Interview, 1972.
60 Easterbrook's notes from these meetings are in file 02, box 001, Accession B1975-0030, University of Toronto Archives. To reduce the number of footnotes, this citation will not be repeated below.
61 These were recorded by Easterbrook for his own use. As such, most are abbreviated or obliquely phrased and require some amount of interpretation.

three seemingly disparate subjects: Innis's use of juxtapositions, his application of Weberian ideal-types,[62] and their mutual interest in bureaucracy.[63] When Easterbrook visited for their meeting on June 26 they discussed the latter and the two agreed that bureaucracies are forged and perpetuated to maintain an organization over time but, in their "real" (non-idealized) form, their means of control typically mediated ways of thinking that are "unstable in the long-run." In reviewing Easterbrook's notes, it is clear that they were addressing what Innis called the spatial bias of bureaucracies involving their propensity to control interpersonal and social interactions. For Innis, bureaucracies mediated thoughts and activities in ways that undermine the kinds of reflective and creative thinking that any society needs if it is to respond effectively to changing conditions. But having said this, Innis and Easterbrook recognized that conceptualizing biased media such as bureaucracies using ideal-types did not itself reveal objective reality.[64] Instead, Innis's concept of bias was used as an abstraction or, more precisely, a heuristic tool applied to identify and help put into perspective universal tendencies while also recognizing an array of real-world conditions and circumstances.

Their discussion then turned to how an understanding of bias could be deepened and how the knowledge derived from its use might become an "active force" in efforts to escape contradictory patterns involving, for one thing, modern society's obsession with spatial control. One strategic response they talked about concerned the use of juxtapositions when presenting their research as this, they thought, might be a way of circumventing the biases of readers. Using the example of bureaucracy, Innis and Easterbrook exchanged views on how to break away from entrenched ways of thinking (i.e., biases) by compelling engagement and self-reflection among audiences, including other scholars. Through the use

62 This refers to the conceptual tool developed by sociologist Max Weber that enabled him to assess historical or contemporary realities and their variations more objectively. By representing them in "perfectly" modeled terms, Weber was able to better understand them in relation to "real-world" applications. Just as ideal-types facilitated Weber's comprehension of a particular social reality, bias enabled Innis to assess a society's orientations and inter-subjectivities in terms of the dynamics and mediations structuring its knowledge or understanding of such realities. Two of Innis's more pervasive ideal-types were the oral and written traditions. Innis made particular use of two books on Weber's method: Max Weber, *From Max Weber: Essays in Sociology*, ed. H.H. Gerth and C. Wright Mills (New York, NY: Oxford University Press, 1946) and Max Weber, *On the Methodology of the Social Sciences*, ed. E.A. Shil and H.A. Finch (Glencoe, IL: Free Press, 1949).

63 Bureaucracy was a predictable subject for conversation given the subtitle of Easterbrook's manuscript: "The Study of Entrepreneurship and Bureaucracy in Economic History."

64 As Easterbrook wrote in his meeting notes for July 3, Innis thought it was "analytically o.k." to conceptualize in terms of ideal-types as long as one does not "carry over the sharp abstractions [these involve] into reality."

of juxtapositions—by, in effect, using ideal-type characterizations alongside contrasting examples and abstract associations—readers might be weaned (or jarred!) away from passively accepting what they read, thus challenging mechanistic and reductionist thinking in the process. One week later, despite agreeing with Innis, Easterbrook wrote that he had some difficulty understanding why his friend was pushing his point about juxtapositions so assertively and reported that he had doubts "about pressing juxtaposition so hard" in his own work. Although Easterbrook recognized that Innis was "concerned with [the] position of [the] observer" and that he believed that the individual's "greater awareness" of their own biases might play a key role in the "process of change itself," Easterbrook admitted that he remained "a little puzzled by his stress on this […]."

Later that summer, Easterbrook appears to have attained more clarity regarding Innis's position. On August 15, the two discussed how contemporary society is characterized by a neglect of time and the role played by linear ways of communicating in perpetuating this bias. For Innis, reports Easterbrook, the "act of writing [for example] is really linear even in [James] Joyce." Revealingly, Easterbrook then noted that "I still think that [the] notion of juxtaposition and attention to [the] shifting position of [the] observer [is] very useful." Easterbrook thus appears to have come round to Innis's views on this strategy. As he later explained to students in *Innis 4b*, "implicit in all this is a *theory of change* although at this unfinished stage of his work this is not always easy to discern […]." Innis, he told the class, amassed and sifted through enormous amounts of research to arrive at conclusions that he "rarely clearly explained." By "juxtaposing apparently unlike things, looking them over, inspecting them," explained Easterbrook, Innis sought to uncover patterns, paradoxes, and "insights into process" while impelling his readers to take part in the search. This championed what Innis called "living" knowledge over the "dead" knowledge used and perpetuated by bureaucracies.[65]

In the months prior to their weekly meetings, Innis's health worsened prompting an operation in May. Following this, he received what Easterbrook called "lachrymose letters" that prematurely mourned his death. But despite these developments, through much of the summer Innis spoke and acted as if he was going to be fine. Easterbrook commented on July 11, for example, that for Innis "death [was] out of the question" and he had "no thought" of making a will, nor for making "plans regarding [his] family […]." On July 25, again, Easterbrook reported that Innis demonstrated "no recognition of his state" and that "continuity"

---

65 By "dead" knowledge Innis was referencing the know-how needed for administration, management, accounting, and similar pursuits. "Living" knowledge instead involves what emerges from mostly reflective and creative endeavors. "The universities," he wrote, "must concern themselves with the living rather than with the dead." Innis, *The Bias of Communication*, 195.

was assumed in relation to him heading the department and his forthcoming tenure as president of the AEA. Even as late as September 19, just four days before *Innis 4b* was to begin, Easterbrook wrote that his frail friend still "planned to begin" the course. But, having said this, Easterbrook also mentioned that occasionally Innis appeared to understand his fate, as indicated by his "strong tendency to reminisce." Moreover, in mid-July, Easterbrook noted that Innis's "reasoning faculties" were "much too sharp [...] not to know."[66]

Easterbrook on Innis after Innis's death

Easterbrook had known Innis for almost twenty years. When he was asked to teach his course, their relationship had provided Easterbrook with an unmatched comprehension of Innis's methodology and emerging interests.[67] At the time of his death, therefore, Easterbrook's status as the scholar best positioned to understand and represent Innis's later work had been established.

In addition to being selected to teach *Innis 4b*, Easterbrook played a central role in preparing Innis's unfinished paper for the AEA meetings in Chicago in December.[68] In 1953, he published both a memorial tribute and a paper explaining to fellow economists Innis's interest in communications.[69] The latter is significant for several reasons. First, the fact that it is an exposition on the development of Innis's communications research reflects Easterbrook's awareness that while most

---

66 There were moments when even Easterbrook found himself "accepting his [Innis's optimistic] attitude." This likely reflected what he reported Mary Innis to have described on July 25 as her husband's "frightening drive and will power" as well as the "aura" that Easterbrook later said surrounded him. It should be added that Easterbrook's records of their bedside discussions also indicate his respect and affection for his old mentor. For example, in his notes for August 1, Easterbrook expressed his amazement regarding Innis's ability to engage in a "long detailed discussion" and that, despite his grave condition, he "seemed very fresh and much less restless [...]. Whadaman."

67 The fact that Marshall McLuhan was Easterbrook's close friend arguably deepened his receptivity to Innis's interest in communications, especially in light of articles McLuhan produced in the 1940s leading up to the publication of *The Mechanical Bride* in 1951. As for McLuhan's awareness of Innis, he may have first read Innis's work in 1936 given that his "Discussion in the Social Sciences" and McLuhan's paper, "G.K. Chesterton: A Practical Mystic," appeared in the same edition of *The Dalhousie Review* 25, no. 4.

68 Easterbrook circulated and subsequently discussed Innis's paper with students.

69 W.T. Easterbrook, "Harold Adams Innis, 1894–1952," *American Economic Review* XLIII, no. 1 (March 1953): 8–12 and W.T. Easterbrook, "Innis and Economics," *The Canadian Journal of Economics and Political Science* 19, no. 3 (August 1953): 291–303. Both are re-published in the present volume. See Appendix III and IV, respectively.

contemporaries did not understand his shift in focus Easterbrook thought he did. Second, as it contains points found in Easterbrook's lectures and given that it was completed sometime in the spring of 1953, his year teaching *Innis 4b* clearly had been an illuminating experience. And third, in mapping Innis's intellectual journey, Easterbrook drew from his conversations with Innis in the summer of 1952 and many occasions before.

Innis's career, wrote Easterbrook, involved four developmental phases and an unfinished fifth that occupied him at the end of his life. The first phase concerned "the antecedents of industrialism in Canada."[70] The second began with Innis's studies of "the new industrialism of mining, pulp and paper, and hydro-electric power" and ended with the publication of *The Cod Fisheries*, "a work which carried him beyond his earlier interest in staples to reflections on the problem of empires, the impact of machine industry in exposed regions, and the broader implications of technological change and marketing influences."[71] Around the time of its completion in the late 1930s, Innis initiated a third phase constituting what Easterbrook described as his "intensive study of technological and pricing factors in the area of mechanized communications beginning with printing and the press."[72] The start of Innis's fourth phase, he continued, was announced by his presentation of "Minerva's Owl" in 1947. At this stage, he worked back "from the industrialization of communications to its antecedents in early empires [...]."[73] Then, in his final months, Innis turned to the monumental (but never completed) task of developing "a philosophy of history."[74]

Given that both men identified themselves as economic historians, it appears that Easterbrook's goal was to explain why Innis seemed to have strayed far from this branch of economics. He did this by arguing that this impression was incorrect, indicating that Innis's communications research sought to identify what was shaping the interests and orientations—the *biases*—of contemporary economists. More generally, he said that Innis was trying to develop a universal approach

---

70 Easterbrook, "Innis and Economics," 291.
71 Ibid., 292.
72 Ibid.
73 Ibid.
74 Ibid., 291. In this effort, Easterbrook added that Charles Cochrane's *Christianity and Classical Culture* (London, UK: Oxford University Press, 1940) was of great significance as, like Cochrane, Innis "was searching for concepts useful in 'the adjustment of order to meet the demands of change' ..." Ibid., 303. Cochrane's influence concerning Greek culture, Roman law, and classical studies was extraordinary in part due to their close friendship in Toronto which lasted until Cochrane's death in 1946. Easterbrook stated that "right towards the end he was turning to philosophy. In the last few weeks, he was reading heavily in that area." Specifically, he cited Innis's interest in Kant. Easterbrook Interview, 1972.

to questions concerning intellectual and cultural capacities. In his research on Canadian economic history, Easterbrook wrote that Innis had "viewed technology and pricing factors as an observer [...]." However, through his focus on communications, Innis became more aware of himself as being "inside or part of the universe he sought to explore, subject to influences productive of bias from which there could be no escape other than through knowledge of the forces which produce bias."[75] Although Easterbrook recognized that Innis was interested in this throughout much of his career, it became explicit in 1938 when he assessed the price system as a communications mechanism that mediates a range of intellectual distortions. Easterbrook told his students that Innis called one such distortion "the disease of economic nationalism."

In his lectures, Easterbrook elaborates that Innis's turn to communications emerged alongside his observations involving the velocity of the production process and developments concerning consumer and corporate preferences. While most economists had treated velocity and preferences separately, Innis realized that the subject of communications could provide a means of assessing them interactively and more dynamically. New technologies, especially those developed in (and since) the 19th century involving newspapers and advertising (such as the telegraph), enabled more than just a substantial acceleration in the rate of economic activity—their use and implications also significantly modified consumer orientations toward evermore fashionable products *and ideas*. More generally, Innis recognized that such applications influenced investments and other activities in ways that enabled vested interests to better control space (i.e. markets). However, their use also undermined long-term stability as the resulting cultural environment severely dampened reflective thought and thus rational forms of decision-making.[76]

Easterbrook wrote that Innis's approach to economics had always involved the importance of cultural capacities and relations: "In the shift of interest from [...] trade routes of commerce to the trade routes of culture, from the exchange of staple commodities to the exchange of ideas or information, there is no suggestion of a break or loss of continuity in thought or interests." The closing sentences of Innis's final paper, although predictably abrupt (as Innis died before its completion), reflect this, as does Easterbrook's observation that Innis's later work was marked by a "tendency to turn more directly to consideration of the interrelations of economic and cultural elements."[77] Here, Innis pointed out that the modern newspaper,

75   Ibid., 297.
76   As Easterbrook told students, "I think this realization made him turn more directly to communications and away from the study of staples in terms of a sharp division between technology and pricing of the sort we find in Veblen's *The Engineers and the Price System*."
77   Easterbrook, "Harold Adams Innis," 8–9, 12.

given its growing dependency on mass advertising, "found itself faced with the problem of finding industries with a productive capacity adequate to the demands of purchasers created by advertising." As such, the newspaper "is concerned in a search for mass production industries to meet its advertising requirements. Its position leads it to take a critical attitude towards trusts as narrowing the market or towards the domination of government by a powerful group." Then, and finally, he references the editor of *Ladies' Home Journal*, Edward W. Bok, who "was said to have changed the physical appearance of domestic furniture, eliminated the parlor from domestic architecture and persuaded the Castles to introduce more and better dances."[78]

Easterbrook told students that he thought it was "curious" that Innis's last written communication "should refer to dance—the catering to feminine tastes." Then again, given what Easterbrook himself argued, it is likely that this was another example of Innis compelling readers to reflect on the relationship between velocity and preferences, alongside the mediating role of the newspaper, advertising, the price system, and the resulting cultural (time-neglecting) contradictions that troubled him so profoundly. In relation to these, Innis had become particularly concerned about the fixed capital investments and overhead costs borne by modern industries in their efforts to control communications and transportation activities. Given these pressures, large corporations became increasingly compelled to dominate more aspects of production, distribution, and consumption. In response to their growing power, competitors responded by using sensual and other techniques to garner the attention of potential customers. For Innis, the example of Bok and the Castles arguably reflected and extended this pattern, in a small way furthering the monopolization of ways of thinking that valued spatial control (i.e., market expansion) to the neglect of time.

Easterbrook recognized that the methodology Innis had been developing constituted an extraordinarily ambitious project. Especially from the early 1940s, Innis turned his attention to transhistorical concerns and, to reiterate a point stressed earlier, the survival of civilization. According to Robert Babe and Edward Comor, arguably, "it was the violence of his time, and the inability or unwillingness of scholars to recognize their contributions to that violence, that constituted the conditions from which Innis dedicated himself to researching communications, media, and civilizational history."[79] As Innis pursued this, influenced by Cochrane and other classicists, he was drawn to a philosophical approach inspired by the

---

78 Harold A. Innis, "The Decline in the Efficiency of Instruments Essential in Equilibrium," *American Economic Review* 43, no. 1 (March 1953): 22. In the early 20th century, Vernon and Irene Castle published widely referenced dance manuals.

79 Babe and Comor, "Introduction," XXXIV.

Greeks.⁸⁰ Babe and Comor explain that one reason for Innis's deepening interest in the Greeks

> is their penchant for dialectical thinking and their insistence on seeking balance between and among extremes. Surely, however, another important factor explaining Innis's affinity for the Greeks was their *quest* for absolutes. [...] This quest for absolutes may seem to be at odds with Innis's focus on dialectical materialist reasoning, but that seeming contradiction is muted when we recognize that one of Innis's enduring truths or 'absolutes' was precisely the necessity to maintain a dynamic balance between extremes.⁸¹

In this context and in response to the fragmentation of pursuits in the modern academy, Innis came to recognize the importance of championing a universal ontology alongside his pursuit of a reflective methodology. The fact that this—what Easterbrook referred to as "a philosophy of history"—was at the heart of Innis's work during his last months is made explicit in his final paper in which he states, "I must begin by pleading for a general emphasis on a universal approach and by insisting as an economist that economic history is primarily concerned with the task of extending the universal applicability of economic theory and of strengthening a central core of interest."⁸² For Babe and Comor, Innis sought "a standard of truth that can stand alongside the dynamism of his historicism; an effort to promote an ontology based on the capacity to reflect and understand the historically produced biases and values of one's own culture and, through this method, the biases and values of others."⁸³

Easterbrook provides more evidence in his lectures for this observation. For one thing, two weeks after Innis's death, he told students that a core reason why Innis had established the course seven years previously involved his quest to examine what history might reveal about "this whole problem of human understanding [...]." During this class, he further explained this goal by linking the concerns Innis had regarding the inability of contemporary economists to communicate successfully (even to one another) with the kinds of international misunderstandings occupying the United Nations.

---

80   Edward Comor, "Harold Innis and the Greek Tradition: an essay concerning his ontological transformation," *University of Toronto Quarterly* 89, no. 2 (Spring 2020): 239–64.
81   Babe and Comor, "Introduction," XXII–XXIII.
82   Innis, "The Decline in the Efficiency of Instruments Essential in Equilibrium," 17. In light of Innis's late efforts to develop a universal approach to economics, had he lived it is likely he would have pursued this in his role as president of the AEA, especially given what Easterbrook told students of *Innis 4b* was the Association's "misunderstandings, broken communications, [and divisions involving its many] splinter groups."
83   Babe and Comor, "Introduction," XXIII.

By way of summarizing the uniqueness of the Innis-Easterbrook relationship, after Innis's death Mary Quayle Innis (herself a capable academic) recognized Easterbrook's knowledge of her husband's work by asking him to help decide which of his papers to include in a collection she was editing.[84] Prior to this request, Easterbrook was part of a special university committee to establish the Harold Innis Memorial Fund.[85] He also was named one of the executors of Innis's estate.[86]

In 1956, Easterbrook co-authored an unprecedented and still-used textbook titled, *Canadian Economic History*.[87] In his reflections on it and Easterbrook's subsequent publications, Mel Watkins—Easterbrook's former student and colleague—called his teacher "the last of his kind" among economists in the Innisian mold: "more economic historian and political economist than economist, as much interdisciplinary as disciplinary."[88] Ian Parker (another former student and Toronto colleague), in his overview of the intellectual influences shaping Easterbrook's career, concluded that Innis's writings had been "the strongest."[89]

What Easterbrook taught in *Innis 4b*

Easterbrook organized the course through consultations with Innis, the use of his reading list, and Innis's past essay and exam questions. At the start of the year, he

84 Harold A. Innis, *Essays in Canadian Economic History*, ed. Mary Q. Innis (Toronto, ON: University of Toronto Press, 1956).
85 The fund was set up primarily to support the republication of Innis's key works.
86 Easterbrook's role included the task of recompiling, reviewing, and revising Innis's files for the University of Toronto archives. Also, with fellow executors Creighton and another Toronto colleague, S.D. Clark, he was tasked to assess the possibility of publishing Innis's incomplete 2,400-page manuscript titled, "A History of Communications." Although, ultimately, it was deemed unpublishable, Easterbrook helped to sort it out, have it microfilmed, and then distribute copies to other universities. Watson, *Marginal Man*, 279 and 473 n. 43.
87 W.T. Easterbrook and Hugh Aitken, *Canadian Economic History* (Toronto, ON: Macmillan, 1956).
88 Mel Watkins, "Personal Reflections," n.d. available at <https://sce.library.utoronto.ca/index.php/Easterbrook,_William_Thomas_James>.
89 Parker, "Introduction," xv. Easterbrook embraced Innis's interest in long-period economic development by extending several of his mentor's concepts and methodological principles. According to Parker, an incomplete list of Innis's influences includes Easterbrook's focus on the sources and dynamics shaping long-term structural development; his historical and structural analyses of the uncertainties and capacities influencing thoughts and activities in particular places and times; and Easterbrook's similar interest in the dialectics of political-economic interaction involving center-margin and core-periphery relations. In each of these, like Innis, Easterbrook placed great emphasis on initial phases of development involving political, economic, and cultural conditions, as well as the relational configurations that shape the institutional developments that mediate historical trajectories. Ibid., xxvi.

told students that they would address three pillars of Innis's approach. The *first* was Innis on the subject of "Communications." Under this heading, the goal would be to clarify "why [there is] so much fuss about it." The *second* subject was "Bias" which would be applied alongside several dialectical pairings: the oral and written traditions, church and empire, Roman and common law, rigidity and flexibility, monopoly and competition, and space and time. The *third* subject for study was "Survival." On this, Easterbrook mentioned three sub-themes: the role and use of *force*, the role played by *values*, and the implications of these and other factors on *culture* (and culture's implications for a society's capacity to survive).

Although Easterbrook did not present *Innis 4b* quite in the way that he suggested he would, he did indeed focus on communications, bias, and survival. For the most part, the lectures presented here are as Easterbrook left them and the editor has retained their ordering in accordance with the dates he provided. In this section, some of what he presented is summarized, beginning with (i) what was addressed from the beginning of the Fall until late October (the eve of Innis's death), (ii) what was discussed after Innis died through until mid-February, and (iii) what the class talked about during its final two months.

(i) September 23–October 28

In his first meeting with students, Easterbrook summarized Innis's approach and objectives. "I have known Innis for twenty years," he said, "[and I have] worked very closely with his approach [...] *yet* to set out his position [...] amounts to an act of courage, though possibly not an act of wisdom [...]." Easterbrook proceeded to trace Innis's interest in communications back to his work on economic history, especially that involving the "presence of heavy fixed costs" and his analyses of "techniques of exploitation." But as Innis turned his attention to modern industrial society, he was compelled to examine developments that more directly involved media and communications. Innis, he explained, found that "technological and price factors [...] *interacted* with other elements, institutional and ideational, and that reference to some larger structure, nation, empire, civilization, was necessary if this *process of interactions* [...] was to have any meaning." Through this complex lens, one that impelled him to assess the implications of the press, radio, and other mass media, Innis came to recognize their "considerable *power to* influence, [and] even *control* public opinion [...]." This led Innis to explore, in earnest, "the issues of *power* and sanction, freedom and monopoly, space and time" as he understood that "[c]ontrol of communications systems *means* power to mould, shape ideas [...]." Furthermore, Easterbrook explained, Innis discovered that "media [...] can produce *biases* in outlook which in the past have destroyed civilizations."

Easterbrook recounted the steps that Innis took on the path to this conclusion. Once he addressed the "omnipresent problem" of bias and its deleterious implications on the capacity to understand, Innis, he said, found himself having to deal more directly with issues such as power and authority, the status of freedom in human relations, and questions concerning stability and survival. In other words, Innis "became a cultural historian, focusing on the rise and fall of civilizations—why for some stability persists over many centuries, why others are comparatively short-lived; a pretty important question today [...] [given that the uncertainty of] our own prospects for survival is apparent."

Easterbrook explained that for Innis bias reflects, essentially, a "lack of balance between [...] contrasting or opposing forces" resulting in "an undue emphasis on the one [to the] neglect of the other." Initially, Innis developed bias to better comprehend the absence of what an economist might call the conditions needed for equilibrium and associated an absence of balance with a "neglect of factors indispensable to survival of a culture or empire." In the mid-20th century, this neglect was discernable in an overwhelming preoccupation with both the short-run and spatial control. These, said Easterbrook, are characteristics of nation-states and the efforts of businesses to access and control markets which, for Innis, reflected and perpetuated a neglect of time or duration. The outcome of this, he added, "may well be fatal."

In October, Easterbrook elaborated Innis's methodology by referencing a premise they both shared: throughout history technologies and techniques emerge and are applied in response to various kinds of survival needs while their application, in turn, entails the construction of institutionalized arrangements involving particular values. From this starting point, Innis then addressed innumerable dichotomies and contradictions and, as such, pursued a "theory of change" that emphasized the "strains and stress in [the] structure of control" yielding a "loss of balance, of disequilibrium in the structure." Easterbrook also made a surprising statement in relation to this: in investigating these dynamics, Innis is studying "the problem of *bureaucracy* in history—why some lack powers of duration, why others have such powers, and why all bureaucracies, sooner or later, rot and give way to other bureaucracies. It is from this postulate that he examines the rise and fall of empires, great aggregations of political and religious power [...]."[90]

---

90 In emphasizing bureaucracy, Easterbrook almost certainly was referencing Innis's analyses of most large-scale organizations, especially states, and empires. In his May 21 response to a letter from Frank Knight dated May 15, 1952, Innis associated bureaucracy directly with monopolies of knowledge. Answering Knight's questions about the tendency for communications to become one-sided, Innis related this to "the universal tendency towards centralization and monopoly" and continued as follows: "The only theory about the whole question which I would like to venture at the moment is that this one-sidedness seems to lead to monopoly and to general

Easterbrook also outlined Innis's concerns regarding monopolies of knowledge, control over space and/or time, endogenous and exogenous threats to status quo relations, as well as the intellectual capacities of those occupying marginal political, economic, and cultural positions. In these first weeks of the course, Easterbrook stressed Innis's values concerning "freedom of thought and action" and associated these with his background in economic history (forged as a graduate student at University of Chicago) and his later self-identification as a "cultural historian" who idealized "the values of Greece and its oral tradition [...]." From these foundations, Innis sought to "answer [...] the age-old problem of [...] reconciling freedom and change with order and stability." For Innis, said Easterbrook,

> Freedom is not the antithesis but rather a necessary condition of order and stability—a successful bureaucracy, i.e., successful in terms of space and time (power and sanction) is, for him, inconceivable without wide scope for free and spontaneous action and discussion. Without it, [...] a hardening of the structure must result in failure to cope with change within or without the area of control, [involving] death of [the] creative spirit. [...] Freedom, in short, is a necessary condition of bureaucratic stability; ordinarily this should be productive of the pessimism most historians are prone to [...]. No such pessimism here. His values are clear-cut, his structural framework equally so, and it is a refreshing change from the almost universal tendency [...] to state such problems in terms of two extremes [...].

Easterbrook implied that the dialectics Innis employed were those of someone resisting reductionist and mechanistic analyses. Late in October, he demonstrated this by referencing Innis's historically informed reflective methodology and the fact that his more sociological writings often critique the unreflective character of "the mass mind, uniform and dead." His approach also involves "a problem which is central to his work"—the "problem of sanctions." Sanctions for Innis are institutionalized forms of faith that, according to Easterbrook, "must be established and maintained if any given structure is to survive." This, he continued, "rests in the end on sanction and sanction is a problem of communication [...]." Innis's interest in this largely unconscious dimension—one concerning shared, taken-for-granted, common sense ways of thinking—involved an elaboration of bias in terms of its implications for contemporary affairs. He raised questions, for example, about public opinion in the United States in light of its more hysterical elements who, in Easterbrook's words, "use force to see that [their] faith is not disturbed." Innis, said Easterbrook, recognized that survival required the pursuit of "greater

> corruption and bureaucracy to the point that it is eventually burned out. I am most grateful to you for your clear statement of what I have tried to say in a bungling fashion. The problem seems to be that of working out a sustained attack on the factors responsible for the one-sidedness." File 06, box 011, Accession B1972-0025, University of Toronto Archives.

enlightenment as to the culture which we take for granted." It was this goal and the need to understand the conditions and mediations undermining self-refection that compelled Innis to champion values concerning freedom over control.

Through the early autumn, Easterbrook brought attention to various capacities afforded by language. For example, he called *Nineteen Eighty-Four* a "very sophisticated book" concerning the use of language to destroy the disruptive implications of creative thought. Easterbrook explained that Innis was impressed by Orwell's association of words with efforts to control space and time, as well as the implications of language on law as a primary institutional mediator of values associated with order and freedom. Unlike many subsequent representations of Innis, Easterbrook thus emphasized that dominant biases involve much more than the materials and technologies used to communicate as he also assessed the biases of broader forms of media, including words and language. As a result, Easterbrook's lectures for *Innis 4b* likely will surprise many as several of the readings he references, drawn from those previously assigned by Innis, address semantics. This, arguably, became increasingly germane for Innis in relation to his later interest in the mediating role of law.[91] By comparing ancient Greek with Latin, English with French, and so forth, and in relating these to power relations and other influential media (from writing technologies to institutions such as economics), Easterbrook demonstrated Innis to have become increasingly interested in how language affected, among other things, what people are able to conceptualize. Once this interest is made explicit, students of Innis will recognize how often he references semantics and the capacities afforded by language.[92]

In sum, Easterbrook underlined that Innis's approach "is not one-factor theorising about history" and added that there should be no notion that a predominant communications technology "is the only element nor always the decisive one."

On the eve of Innis's passing, referencing *Empire and Communications*, Easterbrook explained another key to Innis's methodology—his use of Weberian ideal-types. One of the most important of these was what Innis referred to as the cultural fluorescence of ancient Greece (or what he called the Greek tradition).

---

91   Edward Comor, "Law as a Mediating Institution of History: The Approach and Strategy of Harold Innis," *University of Toronto Quarterly* 91, no. 2 (May 2022): 1–32.
92   In fact, the first paper assignment asked students to assess different legal traditions in light of the capacities afforded by "words." The question sheet for this assignment almost certainly duplicated what Innis had prepared and it indicates that students should use Sir Ernest Gowers's *Plain Words, A Guide to the Use of English*, to complete it (citation provided in lecture notes). By comparing earlier reading lists for *Innis 4b*, it is apparent that this book was only added to the course in 1951. In addition to Gowers, Easterbrook suggested additional works concerning language. For reading lists and a copy of this assignment, see Appendix I.

It constituted for Innis, said Easterbrook, "the polar extreme or opposite from centralized, rigid bureaucracy, with its monopoly of communications." In contrast to this ideal, Easterbrook went on to discuss how the centralization of power taking place in the 20th century was being mediated in part through radio and television, and that Innis referenced the cultural dynamism of the Greek city-state as a means of putting such contemporary developments into stark relief. Innis, he said, sought "freedom from monopolies of knowledge" and, as such, implicitly directed his readers to address conditions and factors in Greece as ideal-type means of comparison.⁹³

(ii) November 18–February 10

Innis died on November 8. Two days later, the University of Toronto held his funeral, classes were canceled, and offices were closed so that faculty and staff could attend. Given that November 11 in Canada was a mandatory holiday (Remembrance Day), Easterbrook did not hold another class until the 18th which he began by commenting on Innis's death, his values, and his concerns about civilization. In making these remarks, Easterbrook emphasized his turn to classical studies and recent interest in law as a mediating factor in history.

Easterbrook again related Innis's assessment of law to the dialectic of order and freedom. Mediating institutions such as law, for Innis, influenced a problem that was common to imperial projects: the tendency for empires to decline due to forces impelling disequilibrium. This was (and remains) a problem often stemming from power being exercised in ways that undermine reflective forms of knowledge. In addressing Innis's concerns regarding these universal tendencies, Easterbrook underlined how Charles Cochrane's reflections on political thought in Rome influenced Innis's thinking on problems concerning time, order, and continuity, especially Cochrane's analysis of "the false doctrine"—the (biased) search for perfection through political action.⁹⁴ In a subsequent class, Easterbrook stressed that Innis's interest in communications involved his recognition that "how [...] people understand or fail to understand one another via the exchange of ideas" is not

---

93   In keeping with this approach Innis recognized that the Greek city-state had a fatal flaw—a flaw that was, in fact, a value that Innis, in the much different context of the 20th century, championed: individualism. In Greece, however, following Plato, Innis recognized that individualism overdone produces tyrants. In what was to be the final class before Innis's death, Easterbrook summarized this position as one in which the need for self-expression had to be reconciled with stability (i.e., the balancing of freedom with order). Greece, from the 6th-century B.C., came closest to this ideal.

94   Cochrane, *Christianity and Classical Culture*, 355.

"merely a problem of different languages and cultural backgrounds [...]." As he put it, "this is what Innis took up as his primary concern—what light had history to throw on this whole problem of human understanding [...]."

Again, rather than straightforwardly articulating his theories, Innis chose to engage readers by compelling them to think about what he was saying. Using history and ideal-types, for example, he sought to spark an awareness of the complex forces and dynamics shaping predominant biases, including the biases of the reader encountering his work. One of Innis's goals in doing this, said Easterbrook, was to help "people to understand themselves [...] since he believed to the end that increasing knowledge of the forces which shape our thoughts and thinking processes is itself an antidote, or at least a hope that we will achieve clear vision in time."

During the first class of the new year, Easterbrook reminded students that Innis's interest in preserving individual freedom developed in the context of his concerns regarding the survival of civilization. According to Easterbrook, the "aggressive individualism" that characterized the activities of the Northwest Company during the fur trade was "fundamentally the same problem" that faced the Greek city-state. Such questions concerning order and freedom, he conceded, were not new, but Innis addressed these differently as he gave "the study of communications a strongly historical bent formerly lacking and in doing this he greatly enlarged the area of enquiry ..." More than this, as Easterbrook put it in his memorial tribute, "communications seemed to be the most effective approach to an understanding of the larger environment of economic activity" as it involves an analysis of a complex of relational factors involving "every avenue of human experience." This then furnished Innis with a possible means of redressing misunderstandings that stem from the multiplication of specializations in the modern academy. For Innis, said Easterbrook, "it was high time that localized monopolies of knowledge [...] were broken down."[95]

At the end of his life, Innis turned his attention to how his concept of bias might be applied to gain a better understanding of the work of economists and, more broadly, the institution of economics. It was in this context, said Easterbrook, that Innis observed that economists working in the world's core nation-state—the United States—often unknowingly embrace an unreflective form of nationalism.[96]

95 Easterbrook, "Harold Adams Innis," 10–11.
96 Innis traced this bias to a complex of factors including the implications of predominant media such as language, law, and statistics. The political-economic and cultural conditions and dynamics here, as in most of Innis's writings, are implicit, as are his references to the rising use of statistics amid a taken-for-granted embrace of efficiency, technology, and growth. "Progress," wrote Innis, "has been defined as that kind of effort that can be measured in statistics. [...] They are collected with relation to specific distinctive problems of states with different constitutions

Easterbrook told the class that for Innis this orientation involved "the process of hardening" that often emerges in a climate of uncertainty, especially one in which the predominance of writing (and neglect of orality) furthers "the process of bureaucratisation [...]."

Innis often used terms and concepts without clear exposition. Words like media, monopoly, knowledge, and capital were applied in ways that sometimes were unclear, even to his closest colleagues. For the most part, Easterbrook again was an exception and the references he makes in his notes regarding these words, the Greek tradition, and Weber's ideal-type method should be read with his relatively intimate knowledge of Innis in mind. In the classes held on January 20 and 27, Easterbrook also discussed Innis's ideal-type *empire*: Byzantium. On these dates, he presented a remarkable summary of Innis's arguments concerning its unmatched success, including its capacity to balance coercive mechanisms with religion through the medium of art.[97] Easterbrook explained that the Byzantines found some amount of equilibrium between stability and individualism by combining an "Oriental authority held in check by Roman bureaucracy and its trained executive supported by Greek democracy." More generally, this propitious tension (involving the use of papyrus by its spatially focused bureaucrats and parchment by a temporally oriented ecclesiastical order) enabled, in Easterbrook's words, "the wisdom of the ancients" to survive. The case of Byzantium also was important as it provided Innis with a means of providing readers with the perspective needed to assess the contemporary American empire and its obsession with spatial control. Like officials in Washington, DC, the Byzantines, said Easterbrook, had "a realistic awareness of the importance of political power" but, relative to mid-20th-century Americans, they were far more aware "of its limitations and the dangers of a one-sided concern with the problems of the moment [...]."

In the last class held in January, Easterbrook returned to Innis's interest in the biases of economists and used his analysis of Byzantium to flip the logic applied by followers of John Maynard Keynes on its head:

> [...]. They are suppressed and distorted for military purposes and their value depends on the literacy of the populations concerned." Innis, "The Decline in the Efficiency of Instruments Essential in Equilibrium," 18–19.

97 Innis compared Byzantium's ability to balance space and time with both ancient Rome and the West. During these lectures, Easterbrook referenced an unpublished paper by Innis titled "Concept of Monopoly and Civilization"—a paper Innis presented in Paris in 1951. Three years later, Easterbrook had it published in the journal edition he helped edit with McLuhan and Carpenter. See Harold A. Innis, "Monopoly and Civilization," *Explorations, Studies in Culture and Communication* 3 (August 1954): 84–90.

> The Keynesians tell us that failure to cope with the short-run means no long-run. [But we] could argue that our failure to take into consideration long-run elements of permanence is a guarantee of an unstable and very brief short-run. This represents much of the difference between the thinking of Keynes and Schumpeter [...] [as we] cannot assume that the long-run will look after itself, and if the pressure is so great that we must concentrate exclusively on the short-run the game is up anyway. Innis's concern was that in the state of communications is to be found the Keynesian's attitudes toward time and [...] [their naïve] faith in the ability of the political machinery to keep things rolling—both biases of a paper civilization.[98]

Classes held in early to mid-February went on to address Innis's treatment of Western Europe and the role played by writing in relation to other factors. Subjects covered included developments in paper and printing, divisions in Christianity, the emergence of the university, the role of Latin and vernaculars relative to heretical writings, and the political-economic and cultural implications of law. Throughout these lectures, Easterbrook framed or related these and other subjects to Innis's dialectical media-focused approach. One of the more important things Innis addressed, explained Easterbrook, was the rise of nationalism, especially as he thought that its role in the violence of the 20th century needed to be much better understood. Innis, said Easterbrook, traced modern nationalism to a "national feeing" that emerged alongside changes in communications (especially those involving the printing press) that accompanied the rise of monarchical power in relation to the Church ("national or state particularism," as Easterbrook put it, had "disrupted the universalism of the ecclesiastical organization"). Monarchies developed monopolies of knowledge through their political-economic organization using paper (involving trade and the development of urban economies) while the Church pursued its power through rural monasticism and parchment.

On the development of the modern press, Easterbrook reiterated and clarified Innis's arguments. The press had a sufficient national and international history to provide insights into its long-run implications while it was modern enough to spark the interest of contemporary readers. Innis paid particular attention to its history in England and Easterbrook's lectures followed this focus. Through this research, Easterbrook said that Innis developed his earlier analysis of spatial control involving European-North American core-periphery relations toward, instead, the time problem involving the changing nature and use of power by ruling interests involving communication and media. Following this shift, Innis also assessed the implications of institutions such as law and the nation. On the latter, Easterbrook elaborated the dynamics that Innis had emphasized and underlined something

---

98 The reader is reminded of the importance for Innis of Cochrane's analysis of "the false doctrine" (discussed above).

that became uppermost in his mind—the relationship of commercial communications with the extreme instabilities characterizing the 20th century.

Easterbrook went on to explain that in Innis's final paper he postulated that unprecedented fixed capital investments and overhead costs associated with modern industry were having a decisive influence on the cultural norms mediated by newspapers, advertising, and politics. Here and elsewhere, one of the great strengths of Easterbrook's analysis is that he never loses sight of how Innis's studies on economic development and decline informed and were interrelated with his communications research. For one thing, Innis associated modes of thinking to his observation that economies typically operate at less than full capacity.[99] Easterbrook referenced commercial radio to provide students with a contemporary example. According to Innis, it emerged in response to the need among businesses to grow and accelerate mass consumption in order to pay down debts and redress unused capacities (mostly those associated with manufacturing and distributional infrastructures). Rather than a transition from printing to orality (or sight to sound), commercial radio elaborated dynamics stemming from these investments, impelling corporations to expand and accelerate the whole production, distribution, and consumption process. For Innis, the space-controlling and time-annihilating biases mediated by radio were very much related to the economics of modern capitalism.[100]

A point emphasized at this stage of the course was that, for Innis, modern media and communications constitute disruptions in daily life that are so fundamental they impel unreflective (if not reactionary) responses. For example, nationalist orientations used in ways that mobilize publics erect barriers between peoples and, in the process, distort or oversimplify a range of issues. Misunderstandings thus had multiplied alongside the use of violence. Put another way, contemporary communications developments were mediating an entrenched state of

---

99 For example, the history of Canada demonstrated that the investments and costs entailed in its development were accompanied by certain rigidities and unused capacities. For Innis, given the often pressing need not only for an economic system to survive (usually a predominant macroeconomic concern among state officials) but also for individual companies to redress potentially wasted investments, he thought that various kinds of fixed capital structures and overhead costs constituted largely unseen forces shaping history. On the relationship between Innis's communications studies and his work involving such economic concepts, see Ian Parker, "Harold Innis: Staples, Communications, and the Economics of Capacity," in *Explorations in Canadian Economic History: Essays in Honour of Irene M. Spry*, ed. Duncan Cameron (Ottawa: University of Ottawa Press, 1985), 73–93.

100 Unlike other political economists, for Innis the economic dynamics involving debt were just as important as the need for revenue. "The economics of losses," he wrote, "is not less significant than the economics of profits." Innis, *Political Economy in the Modern State*, 166.

disequilibrium in which nationalism was undermining what Innis believed was crucial for survival: the capacity to engage in the reflective thought needed to facilitate understanding both within and across nation-state borders.[101]

(iii) February 17–March 21[102]

From mid-February, Easterbrook proceeded with a detailed discussion of Innis's analysis of the modern press. For Innis, the press had become "an integrated part of the entire social organism affecting and being affected by the society of which it is a part [...]." To illustrate, Easterbrook pointed out that the decline in state controls over the press in late 18th-century England "parallels the growth of enterprise and an increase in democratic processes" which "cannot be seen apart from [their] social and political context." Easterbrook also implicitly noted Innis's recognition of vested interests as agents of history—agents who struggled with one another over certain freedoms and who applied (or were subjected to) new methods of manipulation, often involving public opinion.

Easterbrook stressed that one reason why Innis often provided much historical detail in his writing was that he wanted to compel readers to consider the complex antecedents of otherwise taken-for-granted realities. Freedom of the press and representative democracy were two examples. Easterbrook also told students that while Innis assessed both the content of and the form in which communications developments influenced social relations, the latter was more important. He illustrated this by referencing newspapers in the United States. From the late 19th century, given significant new supplies of newsprint and hydro-electric power from Canada—constituting an important dynamic in the context Innis's theories concerning unused capacity—wider circulations were prioritized in order to deliver more prospective consumers to advertisers seeking larger markets. In relation to this, businesses were compelled to produce more commodities for lower and uniform prices. Increasingly, then, news organizations focused on their ability to,

---

101 The university—for Innis, the one institution capable of redressing this crisis—was not only under threat, most of the intellectuals it housed were unaware of their biases and the implications of this for survival. To illustrate, Easterbrook mentioned to students a review of *The Bias of Communication* by E.R. Adair. Innis, said Easterbrook, was "aware that he was going against the current and his pessimism appears to be soundly based, particularly when so-called learned gentlemen can write the fatuous sort of review that appears in the last issue of *The Canadian Historical Review*." Easterbrook pointed out that Adair demonstrated "no awareness of what he was getting at nor the technique he was applying [...]." E.R. Adair, "*The Bias of Communication*," *The Canadian Historical Review* 33, no. 4 (December 1952): 393–4.

102 It is likely that the final class took place on March 21 as students were to give end of year presentations on their essay assignments following that date. The final exam was held on April 13.

in Easterbrook's words, "catch the eye" in ways that might better capture emotions and sentiments. Innis observed that one cumulative effect on American culture was its greater sensitivity to *change itself*. This outcome, he thought, was profoundly significant as newspaper companies magnified relatively isolated developments into potentially world-altering events, and they were doing this at a rate and speed that rendered reflective thought almost impossible.[103]

In his final paper, Innis set out to further his arguments on how the newspaper and other mass media had mediated a disastrous change in intellectual and cultural capacities. Among other things, he addressed how advertising influenced rates of change, as well as how this affected the research and policy prescriptions of economists. The one price system that newspapers, magazines, and commercial radio enabled on behalf of advertisers fueled a dramatic growth in consumer demand. This alongside significant technical advances in communications constituted underassessed factors yielding more production and concentrated (vertical and horizontal) ownership patterns. Among other points, Innis understood that while capital-intensive communications developments compelled monopolistic tendencies among corporations, newspapers and other commercial media were becoming increasingly dependent on such gigantic organizations for their revenues. Modern communications developments, contributing directly to the increasing speed and scale of industrial and commercial activities, were not just undertheorized—according to Innis they had become crucial and dangerous components of complex modern economies and crisis-laden cultures.

Innis believed that a culture of irrational optimism concerning economic growth in the 20th century consequently had deepened and this was compounding the harmful implications of economic downturns. He hypothesized also that certain conditions were impelling a mostly unseen bias in the institution of economics itself, involving its emphasis on case method, a preoccupation with short-run developments, and the failure of most economists to understand the harm they were doing (not just to their profession but also to public policy). As Innis's determination to address these concerns were to have been the bases of his inaugural address as president of the AEA, Easterbrook told students that he was "certain" that its members had been "saved a good wallop [...] by his inability to complete the paper."

In these final weeks, Easterbrook reiterated that Innis's association of economic and communications developments with cultural change did not reflect

---

103 In recognizing this, Innis developed some amount of disdain for mass media. In 1941, he admitted to his wife Mary that he avoided "newspapers and radio like the plague." Quoted in Watson, *Marginal Man*, 236.

the analysis of a technological or media determinist.[104] Innis, he added, always recognized communications to be "inseparable from people's way of life" and, as such, "drastic changes" may be so "upsetting" as to compel "the substitution of thought for action." Significant modifications in the quantitative and qualitative or spatial and temporal dimensions of human relations that can occur in such circumstances may alter the meaning of shared symbols, while new symbols might be hard to find. Innis also recognized that technological advances, especially those related to communications, render time to be an extraordinarily important but undertheorized variable in terms of its meaning and implications. In fact, Easterbrook told students that Innis had considered alternative titles for his final paper. Rather than "The Decline in the Efficiency of Instruments Essential in Equilibrium" (the title used when it was published), he considered emphasizing to his fellow economists that their conceptualizations of time were themselves significant sources of misunderstanding by calling his piece either "The Menace of Absolutism in Time" or "Bias in Economics." Perhaps as a result of Easterbrook's suggestion, the official AEA program for the conference used the latter title.[105]

In concluding *Innis 4b*, Easterbrook emphasized the values needed for a relatively balanced state of order and freedom to re-emerge. According to Innis, mechanized thinking involving price system valuations and the instabilities related to rapid change had, as Easterbrook put it, made "cultural suicide" almost "inevitable." It is in this context that Innis intended his AEA presentation to be more than a critique of mainstream economics. He also wanted to specify how the orientations of economists—most of whom he thought lacked any interest in universal principles or self-reflection—were undermining society's analytical and temporal capabilities. According to Easterbrook, "economics itself cannot be disassociated from human values and emotions, but reflects them to a point where *economic theory* itself changes with *changing attitudes* [...]."

---

104 Innis, wrote Easterbrook, "was too aware of the close interrelations of technology with institutions and physical environment to fall into this trap." More specifically, for Innis, "changes over history in the technology of communications are themselves culturally conditioned, and Innis's writings on law, religion and politics attest to the absence of technological determinism [...]." Easterbrook, "Harold Adams Innis," 11.

105 The full title used was "Presidential Address: Bias in Economics" and at least parts of it were read by Chester Wright. Vincent Bladen and Easterbrook made memorial comments while Joseph Willits presented a paper titled "Contribution to Scholarship." American Economic Association, *Program of Annual Meetings 1952*, 41–2, available at <https://www.aeaweb.org/Annual_Meeting/assa_programs/ASSA_1952.pdf>.

The presentations made by Bladen, Easterbrook, and Willits were published with Innis's paper in the *American Economic Review* (cited above).

In his last formal remarks, Easterbrook asked, "Where was this taking him?" He finished the course with the following response:

> [It is] not easy to say [...] but [there is] not much question, that his main concern was with *the bias in economics induced by the state of communications* [...] [in terms of] the spatial bias of economics; its case method; its preoccupation with the short-run; its failure to understand the forces which shaped the preconceptions and the interests of economists; [and] economics as an aspect of communications, to be understood and improved as a discipline through a better understanding of itself. The theme should be familiar—*one way to freedom is to understand the forces which would enslave us.* [...] [This, Innis believed, is] the beginning of wisdom—everything else is futile without it.

Easterbrook ended by expressing his appreciation "for the cooperation you have shown—not an easy year for any of us—but if you once latch on to the problems Innis was concerned with, you'll probably never be the same again."

Course readings

The archival file containing Easterbrook's notes includes a list of readings inserted among lectures scheduled for October. However, it is apparent that this was prepared at a later date as several of the publications included were not available prior to Innis's death in November.[106] There is no record of a course syllabus and, given that such outlines were not commonly prepared in this period, it might be assumed that Easterbrook wrote the list sometime in the spring of 1953. Below, this list has been reproduced in the order that Easterbrook wrote it.[107]

> Harold A. Innis, "The Strategy of Culture," "The Press, a neglected factor in the economic history of the twentieth century," and "Great Britain, the United States and Canada," in *Changing Concepts of Time* (Toronto, ON: University of Toronto Press, 1953).
> Harold A. Innis, "Industrialism and Cultural Values," "The English Publishing Trade in the Eighteenth Century," "Technology and Public Opinion in the United States," and "A Critical Review," in *The Bias of Communication* (Toronto, ON: University of Toronto Press, 1951).

---

106 For example, Easterbrook's "Innis and Economics" was not likely completed before the spring of 1953. McLuhan's reflections on Innis "The Later Innis" was published in January 1953 and Deutsch's *Nationalism and Social Communication* also was published in early 1953.

107 Readers might want to compare this list with those drawn up by Innis, likely in 1951 (provided in this volume's Appendix I).

J.B. Brebner, "Harold Adams Innis: 1894–1952," *The Economic Journal* 63 no. 251 (September 1953): 728–33.

W.T. Easterbrook, "Harold Adams Innis, 1894–1952," *American Economic Review* XLIII, no. 1 (March 1953): 8–12.[108]

Marshall McLuhan, "The Later Innis," *Queen's Quarterly* 60, no. 3 (January 1953): 385–94.

Lyman Bryson, ed., *The Communication of Ideas* (New York, NY: Harper and Brothers, 1948).

Marshall McLuhan, *The Mechanical Bride* (New York, NY: Vanguard Press, 1951).

Norbert Wiener, *The Human Use of Human Beings* (Boston, MA: Houghton Mifflin, 1950).[109]

Eric Havelock, *The Crucifixion of Intellectual Man* (Boston, MA: Beacon Press, 1950).

Karl Deutsch, *Nationalism and Social Communication* (Cambridge, MA: M.I.T. Press, 1953).

Sigfried Giedion, *Space, Time and Architecture* (Cambridge, MA: Harvard University Press, 1951).

George Orwell, *Nineteen Eighty-Four* (London, UK: Secker & Warburg, 1949).[110]

In several lectures Easterbrook uses or references other books and articles. Chapters from *Empire and Communications*, for example, were read as it was cited extensively. Easterbrook also mentions Cochrane's *Christianity and Classical Culture* and in November stated that "in some ways [this is] the most useful book in the reading list."

Throughout the year, Easterbrook suggested additional readings for the course and to help students with their assignments. References to these can be found in his lecture notes.

---

[108] As Easterbrook used the same title for his subsequent 1953 paper, "Innis and Economics," the editor assumes this to have been an error and has corrected it.
[109] Easterbrook used a different title for this book: "*Cybernetics, Human Use of Human Beings.*"
[110] Orwell's book is listed in square brackets, perhaps indicating it to be of interest but not required.

The contemporary significance of Easterbrook's notes and Innis's approach

It may be argued that among Innis's contemporaries several were well-positioned to understand his work and intellectual trajectory. Marshall McLuhan, Donald Creighton, Irene Spry, Frank Knight, Eric Havelock, or perhaps his wife Mary or son Donald might be listed. But for the reasons discussed above, it was Easterbrook who had the direct knowledge needed of both his economics and communications studies to teach *Innis 4b*. More than this (and to repeat), throughout the summer of 1952 the two met to discuss, among other things, Innis's work and interests going forward. Furthermore, the responsibility of teaching Innis's course (involving his use of Innis's readings and having to explain them to a large group of undergraduates) almost certainly focused Easterbrook's mind on what his mentor was saying with more precision than anyone else had to. Had Innis retained his notes, surely he would have shared them with Easterbrook. But as there is no trace of this, the lectures prepared by Easterbrook constitute the best record we have of what Innis wanted taught in his signature course.

The lecture notes that follow this introduction provide readers with insights into Innis's thinking. On his methodology, for example, they revive key aspects that have been marginalized. By forgetting that many of the concepts Innis developed for his communications research are rooted in (and interrelated with) his work concerning political economy, many have been indifferent to the importance of relating concepts such as bias and monopolies of knowledge to his unique (non-Marxist) dialectical materialism.[111] Easterbrook appears to anticipate such difficulties (recalling, perhaps, his conversations with McLuhan) when he remarked that although "many bright people [...] outside the area of economics [...] are repelled by its [...] materialism," economics itself is "a useful corrective [...] for speculative thinking which can become very woolly at the edges unless cross-checked [...] by reference to the material fact."[112] Easterbrook went on to

---

111 For a widely read example of this not occurring, see Joshua Meyrowitz, "Medium Theory," in *Communication Theory Today*, ed. David J. Crowley and David Mitchell (Cambridge, UK: Polity Press, 1994), 50–77. A more recent instance is the treatment Innis receives in Nick Couldry and Andreas Hepp, *The Mediated Construction of Reality* (Cambridge, UK: Polity Press, 2017).

112 It is difficult to say how much of Easterbrook's direct knowledge of Innis was consciously rejected by McLuhan although, based on his jettisoning of Innis's political economy, McLuhan's receptiveness appears to have been highly selective. Easterbrook and McLuhan were known to argue. Even following the latter's stroke in 1979, when McLuhan's ability to speak had become extremely limited, McLuhan sometimes responded to his friend by turning the volume on his radio up to full volume. Marchand, *Marshall McLuhan*, 272.

say that although grounding one's analysis to "hard items" such as "basic resources and technologies" may be "hard on those who go in for the building of elaborate structures of speculation" (perhaps constituting "a check" on their "imagination"), "it is scarcely a curb on the use of intelligence." The likelihood that Innis would have agreed should be acknowledged if, going forward, the gulf dividing idealist from materialist treatments of his work is to be corrected. Beyond the importance of accuracy, however, is the fact that such divisions were anathema to Innis's methodology, especially given his concerns regarding the role played by intellectuals in perpetuating the crisis he associated with misunderstanding. Of course, this is not to say that others must agree with Innis but, instead, that they should understand what he is saying before representing his work as something to be embraced, developed, or criticized.

Easterbrook explained Innis's interest in studying communications to be, in part, a strategic response to the ongoing march of specialization. Specialization itself constituted a communications problem that Innis responded to by pursuing a more universal approach. To quote Easterbrook from a lecture he delivered in October 1953, for Innis there were "too many voices, talking too fast [...]—coaxing, manipulating, buy this, believe that...."[113]

A common recognition that all social activity requires communication involving media (broadly defined to include organizations and institutions) might, Innis thought, help break down barriers. Moreover, given that changes in communications imply or generate a complex of quantitative and qualitative developments of interest to more than just social scientists (but to those engaged in the humanities and natural sciences also), the subject of communication (not to mention media ecology) should be an attractive area for many going forward. In the decades that followed, however, despite McLuhan's fame and role in making communications and media studies extraordinarily popular, it soon became yet another siloed field in the academy.

Easterbrook's lectures address Innis's use of juxtapositions, dichotomies, and contradictions. Among other things, these provide correctives to the tendency of many to mechanistically reproduce the prescriptions Innis gave regarding the need to balance spatial and temporal biases. Space and time as universal indices of existence structured through media can never and will never exist in a sustained state of harmony. Instead, biases were heuristic tools informed by ideal-types that Innis associated with particular values. This is not to say that Innis was satisfied with using bias only as a concept. As Easterbrook mentions in his notes, Innis participated in several government commissions that, for him, involved investigations into how

---

113 This lecture, dated October 29, 1953, was prepared for the subsequent year of *Innis 4b* and is in file 11, box 014, Accession B1979-0039, University of Toronto Archives.

dominant values might be modified to redress space-time imbalances and related issues (as in his "The Strategy of Culture" which Innis framed as a "footnote to the Massey Report"—Canada's *Royal Commission on National Development in the Arts, Letters and Sciences*).[114]

Innis often asked if the culture being assessed favored living/reflective forms of knowledge *or* dead/mechanized ways of thinking? Such questions were posed in ways meant to shed light on the crisis facing modern civilization, how the intellectual freedom needed to respond to state and corporate power might be pursued and, more abstractly, how media could be used to facilitate conditions and values needed for survival. Just as he recognized that the concept of equilibrium is an ideal yet also an impossible state to realize in the economy, when he referenced *balance* Innis was doing so in both idealized and strategic terms. Similarly, while he understood objectivity to be an important goal for social scientists (as to reject it entirely would yield a bias toward relativism and its deleterious implications), as the concept of bias itself demonstrates he was acutely aware of its impossibility. Easterbrook's notes thus remind us that the tensions and contradictions that Innis associated with power relations (involving not just conflicting vested interests but ways of thinking also) reflected the fact that his approach employed a decidedly anti-reductionist kind of materialism. Easterbrook also portrays Innis's methodology to be more cross-disciplinary and holistic than many realize. By addressing mediations that involve more than just technologies and techniques, Easterbrook demonstrates that Innis requires readers to take into consideration the biases and values related to a given society's pervasive institutions, such as language, law, bureaucracy, religion, nationalism, and even their own professions and specializations (as Innis had with the academy and economics).[115]

One thing that stands out while reading Easterbrook's notes is the prescience of Innis's work. In recent years, for example, given the dynamics and commonsense thinking related to globalization, the resurgence of the nation-state and

---

114 Harold A. Innis, *Changing Concepts of Time* (Toronto, ON: University of Toronto Press, 1952), 1–20.

115 To elaborate a point made earlier, the neglect of Innis's political economy and, more generally, his (non-Marxist) dialectical materialism, may be traced, in part at least, to the influence of McLuhan. Although what Easterbrook published regarding what he learned from Innis and while teaching *Innis 4b* was limited, some of what he might have written was passed down to his graduate students through what Innis called the oral tradition. Several of these became authorities on Innis, such as Mel Watkins and Ian Parker (both of whom are deceased). The editor of the present volume has some experience with this as Parker was his mentor beginning in the 1980s. As a result of discovering Easterbrook's lectures, at least some of what Innis relayed to Easterbrook and what Easterbrook then communicated orally to subsequent generations can be made available to others.

nationalism has surprised many. Arguably, had Innis's approach been more widely and better understood (perhaps with the help of Easterbrook's lectures), the rise of reactionary and extremist forms of nationalism and anti-globalism would have been anticipated. The modern nationalisms that Innis critiqued were directly related to conditions and mediations involving a monopoly of knowledge characterized by mechanistic and time-annihilating ways of acting and thinking. For Innis, the United States in the mid-20th century was a most egregious example of this and he feared that its embrace of values that further space-controlling priorities (sanctioning, for example, an aggressively patriotic brand of militarism) would undermine genuine dialogue and the reflective capacities needed to pursue thoughtful solutions.

Easterbrook also explained that Innis applied the economic concept of disequilibrium to his concerns regarding spatial-temporal and control-freedom imbalances. Rapid developments in communications often lead to crises yielding pressures on dominant institutions and ways of thinking which, in turn, frequently result in entrenched or violent responses. Innis also argued that mainstream economics had become an institution biased in ways that facilitate change in response to the time-space and control orientations of large-scale business interests. Conflicts and the manipulation of public opinion involving politicians and lawyers stemmed in part from such biases and their resulting contradictions. As in his summary of Innis on the history of newspapers, media that dominate space by annihilating time (news organizations then, social media today) have garnered power to make, as Easterbrook put it, a "comparatively small, isolated event [...] a matter of world-shaking importance." But more than this, they have greatly contributed to cultural conditions in which there is a "greater sensitivity to change itself." Almost certainly, the reactionary and extremist forms of nationalism that have emerged amid commercial, state, and even 'progressive' political demands for digital communications infrastructure investments (e.g., redressing the 'digital divide') would not have surprised Innis.

As for Innis's political orientations, the impression given by Easterbrook is that he could not be readily associated with any modern label, be that of a conservative, liberal, or socialist.[116] Put directly, Innis's primary concern was humanity's survival. The then emergent Cold War and threat of nuclear annihilation was what

---

116 In the only overt statement made regarding his political ideology, Innis associated himself (quoting Goldwin Smith) with what he associated with "a Liberal of the old school as yet unconverted to State Socialism" who believes that "the clearest gain reaped by the world from all the struggles through which it has been going through, ... will be liberty of opinion." In his own voice, he continued that "To answer those insisting that sides must be taken is not to take sides." Innis, *Political Economy in the Modern State*, xvii.

he had in mind just before he died but, had he lived in the current century, he likely would have cited the rapidly emerging environmental apocalypse also. In fact, strategically (and thus politically), Innis advocated primarily for values that countered those that were undermining the conditions needed for survival. This focus on what is valued and how values are forged and mediated emerged from and itself stimulated what Easterbrook explained were Innis's sociological and philosophical concerns.

The lectures published in this volume highlight more than Innis's pessimism. To repeat what Easterbrook told students, "he believed to the end that increasing knowledge of the forces which shape our thoughts and thinking processes is itself an antidote" to the biases that prevent humanity from recognizing its own limitations and the importance of cultural vibrancy going forward. Innis thus developed (and was continuing to develop) concepts that could be used to counter disconnected specializations addressing mostly here-and-now issues. Moreover, the crisis facing modern civilization required a methodology that could deal with it in terms of the enormous complexity involved in studying the dialectics of long-term change. Innis concluded that to do this the study of communications and media constituted a superior approach, while many who have since been influenced by Innis might well say something similar regarding media ecology.[117]

Whether the object of his analysis involved empires, nation-states, or cultures, Innis was concerned about how ruling groups think about and exercise power, particularly in terms of their relations with people occupying the world's political, economic, and cultural margins. This is another important corrective for students who have focused mostly on Innis's narrower references to biases and technological capacities. Easterbrook also knew that to properly understand and apply Innis, students and scholars need to engage in an almost perpetual state of self-reflection. In this task, one must be aware of the political-economic dynamics affecting and being affected by the biases and values of any given society, including one's own. Here it bears repeating that, according to Innis, the path to intellectual freedom begins by understanding "the forces which would enslave us." By pursuing this, humanity might rediscover the means of attaining wisdom and possibly, therefore, its long-term survival.

---

117 Lance Strate concludes *Media Ecology* with a statement (and sentiment) that Innis, at least at the end of his life, would have agreed with: "As media ecologists, we are responsible for seeking balance, dynamic equilibrium, sustainability. Media ecology praxis is founded on education, art, spirituality, and the elevation of humanity in harmony with our world. I believe, I hope, that media ecologists will find the ways to extend our understanding of life, the universe and everything, and through that understanding of the human condition, find the ways to heal the world, and ourselves." Strate, *Media Ecology*, 238–9.

Notes on the presentation of Easterbrook's lectures

Easterbrook's lectures were not meant for publication. As such, the notes that follow have predictable shortcomings. Given that Easterbrook was assigned to teach *Innis 4b* just days before the course began and that his mandate was to teach it as *Innis's course,* preparing its weekly lectures was an extraordinarily difficult task. While most of his notes clarify and provide insights into Innis's work, readers should be aware that some deal with administrative matters or constitute summaries of assigned readings. It also should be noted that the titles provided for each lecture are not Easterbrook's—they have been added by the editor.

In addition to Easterbrook's typed lectures, the editor has included handwritten additions and margin comments that appear in many of his notes (where these are decipherable and deemed relevant). Large portions of these lectures were written in point form but as they are, in fact, mostly fragmented sentences, the editor has modified them into proper sentences without notation (as he has done also in correcting misspelled words, obvious errors, and other such issues wherever possible). As for incomplete sentences where Easterbrook's intent is clear, the editor has made alterations (again without always noting these). Words that are underlined in what follows duplicate those underlined by Easterbrook, while words that he circled have been italicized. Other changes made by the editor are explained in footnotes throughout.

Following classes held from September to January, Easterbrook did not always indicate the precise dates for when his lectures were presented. For the latter part of the academic year, the editor has estimated where one lecture finishes and another begins and informs the reader when these dates are unclear. Lecture notes that are not dated, that have been incorrectly numbered (perhaps by someone other than Easterbrook), or that appear to have been haphazardly inserted in their archival files have been integrated into relevant classes and dates, wherever possible. To provide the reader with some context and continuity from one week to the next, the editor provides brief introductions for almost every lecture and makes a small number of direct interventions in several. These introductions and interventions are delineated from Easterbrook's own words by using different fonts.

Most readers likely will approach what follows as students and scholars interested in Easterbrook's contemporaneous explication of Innis's work and concerns. Others, more imaginatively, might proceed as if they are among the undergraduates taking Innis's final course or the first course on Innis. Whatever one's motivation, it is hoped that the reader will find Easterbrook's iteration of *Innis 4b* to be a succinct, nuanced, and often stimulating exploration of Innis's research by the colleague who at the time of his death understood his project better than anyone else.

Tom Easterbrook's Lecture Notes for *Innis 4b*

September 23, 1952: *How best to get at the work of Harold Innis?*

To begin the first class, Easterbrook addresses Innis's illness and how it will affect the course. He indicates that, in light of his "disagreement with [the] medical profession," Innis intends to "be here."[1] However, given any uncertainty, he also acknowledges that "some guidance [is] necessary regarding [the] work of Innis himself, the reading list and the essay [...]. [A]t least some hints as to the best way to get at what Innis is doing, his objectives and method [need to be conveyed]." To help students navigate the course, according to Easterbrook, "A 'key' [is] necessary [...] or at least an outline and introduction."[2] The class, he continues, "will be devoted mainly to a discussion of the work of Innis and others whose researches have taken them in the same direction—the Innis of *Empire and Communications*, *The Bias of Communication*, *The Strategy of*

---

1 Easterbrook typed "Innis 4b: Tues. 10 a.m. (Sept. 23/52)" at the top of the first page. For subsequent weeks he began simply with "Innis." This practice, continued throughout the year, indicates that he was very conscious that *Economic 4b*—"*Economics and History*"—was *Innis's* course.
2 On the page margin, Easterbrook notes James Joyce's *Finnegan's Wake* as an example of another complex work requiring such a "key."

Culture[3] [...]. [T]here is not one Innis but two and it is with the second that we shall be concerned—the questions he asked of history and the technique for getting at some of the answers [...]."[4]

Easterbrook proceeds to introduce Innis and the course as follows:

His work is known internationally and there are signs here and there of some understanding of what he is trying to do—in the past, many of the reviewers of his books were obviously in the dark but light is slowly creeping in. His views are *not* easy to get at, in part because so much of his writings must be taken as a <u>work in process</u>. No neat textbook treatment here, nothing cut and dried, laid out for those who like to memorize, but a hacking through the complex materials of history, with here and there patches of clearing, and then jungle again. His is path-breaking pioneer work and less creative minds may follow to put things in apple-pie order. In any event, at the beginning a shepherd is needed to aid with the guidance of an occasionally bewildered flock through rough territory. A few lambs may still fall by the wayside, but I doubt that there will be many.[5]

[The course will involve a] <u>one</u> hour per week [...] rather informal lecture with some scope for discussion—a review of some of the basic issues raised by Innis and an appraisal of his methods of handling these; also some comparisons of his work <u>and</u> that done elsewhere in the area of <u>communications</u>.[6]

The big question right at the start—how best to get at the work of Innis, his reading list and later, this term's essay? Not an easy assignment. I have known Innis for twenty years, worked very closely with his approach although disagreeing strongly at many points. I spent much time with him this summer on these matters. <u>Yet</u> to set out his position and that of others working in the same field, amounts to an act of courage, though possibly not an act of wisdom, on my part.

---

3   Regarding the latter, Easterbrook is referencing what would become the opening chapter of Innis's posthumously published book, *Changing Concepts of Time*.
4   Easterbrook is referring to Innis's work on Canadian economic history (his so-called staples research) and the "second" Innis who focused on communications and civilizational history.
5   Here, Easterbrook penciled in parentheses, "bleat outside my office door."
6   In fact, the course was scheduled to meet for three hours each week (including the weekly lecture) as students were divided into groups to discuss readings. Occasionally, Easterbrook would take part in these. After explaining why, due to Innis's absence, the course's content would amount to something less than the weight of a full course, Easterbrook told students that other courses will provide extended treatments of some of what won't be covered: "<u>these arrangements are designed to carry on with 4b as Dr. Innis has set it out, to fit in with his program when he returns. It is not going to be easy, but it will be done.</u>"

You would do well to begin with the brief introduction to his *Empire and Communications*. You'll note how he ties-in his earlier work with that of the present. He might have added that in his early work on staples he was applying concepts derived from Veblen and J.M. Clark—particularly the Veblen of *The Engineers and the Price System*[7]—the dichotomy between technology and business, the limitless possibilities of new technologies on the one hand and the limitations or restrictions placed on these by market factors. Fears of obsolescence, upsetting the market, checks on the intent of a new process; opposition between those in close contact with the machine process and those engaged in pecuniary or business employments. [Y]ou may recall this distinction, this conflict between technological and price factors in the history of the fur trade as conducted by the French state [...] [relative to] the English trading companies: (a) <u>techniques</u> of exploitation of staple resources, of transportation, of supplies, and (b) on the other hand, the course of price fluctuations which upset the apple cart and made long-range planning out of the question. The presence of heavy fixed costs, unchanging overhead (J.M. Clark) gave the expansion across the continent its <u>force</u> or <u>momentum</u>.

He held to this approach so long as the economy remained fairly simple—staples, techniques, prices. It was when he turned to the more complex economy of modern industrialism that he found himself in a field of inquiry that is now the central one in my study of change, long or short-run, namely that of communications. This came about when he turned to the study of the pulp and paper industry and found that the earlier and simpler dichotomy would no longer do. When he sought, for example, to examine the place of the newspaper in economic development [...] he found that [the] study of technological and price factors alone was only a beginning, [and] that these themselves <u>interacted</u> with other elements, institutional and ideational, and that reference to some larger structure, nation, empire, civilization, was necessary if this <u>process of interactions</u> of many variables was to have any meaning.[8] So, Innis's study of [the history of the] pulp and paper industry to the economic implications of the printing press and the newspaper led him into the area of communications. In the press, radio and other communications channels there is considerable <u>power</u> to influence, even <u>control</u> public opinion

---

7   Thorstein Veblen, *The Engineers and the Price System* (New York, NY: B.W. Huebush, 1921). Easterbrook inserted a margin note here referencing Harold A. Innis, "On the Economic Significance of Culture," *The Journal of Economic History* Supplement 4, no. S1 (December 1944): 83–4. Also in the margin, Easterbrook writes that this is "one of his lighter bits—having a good time—his presidential address [to the Economic History Association]."

8   Easterbrook here cites Harold A. Innis, "The Newspaper in Economic Development," *The Journal of Economic History* 2, supplement 1 (December 1942): 1–33, and writes by hand that "the shift from Innis I [on staples history] to Innis II [on communications] is here."

and concern with these led him to the issues of power and sanction, freedom and monopoly, space and time. Control of communications systems means power to mold, shape ideas, and the types of communication media and material used can produce biases in outlook which in the past have destroyed civilizations.[9]

[Innis broadened] the scope of his earlier analysis in terms of both space and time: from newspapers he went back to the earliest media[10] by which men sought to exchange information and to exercise control. And his coverage carried him from a study of the earliest civilizations to what passes for civilization today. Again, he found himself moving from concern with industries, empires and finally whole cultures. In a sense this broadening and deepening of his analysis and interpretation was inevitable. Of all the techniques devised by man, those of communications are the most general and pervasive. In any group, from family household to corporation, to government bureaucracy, to international mechanisms of control, authority and submission or cooperation rests on understanding, or the exchange of views, requests, commands, order and obedience of them. We live by words, written and/or spoken. It is difficult to pick up any book in the social sciences today that has no relevance in this respect, and you'll find that every item in the reading list has close and ready reference to this question of communications.

Well, as soon as he had turned to this omnipresent problem Innis found himself faced directly with big issues [involving] power and authority; freedom as fact and criterion in human relations; questions of stability and the survival of structures, big or little; forces which make for equilibrium or lack of it in whole civilizations. In other words, he became a cultural historian, focusing on the rise and fall of civilizations—why for some stability persists over many centuries, why others are comparatively short-lived; a pretty important question today where growing uncertainty as to our own prospects for survival is apparent. Can we learn from the experience of other civilizations, why they eventually collapsed? There are traces of Toynbee here, but not many.[11]

Some of this will be reasonably clear from a reading of an excellent review by Karl Deutsch of Innis's *Bias of Communication*.[12] I don't go for all of it, but it does contain a clear statement of some of the things Innis is trying to do and the impression he has made on others. It is significant that it took an M.I.T. [scholar] to

---

9   After this sentence, referring to Ibid., Easterbrook writes "see p. 33 of December 1942 regarding Veblen." Following this paragraph, Easterbrook added the following handwritten note: "pulp and paper → press and newspaper → communications media → cultural history."
10 Just above the word "media" Easterbrook writes by hand "stone pyramids" apparently as a reference to one of the earliest examples that Innis examined.
11 Easterbrook likely is referencing Arnold Toynbee, *A Study of History* (London, UK: Oxford University Press, 1945).
12 See n. 43 above.

do this, since it is there that the whole area of communications, technological and social, is being most thoroughly explored. [Norbert] Wiener, *Cybernetics*, and his *The Human Use of Human Beings*[13] (Wiener, boy wonder), is concerned with what he calls our second Industrial Revolution. The first replaced manual labor by the machines which can do away with much of our present working force, i.e., technologically possible. He argues that a common interest in communications provides a natural focus for work in the physical and social sciences. The study of control and communications in the animal and the machine promises to restore a unity in the approach to knowledge which is close to what Innis is trying to do. What he [Innis] has done is bring in a <u>strongly historical bent</u> and the use of techniques that emerged from the study of long-range historical change.

In moving into this big and only partially explored field, Innis has broadened this field of analysis, but there are many points of similarity between his earlier work and his more recent writings.

(i) *Substantially,* he has remained a technological historian[14] [as he examines] changing techniques, working on some one resource as the starting point. Here, [he looks at] changing media of communication (e.g., paper, radio), innovations, creative activity, [...] then [their] application and consequences (which include institutional adjustments—some favorable, others adverse to survival). The dynamic of historical change is found here. Closely similar in this respect is the work of Gordon Childe, and Abbott P. Usher whose theory of invention is implicit in most views of change: the innovative act, its application, and consequences.

(ii) Again, the notion of a *dichotomy* never dropped from his analyses, involving] contrasts between opposites or polar types—put differently, [between] space and time, Empire and Church, written tradition and oral tradition, monopoly and competition, centralization and decentralization, civil law[15] and common law. Bias is simply lack of balance between these contrasting or opposing forces, which results from undue emphasis on the one [to the] neglect of the other, and it is the area of communications media that we must search for the sources of bias. In *Bias of Communication*, his chapter "A Plea for Time" develops this.[16]

---

13 *Cybernetics: Or Control and Communication in the Animal and the Machine* (Cambridge, MA: MIT Press, 1948); *The Human Use of Human Beings* (Boston, MA: Houghton Mifflin, 1950).
14 Easterbrook inserted a handwritten note in the margin: "Technology → communication → culture."
15 Easterbrook's margin notes indicate that he used of the term civil law interchangeably with Roman law.
16 Innis, *Bias of Communication*, 61–91.

I would suggest that [to begin read] [...] (i) Innis's short introduction to *Empire and Communications*, (ii) Deutsch's review [of *The Bias of Communication*] [...], and (iii) "A Plea for Time," [Innis's] essay in *Bias of Communication*.

(iii) There is implicit in all this a theory of change although it is not always easy to discern. Change I associate with strains and stress in structures of control. Such strains are the result of loss of balance, of disequilibrium in the structure. This loss of balance is associated with neglect of factors indispensable to survival of a culture or empire—e.g., at present, Innis argues that preoccupation with the short-run, the emphasis on expansion over area or space, which is characteristic of nations or business units (markets), amounts to a neglect of time or duration which may well be fatal. On the other hand, the medieval Church solved the time problem in its emphasis on eternity, but was weak politically in terms of control over territory or space. And it is [in relation to] types of communication media that he finds the explanation of the fatal bias—some favor space, some time. Occasionally, as in the Byzantine Empire, a balance is struck and its survival over long centuries was in part the result.

Two [additional] points before I stop today:[17]

(i) I think that you would do well to take this course as an opportunity to engage in readings broader in scope, of wider application, than is commonly the case in coursework. There is a worldview here, a breadth of treatment, and range of subject matter which should be a refreshing change from a textbook diet. You'll have every opportunity to think for yourself, and some of you may be surprised when all cylinders are brought into play. Some may not like this freedom to roam and speculate and prefer the security of the prison yard or straitjacket, but I doubt that there will be many.

(ii) There are certain to be obscurities and some of these will best be handled individually. I have been freed of worry about graduate programs and will have more office time for coursework. I'll post office hours shortly and whether or not you make use of them rests in part, at least, with yourself.

---

17 The notes for the next (and final) two paragraphs have a single penciled line partially drawn through them that is not as definitive as are Easterbrook's other deletions. As these paragraphs are the concluding remarks for the class's first meeting, the editor assumes that Easterbrook may have drawn the line after he addressed their contents. As such, they have been included.

September 30, 1952: *Main subjects and readings*

The first two full paragraphs of notes prepared for the second class have a diagonal line drawn through them in pencil. At the top of the page, Easterbrook added two handwritten words: "discussion" and "omit." Assuming that he discussed what he typed (perhaps informally), these paragraphs are included and begin what is reproduced below.

One matter to clear up—[I am] <u>not</u> taking over this course. It's still very much Innis's. I will help where I can, but some points should be underlined right at the beginning:
    Concern will be much more with Innis's approach and methodology than with the actual content or detail of his work; the structure he has built and is building, for example, his work on the early civilizations (Egypt, Babylonia). Like most economic historians I have a working knowledge of the literature in this area (there are many interesting parallels with the present—e.g., Karl Polanyi's capitalism with the ancient world), but beyond this I have little interest. The Hittites are very much on their own. <u>Yet</u>, what Innis has been doing with such materials is of the greatest importance and I do not think particularly difficult to grasp once his structure is outlined. Vested interests don't like such intrusive encroachments into their field, and at the beginning his ventures into the study of early empires were greeted with suspicion, open dislike and much misunderstanding. More recently this has changed and criticism has been confined in the main to errors of detail, but there is growing acceptance of his point of view.

The second full paragraph reiterates what Easterbrook told students in the first class, emphasizing that the course will provide them with the opportunity to address their interests using Innis's approach. In the next paragraph, Easterbrook discusses the readings assigned by Innis:

    Now, the problem of the reading list [...]. The reading list may seem formidable at first, but it lists mainly standard works, some of which should be familiar to any reasonably well-educated person. Certainly, if the university has any pretensions of cultivating the intellectual side of life or experience, writings of this sort should be standard diet. What Innis is doing here is taking the professed ideals and aims of university education seriously (seldom done). This makes for some difficulty in communicating with those out for the fast buck, but even many of these are not impervious to other influences and may benefit in spite of themselves, and there is no reason why a balance may not be struck between the practical and intellectual influence and undue bias thereby avoided. The pure vocationalist like the pure intellectual is a very dull fellow even to himself.

Setting down the main divisions of the work with close reference to these readings:

1. Communications—(a) general—I want to spend an hour or two on this field of communications—why so much fuss about it [and on] those aspects which are of special relevance here. This [will be done] without any direct reference at the beginning to the readings [and my presentation will be] designed to make them more intelligible.

    (b) Words—semantics—much on your reading list is on this. The Gowers pamphlet,[18] although I don't like it too much, provides useful notes on usage but we can become too self-conscious about such concerns.[19] I am told that it is possible to become so self-conscious about the mechanics of walking that walking becomes impossible but [Gowers is] useful in illustrating some of the problems of communicating ideas without ambiguity or fuzz. Also, Richards[20] (a very word-conscious individual). Woolner and many others if you want them. [Also,] Quiller-Couch, *On the Art of Writing*.[21]

    [In addition, you may consult] C.E. Montague, *A Writer's Notes on His Trade*, S.I. Hayakawa's *Language in Action*, Stuart Chase, *Tyranny of Words*, and Eric Partridge, *Usage and Abusage* (some of these are referred to by Gowers—H.W. Fowler's *A Dictionary of Modern English Usage* may be known to some of you, but if not, never mind). Some references to semantics in Innis's short paper on "Industrialism and Cultural Values," *AER Proceedings*, May 1951.[22] [It is] pretty good, though not a simple introduction to his work.[23]

---

18 Ernest Gowers, *Plain Words: A Guide to the Use of English* (London, UK: His Majesty's Stationery Office, 1948).

19 For clarity, the editor has changed this sentence from Easterbrook's shortform, which read as follows: "Gowers (pamphlet)—don't like too much—useful notes on usage but can become too self-conscious about such."

20 I.A. Richards, *Mencius on the Mind* (London, UK: K. Paul, Trench, Trubner, 1932).

21 Alfred C. Woolner, *Languages in History and Politics* (London, UK: Oxford University Press, 1938); Arthur Quiller-Couch, *On the Art of Writing* (London, UK: Guild Books, 1946).

22 Paper read at the meetings of the American Economic Association, published in Innis, *The Bias of Communication*, 132–41.

23 A margin note next to this last sentence is largely indecipherable but in one part Easterbrook states that Innis's article is itself "a good illustration of the problem of communicating ideas."

(c) the arts—communication factors—Constant Lambert (*music*); Newton (painting and sculpture); Pevsner (architecture); [and] Wyndham Lewis (*Time and Western Man*).[24]

(d) technology and communications—Innis and others.

Note: in grouping readings, [there are] many cross-references [and] other groupings are possible.

2. <u>Bias</u>: (a) oral and written tradition—references [to these are] scattered throughout the readings. Havelock is useful here.[25]

(b) time and space—a huge literature here, [especially works by] Innis, Giedion,[26] and Havelock. We will spend some time on this.

(c) Church and Empire—Charles N. Cochrane (*Canadian Journal of Economics*, February 1946, Innis review article on this).[27] Also, Troeltsch, and Rashdall[28] (on medieval Universities; the place of law is difficult to place in any one classification).

(d) Roman and common law—Maine, Crandall, and Innis's book in press.[29] [The course's first] essay topic [will address law in relation to] orality and written traditions.[30]

(e) monopoly and competition.

---

[24] Constant Lambert, *Music Ho!: a study of music in decline* (New York, NY: Scribner, 1934); Eric Newton, *European Painting and Sculpture* (Harmondsworth, UK: Penguin Books, 1945); Nikolaus Pevsner, *An Outline of European Architecture* (London, UK: Allen Lane, 1943); Wyndham Lewis, *Time and Western Man* (London, UK: Chatto and Windus, 1927).

[25] Easterbrook almost certainly was pointing students to Eric Havelock's *Prometheus Bound: The Crucifixion of Intellectual Man* (Boston, MA: Beacon Press, 1950).

[26] Sigfried Giedion, *Space, Time and Architecture; the Growth of a New Tradition* (Cambridge, MA: Harvard University Press, 1949).

[27] In referencing Cochrane, Easterbrook is citing his *Christianity and Classical Culture* (London, UK: Oxford University Press, 1944). As for his reference to Innis's review, Easterbrook is citing Harold A. Innis, "Charles Norris Cochrane, 1889–1945," *The Canadian Journal of Economics and Political Science* 12, no. 1 (February 1946): 95–7.

[28] Ernst Troeltsch, *The Social Teaching of the Christian Churches* (London, UK: George Allen and Unwin, 1931); Hastings Rashdall, *The Universities of Europe in the Middle Ages* (Oxford, UK: Clarendon Press, 1895).

[29] Henry Sumner Maine, *Ancient Law* (London, UK: John Murray, 1916). The book "in press" is *Changing Concepts of Time*. It is not clear what the publication authored by "Crandall" refers to.

[30] The first essay assignment is reproduced in Appendix 1 of the present volume.

3. <u>Survival</u>: (a) force—Oman, Mahan, Ridgeway (and Mahan vs. Mackinder on geopolitics).[31]
   (b) values—Dickinson, Jaeger (*Ideals of Greek Culture*).[32]
   (c) culture—Kroeber, Sorokin, Toynbee, Spengler.[33]

All these readings fit very neatly into Innis's structure; the problem is to see how and to get some meanings or sense out of them. This may seem difficult but it is a mistake to think that any serious obstacles face those venturing into this only partially cleared ground. There is no assumption here that many have a large backlog of reading to fall back on, but there is the assumption that some of the readings will strike a spark in the minds of those who read and reflect on what they read.

---

31 Charles Oman, *A History of War in the Middle Ages* (London, UK: Methuen, 1924); A.T. Mahan, *The Influence of Sea Power on History, 1660–1783* (Boston, MA: Little Brown, 1890); William Ridgeway, *Origin and Influence of the Thoroughbred Horse* (Cambridge, UK: Cambridge University Press, 1905). Although unclear, Easterbrook also may be referencing Halford Mackinder, *Britain and the British Seas* (London, UK: Heinemann, 1902).

32 G. Lowes Dickinson, *The Greek View of Life* (London, UK: Methuen, 1914); Werner Jaeger, *Paideia, the Ideals of Greek Culture* (New York, NY: Oxford University Press, 1945).

33 A.L. Kroeber, *Configurations of Cultural Growth* (Berkeley, CA: University of California Press, 1944); P.A. Sorokin, *Social and Cultural Dynamics* (New York, NY: American Book Company, 1937) (or possibly, Sorokin, *Social Mobility* [New York, NY: Harper & brothers, 1927], or Sorokin, *The Sociology of Revolution* [Philadelphia: J.B. Lippincott, 1925]); Arnold Toynbee, *A Study of History* (London, UK: Oxford University Press, 1946); Oswald Spengler, *The Decline of the West* (London, UK: Allen & Unwin, 1926).

October 7, 1952: *Innis's interests and methodology*

The first class in October begins with Easterbrook reviewing previous lectures, including his comment that Innis's move "into the field of communications [...] was less sharp than may appear at first sight." He goes on to say that the "structure" of Innis's thought concerning communications is "not radically different" from that found in his earlier work, although there is a need to keep in mind the "guidelines or sign-posts" mentioned previously. Building on these, he proceeds as follows:

Technology as a starting point is a common approach in <u>long-range</u> history. Most of our historical evidence is of this character—how earlier civilizations met their physical needs. In archaeology [there is the] application of techniques to resources [as past cultures] leave many traces long after their civilization has disappeared. [It is a] problem to reconstruct from these the nature of the social institutions and the <u>values</u> by which early peoples lived.

[Innis applied the] notion of a dichotomy, the setting up of contrasting or opposing reference points [including] such polar extremes as written and oral/traditions, space and time considerations, empire and church, force and sanction, and the meaning of bias as he uses it. [For him] the uncorrected bias, the absence of feedback,[34] is fatal to the continuance or survival. [For example, we] might consider the weakness of the French Empire in North America from this point of view, although for a time a fair balance [had been] struck. [This was] also a problem of the first British Empire and this will be clearer as we go along.

There is implicit in all this a <u>theory of change</u> although at this unfinished stage of his work this is not always easy to discern. [...] One of the difficulties [in efforts to understand Innis's methodology is that he is] an intuitionist [as he engages in the] amassing and sifting out of data, then [proceeding to] his conclusion [...]. [This] process <u>of moving from the one to the other</u>, from evidence to conclusion, is rarely clearly explained and you'll find him juxtaposing apparently unlike things, looking them over, inspecting them (a method fairly common in the field of aesthetics), searching for insights into process.[35] [This method] cannot be defined as a purely rational procedure of <u>creation</u> [...] [as it also involves] an aptitude which few possess. This is followed by testing, reinterpretation, and new moves forward. But getting back to his theory of change, [for Innis] change or movement is associated with strains and stress in structure of control. Such strains are the result of loss of balance, of disequilibrium in the structure. This loss of balance

---

34   Easterbrook wrote "cybernetics" above this point.
35   In the margin beside this line, Easterbrook wrote the word "paradox."

is associated with neglect of factors indispensable to the survival of a culture or empire; for example, at present, he argues that preoccupation with the short-run, the emphasis on expansion over space, the passion for logistics, which is characteristic of modern states or business units (markets) amounts to a neglect of time or duration which may well be fatal. On the other hand, the medieval Church solved the time problem in its emphasis on eternity (a fairly long timespan) but was weak politically in terms of control over territory or space. And it is in types of communication media that he finds the explanation of the fatal bias—some tend to an emphasis <u>on space</u> (and his work is replete with illustrations of these), [and with] a few, <u>time</u>. Occasionally as in the Byzantine Empire a balance is struck and its survival over long centuries was in part the result.[36]

Looking at his work a little more broadly, his main concern is with the problem of <u>bureaucracy</u> in history.[37] [Innis asked] why some lack powers of duration, why others have such powers,[38] and why all bureaucracies, sooner or later, rot and give way to other bureaucracies. It is from this viewpoint that he examines the rise and fall of empires, great aggregations of political and religious power and this is the theme throughout.

However, in the empires he studies, this much seems to hold true, that in each instance there emerge monopolies of knowledge (communications) based on the dominant written medium of communication, that via such monopoly control over space and/or time is achieved, success in this direction varying with the degree of time or space bias present in the minds of those who actually do the controlling. But for even the most successful to survive they must cope effectively with the threats present in new and competitive media of communication which, unless checked or absorbed, will bring about new political alignments detrimental to the powers that be.[39]

Threats to dominant structures of control may appear on the margins where control is weak ([as in] English economic history, also Holland's, or even the United States) and/or in the interstices of the imperial structure itself where central control weakens or even breaks down. Structures whose control over space (political power) weakens and whose control over time (religion and sanction

---

36   The reader will note that some of what Easterbrook says in this paragraph repeats content from his first lecture.
37   In the margins, Easterbrook suggests that students "consider bureaucracy and Innis's emphasis on time insights."
38   The editor has replaced the word "lack" for "have" as Easterbrook almost certainly did not mean to repeat the first part of this sentence in the second.
39   At the end of this paragraph, Easterbrook makes a few succinct points. The only one that is discernable asks, "newspaper—loss of influence?"

breaks down, which is another way of saying, fail to avoid undue bias) are open to threats of internal breakdown and to pressures exerted by aliens pressing on the borders of empire.

This is not a fair outline but it will do as an introduction. It leaves untouched the values Innis has in mind. [But] this much may be said, that this preoccupation with bureaucratic structures and their problems of survival stems from his concern with the preservation of the liberal values of individual freedom of thought and action.

Steeped as a young man in the economic literalism of the Chicago School of Veblen and Clark, and later Frank Knight and Henry Simons, associating himself as a cultural historian with the values of Greece and its oral tradition (discussion, freedom from the grip of the written or printed word) he seeks an answer to the age-old problem of some who [sought to] reconcile freedom and change with order and stability.

Freedom is not the antithesis but rather a necessary condition of order and stability—a successful bureaucracy, that is, successful in terms of space and time (power and sanction) is, for him, inconceivable without wide scope for free and spontaneous action and discussion. Without it, dry-rot sets in, or putting the matter in another way, a hardening of the structure must result in failure to cope with change within or without the area of control—the death of the creative spirit. If we were to put this problem more narrowly, say, in economic terms, it would amount to a search for the values of free competition in a world in which large structures of control in economic life are the rule and, in fact, a necessity unless it is an unusually secure world. Freedom, in short, is a necessary condition of bureaucratic stability. Ordinarily, this should be productive of the pessimism most historians are prone to (Toynbee throws up his hands and heads for the sanctuary of religious quiet, others commit suicide). No such pessimism here. His values are clear-cut, his structural framework equally so, and it is a refreshing change from the almost universal tendency [...] to state such problems in terms of two extremes, with the solution that of seeking a happy middle-way between them.

October 14, 1952: *Why so much fuss about communications?*

Easterbrook continues his introduction by addressing Innis's interest in communications. As the lecture proceeds, he provides several insights (mostly through examples drawn from *Empire and Communications*) that aim to help students comprehend the relevance of Innis's work on ancient civilizations. Although his presentation is uneven and in places condensed, he summarizes Innis's work on this history and raises questions that Innis was unable to fully answer.

Innis's set of values: Best reflected in his attitude toward what he refers to as the oral tradition. [By this he is referring to] freedom from the grip of the written word and spontaneity in discussion. The real creative act [is possible] here—the individual free to work, think, and develop on his own. David Riesman's work is helpful here [concerning people who are] inner-directed (gyroscope) vs. the out-directed (radar). [His book] *The Lonely Crowd*[40] [categorizes these as cultural types in which the inner-directed are characterized by] an inner drive of the individual posited goals, strong resistance to demands for external conformity—the Calvinist personality. [An example of this type is] the 'pure' entrepreneur [...] whose internal drive is working to alter the material environment and self. [It is a social type that is] associated, historically, with rapid change. [...] The other [the outer-directed] exhibits craving for the approval of others, the sale of self on the personality market. His success is dependent on what others think and is measured in terms of the goals others follow. [This individual is characterized by] a lack of self-assurance (*Death of a Salesman*). [He is] a more vulnerable, less creative personality type [who is] less dynamic because of the stress on conformity and adaptation. This is the personality most likely to be found in the bureaucracy. Historically, [there has been] a shift from the (a) to the (b) group [or, in terms more relevant for this course, from] Innis [and his creative ideal] vs. institutionalized research. Innis has contempt [for the latter and has sought to] find the individual and help him make his own way. For Innis, group effort [that is bureaucratized often leads to] the negation of creative thought.[41]

[Previously, I] mentioned the problem of the reading list. It is not as bad as it looks. [It involves] three divisions: Communications—general, words, the arts,

---

40   David Riesman, *The Lonely Crowd; a Study of the Changing American Character* (New Haven, CT: Yale University Press, 1950).

41   The last typed sentence is somewhat cryptic. It reads as follows: "Ford fdnt. Research Center ent. history." In pencil, Easterbrook adds that the "Individual in his study can starve."

technology and communication; Bias—oral and written, time and space, church and empire, Roman and common law; and Survival—force, values, culture.

All these readings fit very neatly into Innis's structure. The problem is to see how and to get some meaning or relevance out of them. [There is] no assumption that many here have a large backlog of readings to fall back on (the book is dying), but there is the assumption that some of the readings will strike a spark in the minds of those who read and [that they will] reflect on what they read.

Well, why so much fuss about the communications problem? Why this going back to an interest in language, the subject matter of which was identified with formal education?

Man has always had to exchange earnings unless he chooses to exist alone, yet the feeling now seems to be that technology has added an element of urgency to this problem that was formerly lacking. Very few voices now speak to tens of millions and the babbling never ceases. Hollywood, magazines (preferably pictorial), radio, and now TV. Many have written[42] of the mass production of ideas via the use of visual and audible symbols [and with these] the new possibilities of manipulating individuals. The nightmare of the mass mind, uniform and dead.

Obviously, there is much in this, but widespread concern about it seems to go deeper, to a problem that is central in Innis's work—that of time or the duration or survival of given civilizations, in this instance our own. And this, I suggest, is fundamentally a problem of sanctions which must be established and maintained if any given structure is to survive. That expression, "without faith the people perish" may be interpreted very broadly. Control over space may be established by conquest, but perpetuation of this or that system however established is quite another question. I think that awareness of its implications has been heightened in the United States by the failure of its efforts to convince the Japanese of the virtues of a system which seems sound and good without question.[43] Surely the benefits are obvious in both real and value terms and yet others do not buy [into it]. Have the [communist] Russians a better understanding of the communications problem and is Asia really falling for their line of persuasion? And what of the U.S. public mind itself and its beliefs? The more hysterical elements would use force to see that

---

42 For clarity, the editor has changed the first words of this sentence from "Bryson has written" as the word "Many" is handwritten above "Bryson" and "have" is handwritten above "has." Easterbrook is referencing Lyman Bryson, *The Communication of Ideas* (New York, NY: Harper, 1948).

43 Here Easterbrook writes by hand (assumedly as part of his lecture) what appears to be the following: "yet military recognition a 5-R solution."

faith is not disturbed, but many more are coming to realize that something[44] more than the witch-hunt is needed. Survival rests in the end on sanction and sanction is a problem of communication which itself calls for greater enlightenment as to the culture which we take for granted. That is why McLuhan's *Mechanical Bride* should be added to this readings list [as it] takes advertising seriously. These [advertising] boys probe the mass mind and know a good deal about it [as they] have to. [Advertisers know] how to shape, influence, sell—persuade—[and as such McLuhan's book is] a very useful piece of work [as it contains] some quite remarkable insights [especially in relation to] his view of culture [...].[45]

Now, [to address what] I had in mind in looking over the general literature in the field of communications and then tying this in with Innis. Judging by questions that have been raised and having in mind the problem of [how many] readings [might be added], I think that I'll change this somewhat. [Instead, we will] look at a few points in *Empire and Communications* [in order to] get some points clear at the beginning. This certainly [will be] much simpler than commonly assumed. [Although there may be] some fear of quicksand, of dangerous and unknown territory, [this is] not borne out by the facts.

Innis's article, "Industrialism and Cultural Values," [...] is a condensed summary. [It is] not simple but worth skimming over just to get placed [in his] semantics. Then review, skim [what Innis writes regarding the] Greek and oral tradition, p. 205: the influence of Greece, p. 207, [and on the] eye and ear, pp. 207, 208. [Also review what he says regarding] Laski on education, p. 208, [concerning the] search for balance and proportion and stability as a prior condition.[46]

Before looking over *Empire and Communications* [we might compare it to] a very useful book, a popularization of much the same theme, Orwell's *Nineteen Eighty-four*, on how an extreme variant of bureaucracy, dictatorial and ruthless, might use control of communications to solve space-time problems. Regarding space: preservation of internal order and defense vs. external enemies, and time: the infallibility of the state, the deification of Big Brother, the complete monopoly of the written word, and of the oral too via the omnipresent microphone and television (two-way), and more important the device of Newspeak. [This monopoly] destroys creative aspects of the oral tradition by elimination of all words which can

---

44   The word "something"—located at the start of a new page in the notes—is at one end of a diagonal line drawn through what remains of this paragraph. The editor has included this content as he sees no substantive reason for their omission.

45   At the end of this sentence, Easterbrook adds "Obeck" but it is not clear who or what he is referring to.

46   The numbers included in the text are page references to Innis's "Industrialism and Cultural Values," *American Economic Review* 41, no. 2 (May 1951): 201–9.

express other than the most obvious notions. Very interesting reflections here on the power of language—also on law. It is a very sophisticated book [as it addresses] the problems pointed out here, and [these are] worth reflecting about.

In all Innis's books, you will note the heavy emphasis on the physical setting [as in his work on] economic geography [...] [concerning] (i) the implications of rivers [such as the] Nile, Tigris, Euphrates, Indus, St. Lawrence; (ii) land civilizations (Phoenicians [and their] simple alphabet), North Atlantic and North American continental expansion; (iii) his concept of physical margins—areas of greater technological change rise to attack an older center; (iv) geographic isolation [...] [involving] bodies of water; (v) topography—[including the] physical environment of Greece, regionalism, valleys, problem of centralizing vs. geographic localism (Spain is a more modern example).[47]

In *Empire and Communications* Innis is posing a <u>political problem</u>—that of maintaining authority with the instrument of control, that of communications networks. The road to collapse [involves a] loss of the flexibility of the oral tradition as the written tradition, with its tendencies to monopoly and rigidity, comes to dominate. Signs of weakness include (a) the closing of lines of communication between rulers and ruled (including [an increased] reliance on force) [which] results in (b) [internal] weakness and a resulting inability to cope with threats from outside the borders of empire.

Innis frequently expressed fear that science, technology, and the mechanization of knowledge are destructive to freedom of thought. The cruelty (impersonality) of mechanized communication [implies] passive reading, loss of creative force.

Summing [up Innis's] section on Egypt, [he addresses its] political weakness regarding control over space but [also the] great tenacity of its religious monopoly [which] broke conquerors (e.g., Assyrians and Persians in the end).

(a.) [rule by a] <u>King-Priest</u> (a stone-[clay] fusion) from 2895 B.C. (papyrus was introduced in 2600 B.C.). ([This constituted a] monopoly of the means of communication.)
(b.) democratization [began] centuries before [...] and [continued] after [...][48] [involving] competition of the new medium [papyrus].
(c.) rise of a priestly monopoly [took place from the] 13th to 10th centuries B.C.[49]

---

47 At the end of this paragraph, Easterbrook references an exchange Innis had with Jan O.M. Broek at a meeting of the Association of American Geographers: Harold A. Innis, "Geography and Nationalism: A Discussion," *Geographical Review* 35, no. 2 (April 1945): 301–11. This reference is accompanied by the following: "controversy with Broek—problems of continents vs. maritime areas."
48 Here, referencing *Empire and Communications*, Easterbrook inserted "p. 17."
49 On the margin, Easterbrook wrote next to (a.), "stone," beside (b.) "papyrus-stone" and by (c.) "papyrus."

[Regarding] (a.), the use of stone as [the dominant] medium, [given] its characteristics, problems [emerged related to the use] of complex script.

[As for] (b.), the weakening of absolute kingship with its aspect of divinity coincided with the introduction of papyrus, [especially given that it is] light and [lent] itself to more flexible script [which facilitated a] more generalized use of writing [that enabled] greater efficiency in advances over space. [This led to a] weakening of the old monopoly based on the earlier medium and a democratic revolution [involving the] extension of religious and political rights, but [such developments] included disequilibrium [...] [followed by] invasions [from the] 17th- to 10th-century B.C.

[And as for] (c.), the growing political instability [that emerged] with the disappearance of the earlier [state of] equilibrium [enabled the] triumph of a religious monopoly based on written instruments, but [this entailed] weakness before invaders.[50] The <u>theocracy of the 13th century</u> was unable to check such invaders as Assyrians and Persians, although these conquerors in turn were unable to overcome the tenacity of religious monopoly. [As such, a] strong and durable imperial unity was out of the question.

[Innis points out that an] escape from older bureaucracies only [took place] on the fringes of empire, in maritime areas where the oral tradition was stronger. He dealt with this in the later chapters [of *Empire and Communications*].[51]

[Innis is] posing the problem of liberalism. Its values are those he associates with Greece: the creative individual and his freedom. <u>But</u> the weakness of Greece and its city-states, of maritime areas, [was that they] lack the duration powers of larger aggregates [...] [nor] any real cohesive force or cement.

Now,[52] as an easy exercise you might to set up a diagram, for simplicity's sake, say,

---

50   In pencil, directly below point (c.) Easterbrook cites *Empire and Communications* by inserting "p. 29."
51   A handwritten comment in the margin beside this paragraph states that "[a] monopoly control of communication defeated attempts at constructing empires."
52   On top of the page on which this sentence begins, the word "omit" has been added but, as it is written in pen (unlike virtually all of Easterbrook's other margin notes) and the text on the page does not have lines drawn through them (as do others in his notes), it is assumed that what follows was used in his lecture (and perhaps drawn on a blackboard).

Material – Place – Period – Significance (Time or Space) – Why Time or Space[53]

[Regarding the] case of Egypt, [its dominant media were] the Nile, use of stone,[54] Kings as Gods, and the pyramids as prestige factors that reflect control over time (eternal as well as over space). Divine rights of a king whose power was mainly religious [involving] hieroglyphics, sacred writings, a priestly cult, and the written instrument (one which was heavy, durable, religious, permanent) but that raised difficulties of space control—difficulties of using a generalized instrument of communication. Then after 2000 B.C. [this rule] included the use of papyrus as a writing medium, [and this] coincides with a weakening of absolute kingship, a shift to equality, political rights, [and a] move to democracy. Papyrus is light,[55] easily transportable over great areas, and lent itself to less formal more flexible script. Greater efficiency in administration [then became possible facilitating a] more generalized knowledge of writings. The resulting institutional changes, particularly religious, are traced [by Innis such as a] continued strong priesthood based on more complex script including instability regarding an unsettled King-Priest relationship. [These conditions] added up to administrative weakness and failure before invaders. The Syrians later were expelled and the New Kingdom emerged only to collapse as kings (political power) lost control to priestly theocracy. [This theocracy was] weak in relation to control of space and unable to check the Assyrians and Persians, although [this also] raised difficulties for conquerors due to powers of persistence based on strength in terms of time. Monopoly of communication in the hands of priests made it impossible to maintain a strong imperial unity. [As the] King is not God, tensions and decline [took place as the] monopoly was conservative and divorced from the oral tradition. Escape from monopolies emerged on the fringes of empire where the oral tradition was stronger.[56]

This is not a very difficult thing to grasp. There is a point in [Karl] Deutsch's review[57] I should like to refer too—his feeling that there is much technological

---

53 Directly below these five headings, Easterbrook typed examples but deleted them. What he deleted began with the example of "Egypt" for which, under Material, he wrote "Stone" and "Clay"; under Place, "Mesopotamia"; under Period, "Before Rome"; under Significance (Time or Space), "Time" and "centralization"; and under Why Time or Space, he wrote "Heavy and/or durable—difficulties re. space control."
54 In a margin note here, Easterbrook writes, "not so much balance or fusion."
55 Two words are penciled in here. The first is illegible, but the second is "library."
56 On the left margin, Easterbrook penciled in the following: "note 1. weakness of place 2. great tenacity of religious monopolies—broke conquerors, e.g., Assyrians & Persians in the end."
57 See n. 43 in the present volume's Introduction.

determinism (determination) implicit in the book. I think that there is some misunderstanding here. This is not one factor theorizing about history, even though on the surface it looks like it (i.e., picking out one factor and writing all historical change in terms of it). Innis set out to see what difference resource and technological elements in communication [...] make [but there is] no notion that this is the only element nor [is it] always decisive. I do not think there is any question that on occasion other forces were the decisive ones. There is one dynamic element which at times, particularly [in relation to] substantial or large-scale change, has been of major significance.[58] [...] [This is] not a matter of defending Innis in detail—I lack such competence—but of getting at what he was trying to do. As I indicated, technology is only a starting point, but his emphasis on the historical significance of communications may be broadened and errors [may be] corrected without any noticeable damage to his method. Innis has thrown much light on many dark places in history. While some of it needs refocusing, I think it needs <u>broadening</u> (other factors such as uncertainty in history [should be] considered) but he has done the pioneer job of hacking out a path—others can widen and harvest.

Now, I do not propose to trace in detail his discussion of Babylonia, Greece, Rome and so on, and the chapter on Babylonia may be set aside since it is covered more clearly in *The Bias of Communication*. His treatment of Babylonia makes for very rough going [as it is] enormously condensed and at several points the argument is extremely difficult to follow. [While this is] a problem in communications [there are some] points [to mention] here[59],[60]

(1) The early Sumerian civilization used clay and a <u>complex script</u>. Writing was introduced about <u>2900 B.C.</u> (Time). The medium was durable, heavy, and supported a complex language involving priestly monopolies [that were] <u>never broken</u> by a whole succession of invaders. [This reflected the] great power of survival of then a monopoly of communications as monarchs came and went. [For the] Semitic [invaders], the emphasis was on the use of the medium <u>stone</u>, sculpture, and architecture. Invasion

---

58 At this point Easterbrook cryptically listed several examples: "touch on case of China later; Egypt—disequilibrium, political weakness; <u>Greece</u> and what was its characteristics, [Innis] did not rule out other media; spread of Christianity; Church linkage with political power; Eskimos, oral tradition not out of line with permanence where forces to change weak, factor of isolation; Vikings and Turks, media not the only dynamic."

59 In parentheses at the end of this paragraph, before the colon, Easterbrook included what appears to have been an instruction or reminder to himself: "his [Innis's] references to force regarding iron and the horse leave aside at this point."

60 In the margin, just before (1.), Easterbrook wrote the following: "Another case study. Jottings. A first point."

made rule easy [due to the] political weakness of [the Semitic] priestly cult, and yet the rites, beliefs, and script of the Sumerians, used in legal forms, was never dispensed with. Divinity was associated with the law. The Akkadian invasions (led by Sargon) in about 2500 B.C., were followed by the Elamites (2200 B.C.). [The Amorite king] Hammurabi appears as the great unifier about 1955 B.C. [and had] great success regarding control over space. The Hittites [military success was] aided by iron, about 1950 B.C.

The most enduring dynasty under the Kassites (1750–1200 B.C.) [involved a] heavy emphasis [...] [on a successful] balance based on clay (religious) and stone (kings, political). [It was] finally succeeded by the Assyrians and their efforts to control Egypt and Babylonia, [until the] break-up of the Assyrian empire in the 7th century (612 B.C.). Then the Persian [empire emerged] (ended about 330 B.C.). Apart from the Kassites, [this history was characterized by] persistent difficulties with control of space in the face of the old religious monopoly of Babylonia. This was a recurrent theme throughout—Kings were unable to take on divinity, and unable to come to terms with those who spoke for divinity. The Kassites accepted the Sumerian language as sacred but freed law from religion, and the king [acted] as the secular authority within his own jurisdiction. This achieved strong political control but [it required a] working compromise with religious forms.[61]

So [concerning] the first point, apart from one instance of balance regarding compromise on religious and political jurisdictions, [there were] continuing difficulties [...] [involving the] strength of a religious monopoly of knowledge, for example, control of communications. Kings were never able to dominate or absorb these long-established traditional forms with their grip of communications media (clay and a highly complex script), and the latter was too weak politically to achieve an enduring theocracy. The problem can be seen as one of balance (Kassites) or of fusion, [as with a] King-Priest in one as in early Egyptian dynasties. We should note that these are river civilizations [that experienced] great pressure [...] [to further their] centralization, yet political unification was always a problem. And even the strongest political power found in stone a check to easy control over space [...] [due to its] weight and difficulties in transportation. So this prolonged disequilibrium, [yielding] invasions and counter invasions, [constituted] a very involved history and a course in itself.[62]

61   On the margin, Easterbrook writes, "Stone—difficulties regarding control of space (territory)."
62   The next paragraph in his notes likely was relayed to students only in passing. As such, the editor has not included it in the main text of this lecture. It reads as follows: "There are various asides. On time, (1) sidereal and solar [calendars] which may be left aside; I want to look at these under

(2) Escape from monopoly on the fringes. The Phoenicians and Armenians were commercial peoples who emphasized simplicity rather than complexity in writing: (i) their use of simple, flexible alphabet, and (ii) use of papyrus and simpler script. [These provided them with] greater scope for the oral tradition among trading peoples as the medium's lightness [facilitated its] greater ease of use over wide areas. In the 12th century, Phoenicians importing papyrus from Egypt [...] [was an] important [factor] in weakening the control of priestly monopolies.

On p. 52 in *Empire and Communications* [Innis writes that] "[t]he Phoenicians had no monopoly of knowledge in which religion and literature might hamper the development of writing. The necessities of an expanding maritime trade demanded a swift and concise method of recording transactions and the use of a single shortened type of script." Commerce and the alphabet were inextricably interwoven [and this] aided cities and small nations rather than empires. The Phoenicians and Hebrews used the dialects of a common language (facilitating greater simplicity and vigor of language). [In relation to this,] see "The problem of Space" [pp.] 102–3 [in *The Bias of Communication*] on the significance of poetry [...] [as there is] much on Palestine and the strength of the oral tradition [in these pages] [...] (it was free of the monopolies of Babylonia in Egypt). The Greeks <u>took over</u> the Phoenician alphabet, and this whole notion of freedom from centralized monopoly is discussed in full in his [subsequent] section on Greece.

So [Innis directs us to consider] the concepts of center and margin, monopoly and competition, freedom and control.

The section on Greece—his ideal-type—[addresses how] for a time [it was] the polar extreme from centralized, conservative bureaucracy with its centralized monopoly of communications. [Greece was] free of the "centralizing tendencies of the river civilisations"[63] [as it was] separated by a body of water from these civilizations. [The Greeks borrowed and adapted] [...] the simple, flexible alphabet of the Phoenicians. It is difficult for us, mired in the written tradition, to grasp the meaning and virtues of the oral, as our bias is a deep one. [As Innis observed,] "Greek civilization was a reflection of the power of the spoken word."[64] <u>Socrates</u> was the "last great product and exponent of the oral tradition" [and supported]

---

another heading as I indicated; also his remarks on the alphabet (2) and on the use of force (3); one thing at a time and that is difficult enough." A margin note beside this paragraph includes several words that are indecipherable but those that can be read include "Time," "alphabet," "force," and "power."

63 Innis, *Empire and Communications*, p. 68.
64 Ibid., 67.

the discovery of truth through the "well-planned conversation."[65] Plato sought to preserve the power of the spoken word on the written page [arguing against a] [...] "closely ordered system" [...] [and] refused to be bound by what he had written. Then Aristotle and his systematic treatises—the extension of the written tradition—can be put down as a shift from the dominance of poetry in communication to prose. The tragedy of the oral tradition [...] [is recognized by Innis in his assessment of] the fall of Athens and the execution of Socrates—after Aristotle, the eye rather than the ear.[66]

The final page of this lecture was completed by hand. Despite difficulties reading it, with minimal modifications the editor has included it below primarily due to the questions raised by Easterbrook.

Lunch[67]—Regarding technological determinism, [according to Innis] the fur trade determined our national boundaries. [It] changed [indecipherable word] politics [indecipherable word] and [indecipherable word] reflected choices in regards [to] space. All change [was] determined by changes in [indecipherable word] of the fur trade.

Yet in the fur trade [Innis used] technology as a starting point but the outcome was a product of a whole complex of forces. Institutions ([such as the] French state, and English mercantilism) [reflected and shaped its] organization and values. Geography and [indecipherable word] and in a single [indecipherable words] and a single staple [it is] difficult to avoid the conclusion that the development [of] fur [indecipherable word] basis. [...] [The fur trade was important] in preventing U.S. inevitability.

And what of more complex societies bound together by communication systems? Technological determinism here?

[Regarding] stone and alphabet writing. The use of these needs [some] discussion as social and political spheres? Is change a mere matter of accident of the medium use? [Indecipherable words] Yet [there is] interaction. Use of this or that medium reflects its type or the stage of a civilization able to use it. Communications

---

65 Ibid., 68.
66 In the margin, Easterbrook adds, "Spread of writing—latter part of 5th into 4th centuries." Below this, he lists the following philosophers and dates: "Plato 4th century," "Socrates 469–399 B.C.," "Aristotle 384–22" and "Plato 427–34?"
67 "Lunch" may indicate that these handwritten notes were made after class (which began at 10 a.m.). On the margin, Easterbrook writes, "a brand of technological determinism" and in the right margin adds "Deutsch" (perhaps reflecting his earlier comment regarding Deutsch's reading of Innis as a technological determinist).

produce [...] an <u>institutional</u> effect which interact with communications. If [this] emphasizes space, [it] explains [indecipherable word] time problem, and [the] search for other media which compete with marginal ones.

What of values? They're determined too? Or [are they] taken as given? Communications systems stress certain values, but these in turn are more than a product but [also they are] an active force which impinges on its communications [indecipherable words].

The case of Greece is very interesting. His [Innis's] values are rooted here. What of media are determinants of values here? A one-way relationship?

October 21, 1952: *Receptivity to Innis*

Regarding Innis's place in his field, he began to break new ground in the early 1940s. Up to that time, his reputation was based on works in Canadian development. Then [there was] a shift in gears [in which he spent] four or five years in the wilderness. [During this period Innis was] little understood and plowed along alone [as what he was doing produced] mystification. [He had a] feeling that something very important [was unfolding] here but [there was] little [clarity] as to what it was. It didn't seem to be economic history and the papers he read to economics meetings on early civilizations seemed to be dealing with material very remote from the interests of economists. The book *Empire and Communications* marked the end of this period. The stuff [of what he was trying to do is] there but it is extremely hard to get at [in part because of his] supreme contempt for the written tradition. Most authorities in the field simply reserved judgment. Since then, [there has been] a pulling together of many loose threads—a retracing of steps to show how he got from here to there. His *Bias of Communication* is a long step forward in intelligibility. Although it is still far from clear-cut in its argument or approach, [...] [by reading it, it is] possible to see the argument as a whole and this book along with the articles built around it has firmly established him in the top rank of cultural historians. With another five years, like the last five, [...] the edifice [he is building should be] complete. It is a very real tragedy that this progress is being held up for at least the time being, but there is no doubt of the impact [he will have] in thinking in the United States and Europe. I saw some of the correspondence addressed to him this past summer and in essence much of it amounted to a spontaneous acknowledgment of the contributions he has made to historical understanding.[68]

---

68 Knowingly or unknowingly, Easterbrook was exaggerating how well Innis's communications research was being received (see this volume's Introduction). Nevertheless, one example of a positive response that Easterbrook was aware of is found in a letter that Frank Knight wrote to Innis on May 1, 1952. In it, Knight told Innis that after a two-year delay, he read both *Empire and Communications* and *The Bias of Communication*. Although he said that they were "not easy to read," he thought them to be "enjoyable" and "educational." Innis, writing back ten days later (following his surgery for prostate cancer), told Knight that "I cannot say how much your letter meant to me [...]" File 06, box 011, Accession B1972-0025, University of Toronto Archives. Another (but indirect) example was discernible from a letter Innis sent to Easterbrook (also on May 11) in which he implied that great minds are thinking like him: "I had a letter from Gerald Graham at Princeton referring to conversations with Einstein and Bertrand Russell, both of whom seem to regard technology or techniques as the great enemy for the future." File 01, box 001, Accession B1975-0030, University of Toronto Archives.

There seems to be the impression, particularly in Canada, that it is surprising that a Canadian working with inadequate library and research facilities, faced with difficulties of communicating with other 'experts' in the field, should have contributed so much. I'm surprised at this surprise. Unlike many other nationals, the Canadian who is writing more than narrative history is forced to think <u>internationally</u>. The U.S. historian, faced with the complexities present in the development of his country has for the most part written of the United States alone and quite frequently with only one other. The English historian obsessed with the Industrial Revolution and tragedy of the 20th century has, again, written mainly of his own tight little island. This concentration on single political units (even with the colonies thrown in) has frequently led to interpretations of all history on the slender basis of the experiences of one area or empire. The character of economic change in an economy so vulnerable or sensitive to external influences [such as Canada's], forces one to move beyond the boundaries of his own country, to <u>compare</u> and contrast changes here with elsewhere, in short to take a world view, whether he likes it or not. He cannot be an academic isolationist.

The Canadian, I think, is also able <u>to stand back</u> a bit and frequently to see issues in the large, something much more difficult when one is in the center of strenuous economic and political change. I think that the U.S. economic historian, in particular, works under great difficulties in this respect. I have the impression that he has <u>less opportunity for reflection</u> and is more subject to the pressure of immediacy. Also, it may be that the academic elsewhere is taken more seriously than in Canada—he is under more pressure (book a year, always the same book)[69]—to deliver the goods, pronto, now. Elaborate research centers only add to this pressure. Unfortunately, delivering some types of goods takes <u>time</u>, and some measure of <u>quiet</u>. As Canada moves into <u>her</u> century, this situation is changing; I doubt that it is changing for the better in this respect.[70]

Now a look at some of Innis's readings.[71] We will glance at his *Empire and Communications* although hesitate to place it on any reading list. I have mentioned some of his later essays you might be looking at—those dealing with modern times

---

69   Easterbrook adds by hand, "read every semester."
70   The next paragraph, forcefully penciled out by Easterbrook's hand, reads as follows: "I touched on the section on Egypt in *Empire and Communications*—the difficulties of political (space) powers unable to handle the issue of time as reflected in the Sumerian religious monopoly of knowledge—conquest relatively easy but difficult to establish continuity of empire."
71   A list of "readings" was inserted among this week's notes. However, as noted previously, it appears to have been prepared later (perhaps for a subsequent iteration of *Innis 4b*). For this list, see editor's Introduction above.

are the easiest to get at. Hence, the first, fourth and fifth chapters in *Changing Concepts of Time*, and the last four chapters in *The Bias of Communication*. We will take them up at a later point. For now, [we will conduct] a survey of his work on the early empires and civilizations. In *Bias of Communication* [we will read] a short essay on "industrialism and cultural values"—[it is] not free of difficulties but we should go over it and later reference to it will be made on the assumption that you have spent some time on it. Following that, his "A Plea for Time" expands some of the ideas in the shorter essay. Finally, his essay "Bias of Communication" should be looked at. Once I have surveyed the leading ideas of his *Empire and Communications*, I'll go over these essays in *The Bias of Communication* in the order named. This will take some effort on your part as he wasn't writing for a general reading audience, as you'll find.[72]

---

72 This page of Easterbrook's notes ends abruptly with the following: "In all Innis's books—" The remaining notes for this week's class are missing.

October 28, 1952: *Greece—Innis's ideal-type culture*[73]

Raising various factors addressed by Innis (geography, language, law, communications technologies, and others), Easterbrook proceeds to outline his conceptualization of ancient Greece as an "ideal-type" culture. Readers who have not reviewed parts of the editor's Introduction to this volume regarding Max Weber's ideal-type methodology may wish to do so to grasp its importance (as well as subsequent lectures Easterbrook presents concerning Byzantium as Innis's ideal-type *empire*).

Now, those chapters on Greece and Rome. I'm inclined to feel that unless you are something of a classical scholar, it is best to omit most of the detail in these chapters in *Empire and Communications*. The principal essays in *The Bias in Communication* cover the main points. However, I shall touch on the main ideas developed in each chapter and at a later point I intend to call upon some of the faculty who are specialists in this and related fields [although I am] not quite certain at the moment what time I will have at my disposal.[74]

Well, Greece [is] his ideal-type—the polar extreme or opposite from centralized, rigid bureaucracy, with its monopoly of communications. [We have] difficulties understanding Greece and the oral tradition of its best days since we are so hopelessly mired in the written tradition. An interesting quote from Plato on p. 44 in *The Bias of Communication* [in relation to this is as follows:] "no intelligent man will ever be so bold as to put into language those things which his reason has contemplated, especially not into a form that is unalterable—which must be the case with what is expressed in written symbols."[75] The written word is frozen, fixed. [A question for Innis was] how to break its grip? [This is] a particularly difficult [task] when we are not aware of its grip.

Radio and television do not [entail a] loosening of this grip since what is put on the airways is the written product in spite of all the talk about it being free, spontaneous, and unrehearsed (this is my experience). The dilemma is that oral discussion and the bull session are possible only in the small group or such small political entities such as the city-state. What of the large group, the vast empire?

---

73 On the top of the first page of his notes for this class, in pencil Easterbrook reiterated what he had previously addressed: Innis's supposed technological determinism. Here he referenced previously posed questions about Innis's analysis of the fur trade and the newsprint industry, relating these to societal and political factors.

74 The only person that Easterbrook appears to have brought in was Karl Deutsch who, according to his notes, visited Toronto from late February to early March 1953.

75 Innis is quoting Plato's *Seventh Letter 343a*.

Well, at the least, we should be aware of the values of spontaneity and the dangers of fixity, the loss of creative power. Big university classes [are like] a big sausage machine. There is no interchange [and it is] easy to forget [the true] meaning of education is its fostering of creative independent thought.[76]

So, the ideal, the "discovery of truth through the well planned conversation."[77] Why Greece? Because the oral tradition was protected by the late development of writing (7th-century BC). This lateness was the result of a number of factors.[78]

(1) Especially from a body of water from Eastern civilizations, free of the centralizing tendencies of river civilizations. (2) Topography of country helps to explain the presence of the city-state as the dominant political unit—pressures for centralization were not great. (3) Use of the simple, flexible alphabet of the Phoenicians. (4) Limited use of papyrus—no large and regular supplies from their source in Egypt. (5) The medium, stone, cumbersome and not very durable—it delayed, although could not by itself prevent, the introduction of writing. (6) Stone, not a satisfactory medium—limitations regarding type of alphabet and the needs of Greek trade.

[These factors] added up to [enabling the conditions for its] freedom from monopolies of knowledge with results which we, with a very different bias from that of the Greeks, find difficult to grasp. Such statements that "Greek civilisation was a reflection of the power of the spoken word"[79] take some thought. Even though this was a civilization with a language structure beautifully adapted to fine and subtle shades of meaning, its great discovery was the possibilities inherent in freedom of inquiry, free discussion. Spontaneous utterance as in poetry had enormous influence over public opinion. There was no sacred book, no powerful priesthood, no all-embracing dogma. [Greek thought enjoyed a] freedom from absolutism [as found in] the Babylonian priesthood and the Egyptian monarchy. [These factors enabled the] production of new outlooks and values, a decline of belief in the supernatural, and the discovery of uses of abstract intelligence and rational procedures that escape [...] traditional limits or curbs [such as one's] detachment of self from object. [They also facilitated a] growing interest in science, natural laws—in navigation, astronomy, geometry, new notions of the universe—and an appeal to rational authority. The science of man as man [led to a] reliance on unwritten customary law ([Innis referenced] frequent contrasts [in relation

---

76   In the margin, Easterbrook writes: "p. 68 [in *Empire and Communications*] Socrates the last great exponent of the oral tradition. Plato—read p. 68. Aristotle—shift to written—his school founded in 4th century."
77   Innis, *Empire and Communications*, p. 67.
78   Several largely indecipherable points are handwritten immediately below this paragraph.
79   Innis, *Empire and Communications*, p. 67.

to this] regarding the U.S. written constitution and the absence of the same in England). Demands [in Greece] for written law in the interests of uniformity were kept within limits by the absence of a written authority. [Thus, there was a] very slow development of legal codes, an emphasis on compromise and on the responsibility of the individual, and the flexibility in law was reflected in its emphasis on personal freedom as a right. [In Greece, therefore, there was a] continuous adjustment to conditions rather than appeals to authority fixed and unalterable [involving an] emphasis on the virtues of popular assembly and the right to appeal from magisterial decisions to the assembly. [This resulted in a] greater freedom for the commercial class and the support of individualism in the economic sphere.

Yet the flaw of unrestrained individualism[80]—of neglect of order in the emphasis on freedom and [the dictum that] individualism overdone produces tyrants—[led to] political drawbacks as apparent in the struggles of the 6th-century B.C. [In this] release of individual energies, […] [the Greeks were unable] to reconcile this with [the need for] political order—[a contradiction] not solved yet.

Some of these problems are present in the area of religion also and he makes a few references to the rise of mystery religions such as Dionysian rituals involving orgiastic[81] ecstasies, and a lack of balance and restraint—God of grapes and wine [worshipped through] organized religious frenzies.

Although this is touched on at later points, his [main point] is that the oral tradition proved to be strong enough to hold in check the worst excesses of each.[82] In the 6th century, balance was achieved [in that] (a) the rise of tyrants was displaced, although no satisfactory machinery of succession was evolved; and (b) the influence of Apollo in religion with its closer reference to order and authority […] provided for a reconciliation of the needs of self-expression with demands for the stability lacking in [cases of] individualism gone wrong. A more constructive political philosophy emerged, one which curbed the independence of religion as an independent element on the one hand, and the unrestricted use of force or political power on the other. This balance gave [the Greeks] powers of resistance to such invaders as the Persians. There was neither an absolutism of religious form or state and a cultural flowering in the 5th century followed.[83]

80 Directly above "individualism" Easterbrook pencils in "McLuhan."
81 Easterbrook wrote the word "religious" directly above "orgiastic."
82 The editor has not reproduced several deletions and minor revisions made by Easterbrook to the first few lines of this paragraph.
83 Handwritten notes were made along the margin and, although some are indecipherable, the following are legible: "absence of extremes where [there is] feedback. Themes of governing a system emerged—[indecipherable words]—correction not allowed. Self-correcting mechanism—[indecipherable words] feedback failed—can't argue with a book."

November 18, 1952: *The value of studying antiquity*

There is a gap of two weeks in Easterbrook's notes as the class appears not have met on November 4 nor the following week (an official holiday in Canada—Remembrance Day). Innis died on Saturday, November 8. In his honor, classes were canceled and offices were closed on Monday, November 10 to enable members of the university community to attend his funeral held in Convocation Hall.

To begin the first class after Innis's death, as indicated by hand, Easterbrook told students that he had "hoped for at least one more [indecipherable words] like [indecipherable word] summer—but not to be—no acceptance of [indecipherable word] final." Then, with typed notes, Easterbrook recognized that with the "loss of Innis" there are questions as to "what line to pursue" in the course, and that this would be determined "following department meetings."[84] He then proceeded with his lecture.

Karl Helleiner—on Henry Sumner Maine[85]—[addresses] differences in educational traditions as illustrated by Maine's interest in metaphysics and his grounding in classics. His interest in speculations about the meaning of things tends to be foreign to the Anglo-Saxon mind with its more pragmatic, practical bent. Innis, in moving back into the classical world, was venturing into alien territory—[one dominated by] experts on questions concerning antiquity. [This is] a highly dangerous world for economic historians and it is very commonly avoided by them. It took courage to move into this hostile territory. For example, his experience regarding the Oriental Club[86] who raised questions with Innis as to the risks involved in this invasion. His answer [was that he was] giving full value to their researches [as, unlike his efforts, there was] nothing being done in relating these to general economic history. [Instead, Innis valued] antiquity for its own sake. Yet there is much here of value to understanding of problems of the present day—not only the question of value itself but pressing problems of the survival of Western civilization. We need the eager beaver specialist in this or that area or epoch but, in addition, we need concepts that relate their findings to the present. Spengler, Toynbee, and Kroeber have worked in this direction, but even a glance at the work

---

84 Easterbrook likely was telling students that he was unsure about how the course would proceed given that Innis would not be returning.
85 Henry Sumner Maine, *Ancient Law: Its Connection with the Early History of Society and Its Relation to Modern Ideas* (London, UK: John Murray, 1888).
86 Easterbrook likely is referring to a group of orientalists, classicists, and medievalists at the University of Toronto who specialized in the languages, history, and culture of the Near, Middle, and Far East.

of these will reveal a sad neglect of those factors which Innis wished to underline and I hope to make this clear at a later point.[87]

So, the space-time solution of the city-state [involved] the absence of a monopoly of communications, and its free and spontaneous communication of ideas. Its great innovation was the free play of rational powers as reflected in developments in the university, science, and the arts. [This constituted] a successful though temporary attack on absolutism [and it had] an enormous impact on the whole Western world [in terms of valuing] the free play of critical intelligence. These traditions of 5th-century B.C. Greece were preserved and were handed on via the written forms (libraries) in later Hellenistic Kingdoms of Macedonia, Egypt of the Ptolemies, and the Seleucids. The significance of Constantinople [should be assessed] in this respect. Later we will deal with its reawakening or revival in the late medieval world. This freedom was one element of the balance necessary for continuity, yet only one. [There is a] one-sided emphasis here with its neglect of stability and order and uniformity [as the free play of critical intelligence] cannot [itself] yield the balance Innis had in mind and without it large-scale political organization of any duration is out of the question, whatever may be said of the city-state as a smaller unit of administration with its greater scope for free and frequent discussion. In short, there remains the question of empires. For these, Greece had

---

87 Two paragraphs that follow were crossed out but are reproduced below:
"A question—what to do about the essay? [...] I cannot expect you to turn in much this term. However, despite certain difficult problems it raises, it is highly useful in providing one central reference point for most of the problems Innis has raised in his work, particularly those [...] [concerning the] oral and written traditions. [In Innis, we] cannot separate out law from politics or religious factors. This dichotomy, [involving the] oral and written [traditions], cannot of course be handled without qualification [...] with respect to Roman and civil law. [There is] more flexibility in Roman law and less of it in common law than this parallel would suggest. However, the basic antithesis between freedom and control remains. I think that if we push ahead with points such as these in mind, the subject of the essay will become clear or intelligible enough to a point where a fairly substantial essay may be expected of each of you some time next term. I cannot set a deadline at this date but you would do well to think and read about it as we proceed. It will be heavily weighted as far as the course as a whole is concerned.

For the remainder of this term, and possibly the early part of the next, I plan to push ahead with the general theme of what Innis was driving at and I expect to have 'experts' in various fields [address our class] from time to time. The problem is to provide some continuity as we proceed—not always easy since Innis did not proceed in any continuous or straight fashion. [Instead, he conducted his research through] the amassing of evidence, the intuitive flash, frequently without the connecting links, then the working back from conclusion to premise. This last was a task which he was unable to complete."

In the margin next to the first of these two paragraphs Easterbrook asks, "why his emphasis on law? [Note Innis's] work with Royal commissions."

its values and contributions but no adequate solutions of the space-time problem with which he was so concerned.[88]

It was when he turned to Rome that Innis began to emphasize the factor of law in history (his book still not out[89]). "Contrast the demands of Roman Law and of Common Law on Words."[90] Book technology as a cause of changing attitudes toward time [will be the subject of] the first essay question. Without doing anything on this theme at this point of the course (we are waiting for his book), you might note that in his work common law, broadly speaking as compared with Roman law, is taken as the more flexible legal form, less formal, less dogmatic, less absolute in its interpretation of legal questions. Its stress is on interpretation according to the facts of the case rather than to abiding principles formulated in advance. This enabled greater scope for continuous as distinct from revolutionary or radical change—less reliance on tradition and authority or on prestige factors. Obviously for him it has values that were closely associated with this oral tradition and his preference clearly is here. Roman Law, on the other hand, appealed to principles formulated in advance that are universal and lasting, authoritarian and relatively unchangeable. In essence, [this is] a contrast between written and unwritten law and written and unwritten constitutions—unwritten with its greater scope for individual freedom, and the written with its emphasis on the supremacy of law over individual behavior. The contrast needs qualification, however, as the distinction is not as clear and sharp as this, as he knew, but this will do as a starting point. There are no pure types anyway in reality, although [ideal-types are] useful for conceptual purposes. One minor point [is that] some confusion is possible regarding civil and common law (from looking over certain essays handed in last year, this confusion is not uncommon). Civil law sometimes [...] references [...] the whole Roman legal system. Under Roman Law, [civil law] originally was referred to as local law (for Roman citizens) as distinct from the law pertaining to their intercourse with aliens. Now, however, civil law usually refers to the body of private law developed from the Roman law in states where the legal system is substantially Roman.[91]

---

88 In the margin, Easterbrook writes, "Contrast [George] Orwell. Life—[indecipherable word]—prisons."
89 Easterbrook is referring to *Changing Concepts of Time*.
90 As reproduced in Appendix I of this volume, this instruction was the basis for the first essay assignment. It was almost certainly written by Innis.
91 Along the margin of this paragraph, Easterbrook added several sentences that are largely indecipherable. Words that are readable include, "18th century enlightenment," "trade," "problem of Labrador," "reliance on state or political [...] to provide ballast," "curbing of powers of state," "question of its freedom as an end [in] itself?" In the next paragraph, with typed notes, he addresses the essay topics: "For essay purposes, a very large number of references possible— Maine only one; Randall, *The Creative Centuries*, particularly ch. 29; Lord MacMillan, *Two Ways*

Now a few general points on Rome as dealt with in *Empire and Communications* by way of distinguishing between the forest and the trees:

(1) Begin with the rise of an aristocracy of patricians, a republic, in the 5th and 4th centuries [when there was an] absence of a written body of law and the oral tradition was strong [and there was the] presence of deliberative assemblies. The importance of trade with other commercial peoples led to the development of commercial law with its greater flexibility (as with the later Law Merchant was so important in the trade of medieval Europe). Although there was recourse to the written document in intercourse with aliens, as with the use of treaties, etc. (laws of the provinces, Lex Provinciae), the oral tradition was strong in civil law pertaining to Roman citizens.

(2) The expansion of empire—particularly in the 2nd-century B.C.—[led to the] sad end of Carthage and of the Macedonian kingdom and of Greek resistance. Papyrus was the basic medium of communication. [It was] adaptable to this expansion over space and to the purposes of a centralized administrative bureaucracy.

(3) With expansion east, [there was a] renewed influence of Greece of the late classical period [in which the] written tradition was very strong. You'll note in various sections in *Bias of Communication* the stress in the Hellenistic kingdoms on libraries and archives. Under this impact, oral communication gave way to the written—increasing inflexibility and heightening tensions within the Republic reflect this. [There was a] growing rigidity in the administrative sphere, and this led to the collapse of the republic and the rise of Empire and the Pax Romana of the first two centuries A.D.

(4) The unsolved problems of the Republic writ large in the Empire: the difficulties of a vast bureaucracy under the spell of the written tradition led to such solutions as the return of emperor worship. Kings as Gods was a reflection of the effectiveness of the written tradition as a means of incorporating the influence of the religions of the east. Emphasis on the written instrument was seen in the codification of the law, reliance on the dead letter, and the growing inability of the Western Empire to cope with threats on its borders or with strains within […] [leading to]

of Thinking—short and sweet. Useful references in Cochrane, *Christianity and Classical Culture*, in some ways the most useful book in the reading list. Somewhat more specialized works, F. Schultz, *History of Roman Legal Science*; R.W. Lee, *Elements of Roman Law*; C.P. Sherman, *Roman Law in the Modern World*; N.S. Timasheff, *An Introduction to the Sociology of Law*; S.P. Simpson and J. Stone, *Law and Society*. The main problem at the beginning is to get at the difference between Roman and common law systems, and the values Innis is driving at—freedom and spontaneity but reconciliation with order and stability."

its collapse in 476. Neither the later republic or the western half of the empire achieved duration [and this involved the] weakness of the oral tradition and a lack of balance among communication media. Cochrane's reflections on Roman political thought are very useful at this point.[92] The false doctrine, that is, the search for perfection through political action, is not unknown today. Secular pride in political power, in reason alone, as the source of the solution for problems of order and continuity, [and with it] the tendency to overlook individual human values. On p. 355 of *Christianity and Classical Culture*, this is the underlying theme of the book. The fall of Rome was the fall of an idea, or rather of a system of life based upon a complex of ideas which may be described broadly as those of Classicism—the dominant idea that it is possible to attain a goal of permanent security, peace, and freedom through political action, especially through submission to a political leader. [This was] the error of envisaging faith as a political principle—temporal power [through means of] an empire held together by force.[93]

(5) The story was different in the eastern half of the empire, and from Innis's standpoint more interesting: the rise of Constantinople (Burckhardt on Constantine[94]) dedicated in 330 A.D. [Here there was] more success with the problem of balance based on (a) papyrus in the administration of empire—space—political, and (b) parchment in the service of early Christianity. This balance was productive of a strength and resilience great enough to throw back the Goths who then turned to attack the west. The Byzantine empire collapsed only in the 15th century so it had enormous powers of duration. This empire and the case of the Kassites to Innis were the best examples of space-time control. The contrast between the administrations of western and eastern parts of the Roman empire throws a good deal of light on the whole Innisian approach. Keep this in mind when looking at these in more detail. It is clear when we look later at early Christianity.

(6) A few points on law emerge from this chapter.[95]

---

92 Easterbrook is referencing Cochrane, *Christianity and Classical Culture*.
93 In the margin Easterbrook writes, "papyrus & concern with space."
94 Easterbrook almost certainly is referencing Jacob Burckhardt, *Force and Freedom: Reflections on History* (New York, NY: Pantheon Books, 1943).
95 It can be assumed that the chapter Easterbrook is referencing is Innis's "The Written Tradition and the Roman Empire," in *Empire and Communications*. From this point in the lecture, Easterbrook covers material used in a subsequent class (January 6). To avoid unnecessary repetition, here the editor has deleted this content, especially as Easterbrook's January 6 presentation is a more detailed iteration.

November 25, 1952: *Innis's transition to the subject of communications*

On this day, Easterbrook discusses ways in which the class represents Innis's teaching and intellectual project and how his death will affect it going forward. Easterbrook emphasizes how difficult it has been to teach Innis's course and thanked students for their understanding. Likely reflecting on the moment when he was asked to step in for Innis, Easterbrook admits that "I felt more or less on the spot" and added that it "takes time to build a course and more time when the material concerns a span of many centuries and a method as unique as that worked out by Dr. Innis." Easterbrook goes on to tell the class that, given the un-realized assumption that Innis would return, *Economics 4b* would no longer be a required course for honors students and those who wished to drop it could. In saying (or suggesting) this, Easterbrook recognizes that the course's contents and Innis's approach are not to everyone's liking: "I know that many have no love for other than tried and true ways of looking at things [as opposed to] speculative thought with its emphasis on interpretation of complex materials and its absence of final and conclusive answers. Sailing in uncharted waters doesn't make for peace of mind and I think that in many ways we do our best to knock the spirit of adventure in the realm of ideas out of the minds of students from their freshman year onwards." Easterbrook then encourages some to leave the course thus reducing enrollment to a number that might allow the class to proceed as a seminar: "In listing this as a course at all I made one assumption which I most fervently hope is sound—that only a small proportion would remain and that, with a small group, [it could be] handled by the seminar method, i.e., discussion, flexibility in procedure, the oral tradition [and as such] a good deal might be done that could be done only with great difficulty in a larger group. And I proceed with this assumption very much in mind."[96]

As this class meeting was, to repeat, largely an administrative discussion, below the editor has reproduced only what Easterbrook said regarding course content, Innis's thinking, and his intellectual contributions.

---

96 This passage reveals some confusion regarding Innis's terminal condition. Had there been confidence in his recovery, it is doubtful that Easterbrook would have anticipated that students might leave (while it was Innis's course, it was mandatory). This uncertainty likely involved Innis's overt refusal to accept his fate and, as he was Head of the Department of Political Economy, others had limited authority to address this directly.

Where to go now? Well, some of you will recall with nostalgia course *3f* ["Economic History of Canada and the United States"]—the Innis of the staples and the technologies and institutions that were associated with them against a geographic background which interacted with these. Although Innis pioneered in this field, many others have followed or worked with concepts based on his early work. He more or less determined the direction of research and teaching in Canadian economic history and I doubt that in our time we will go much beyond building on the foundations he laid and, of course, much building still remains to be done. It has the advantage of being a well-defined area in which Canadian scholarship has a complete monopoly, although there is danger that too close a preoccupation with the development of this one small nation could lead to a distortion of the views of researchers in the larger field of general economic history—a danger which may be avoided only by close and constant reference to the external forces which have shaped so much of our economic history, which is not to say that we have not had any influence on such other areas as the British empire and the United States. On occasion, we can rock the boat too.

You may recall the process by which Innis moved on from the fur trade and cod fisheries, lumber and mining, to pulp and paper which took him to the large, relatively new and extremely complex field of communications—how in fact people understand or fail to understand one another via the exchange of ideas [which is] a problem of the firm as well as the empire, of the family, and the university. This is not only a problem of how the Frenchman understands the Englander's way of looking at things, i.e., not merely a problem of different languages and cultural backgrounds, but of vocational differences too. Mix up a few professors and business types and watch the misunderstandings grow. And within or between organizations of any kind, such misunderstandings easily end in conflict and threats to continuity or survival.

Working with graduate students from areas not steeped in the culture of the west brings home the difficulty and importance of the problem. A man may spend several years struggling with a subject, knows all the names, all the words, be able to talk about progress in economics from Alfred Marshall to William C. Hood and yet in a PhD oral examination the same words just don't add up to the same thing as they do with us. There is something missing, mutual understanding, a common way of looking at things and using words has not resulted in this. [Such misunderstandings can be] very dangerous when put in the larger setting of differences between the way the Asiatic and the North American looks at things. The United Nations are concerned with problems of this sort—one Bloor Street [in Toronto], a Center for Communications Research (Al Shea) aided in working on this sort of problem. And others here and elsewhere are more and more focusing on what has become an extremely urgent problem of the present in view of the enormous advances in techniques of informing and confusing the multitude.

Well, this is what Innis took up as his primary concern—what light had history to throw on this whole problem of human understanding based as it must be on the transmission of ideas, information, commands, and so on. And so he moved from *Economics 3f* to *4b*—from a small clearly defined field which he helped to make so [influential] to a much more difficult and demanding field of research, one in which scholars of many nations are becoming interested, and it is because of his real and genuine contributions to this problem that he has become internationally known. It took courage to step out from a sheltered position in the staples field into areas in which no one could pretend to monopoly advantages and in which criticism could be sharp and devastating at the hands of 'experts' and 'specialists' who resented intrusion into their well-established preserves. The dangers of misunderstanding were very great and early reviews of his work make this very clear. It is only now beginning to be grasped in its meaning and content, although many continue to argue his major work for which he will be known is his early work, which is so much bunkum. It is important to know his early work to get at the later advances, but we cannot stop there (Hancock at lunch—mouth full[97]). In sum, Innis of the staples is but part of the man.

With Easterbrook's next point, he makes elaborations regarding course readings, stating that his focus going forward will be on the contributions of Innis and others concerning the subject of communication. This will include "an <u>outline</u> sketch of his *Empire and Communications* and *The Bias of Communication*—enough to give us perspective" followed by "a more detailed treatment of his recent volume [...] *Changing Concepts of Time*" [...] mainly concerning "Canada-U.S. relations [...]. You will find in looking at this volume that he could write with great clarity when he chose although as he worked in this field his increasing mastery made this much less a problem. Exploratory writing is much more difficult as a problem of communications than the revision and reformulation of ideas worked out in earlier stages. And you will note his lethal sense of humor—not a dull or stodgy page in the lot. Also note how hard he could hit at things he did not like. [There are] few punches pulled when words like freedom and liberty are abused or put to shady uses." The course, Easterbrook continued, will address readings by Karl Deutsch and Norbert Wiener "and others as we go along and time permits." It will end, he says, with some recent literature "on the impact of radio and television [and their implications for] the speeding up [of relations and activities] and the new possibilities of mass manipulation in these

---

97   Easterbrook likely is referring to historian W.K. Hancock.

new media. [These involve the] problems of advertising and propaganda in our time." Easterbrook goes on to discuss course readings and proceeds as follows:

Havelock's *Crucifixion of Intellectual Man* is a must. Cochrane's *Christianity and Classical Culture* I shall refer to as desirable in the sense that it is a great book and helpful in throwing light on some of Innis's reflections on the Greco-Roman world. Gowers helps with the problem of Semantics. But apart from these, I do not press for any on the list. I shall refer to some here and there where relevant but unless you have a keen interest in one or more of the rest [they are] to be regarded as supplementary ammunition. I shall expect you to become acquainted with Norbert Wiener's *The Human Use of Human Beings* (his *Cybernetics* also is useful but it is more technical and the more useful points are in *Human Use*). And D.C. Somervell's summary of Toynbee's *Study of History* [is helpful also].[98] I shall have something to say about Kroeber in this context but hesitate to [...] suggest that it is an interesting book.[99] There will be a few minor additional readings to be dealt with but I shall not detail any elaborate reading list here. Careful reading rather than discursive reading is what is needed—and the total amount will depend on the rate at which we proceed.

Easterbrook then turned to discuss the first essay assignment which constituted a choice of three topics.[100] Although the first, he said, "looks very formidable" concerning law as an aspect of "the communications problem," *Changing Concepts*

---

98 Easterbrook probably was referring to Arnold J. Toynbee, *A Study of History*. Abridgement of Vols. I–VI by D.C. Somervell (New York, NY: Oxford University Press, 1947).
99 He is referencing A.L. Kroeber, *Configurations of Culture Growth*. Berkeley and Los Angeles: University of California Press, 1944. In his 1949 paper "The Bias of Communication" Innis writes that "I do not propose to do more than add a footnote to [...] [Kroeber's volume] and in this to discuss the possible significance of communication to the rise and decline of cultural traits." Innis, *The Bias of Communication*, p. 33.
100 Easterbrook tells students that it must be 15–20 typed pages in length and submitted by February 29, 1953. "I want something turned in that you have thought about," he says, "not scrambled together the night before—read, talk and reflect, but don't try throwing a line—[you] might do it in a large class regarding the fur trade, but not here." Easterbrook's final version of this assignment has not been found. However, what likely was a draft prepared prior to Innis's death (containing Innis's questions from the previous year and a December 1 due date that Easterbrook subsequently altered) is reproduced in Appendix 1 of this volume. Not only did Innis's questions frame what Easterbrook taught, the due date given by Easterbrook on this draft (February 29) was incorrect (as 1953 was not a leap year, but 1952 was) indicating, again, that Easterbrook made direct use of Innis's course materials.

of Time contains an essay that "may give some courage"[101] while the question of communications should "throw light on present-day difficulties [as it may prompt you to address] where you feel his [Innis's] work to be adequate and where [it is] incomplete." Finally, while he told students that the essay topic is to be worked out more fully through class discussions and in his office hours, Easterbrook provided more ideas for their consideration, such as how American-Canadian relations are "affected by technologies of communication"; "advertising as a force in modern society"; "propaganda devices and their implications for the present"; "sanction as a problem of the large corporation, and so on."

---

101 Harold A. Innis, "Roman law and the British empire," in *Changing Concepts of Time*, 47–76.

December 2, 1952: *Capacities involving Roman and common law*

The editor assumes that the following is what Easterbrook presented for this lecture as, despite not being dated, the notes reproduced below are a continuation of his brief November 25 references to law (and were filed immediately after that lecture).

[In common law] the facts are those of the case, of the moment. [Among the] advantages of common law [...] [is its focus on] facts and the scientific tradition, but [there is also a] strong tendency for considerations that relate to the short-run and [thus] the long-term implications are neglected, i.e., the problem of continuity in time is neglected. The emphasis is on practical problems to the neglect of theoretical principles and there is little place for philosophical theory or theoretical speculation of any sort (e.g., Harvard Business School with its case method as the 'intellectual center' of Harvard[102]). [At Harvard, there is] not much interest in general principles as in the Roman law tradition and it is much less tied in with the academic field with its interests in speculation. [This is] very different from the situation in Roman Law France. In common law countries the close connections are not with universities but with politics which reflect the power of the legal profession.

[There is an] interesting footnote on p. 59 [in *Changing Concepts of Time*]—the common law [tradition] tends to mold facts to suit words and the Roman law [tradition] to mold facts to suit writing. In the former, the interpretation of the fact is the thing and no two situations are exactly alike. [...] Facts may be molded with the situation and words themselves undergo changes in meaning over time unless there are defenses against such change—for example, the code, or written form of Roman law is such a defense [as] the static word is an essential [feature] of the unchanging principle. Canon law is strong in such a defense as if laws are the will of God and as He is perfect such laws cannot change. With secular law, the absolutist state or imperial absolutism means a similar imperial control of law, with interpretation only by edict. In Rome, the shift to codified law accompanied the shift to despotism. [There was] no such codification with the Greeks; much of their law was customary throughout with faith in the person and justice of the lawgiver. It has been argued that language itself is important to the legal form.

---

102 Although he attended Harvard to pursue his doctorate (but transferred to Toronto to complete it under Innis's supervision), Easterbrook told students that he garnered the status of its business school from a remark made by a "Toronto law school man."

The Greek language, more artistic and less formally precise, did not lend itself to comprehensive codes. [It is] no accident that written or code law developed where the Latin language was supreme [as it was] a language of great formal complexity in which ideas may be classified and distinctions made with "considerable nicety."

Latin was the official language in French law courts until the 16th century. In northern France [there was the] greater influence of Teutonic language and a stronger oral tradition. And English, like the Teutonic language, is not suited to the fine distinctions and precise meanings demanded of language in written law. Early England was a country of rapid change, a succession of conquerors, rapid changes in language, and the absence of a stable language necessary for code law. Even the Magna Carta was not a matter of a code of specific laws but of legal procedures. English law is not the law of a code but an account of an accumulation of precedents, involving some modifications by the state but fundamentally decisions are those of the judges rather than of written legislation. England received Roman ideas in distinction from continental countries which received Roman codes. The English vernacular lacked the precision and subtlety sufficient to ensure the general applicability of code laws and where language is vague, the latter may be observed while the spirit is violated, hence [there has been a] constant need for court interpretations to preserve the original intention of the legislator (Lipsay's essay[103]). In this situation interpretation and precedent are the thing. From individual decisions to a principle of justice rather than from abstract principle for application to individual cases.

It is probably fair to say that geographic elements are not absent in these decisions. Small compact areas, like Greece and England, lend themselves to oral customary law as consistency is more easily achieved via the ease of communications. Large continental areas of empires such as Rome and France could not afford a customary law that stresses divisiveness of localities […] [that might] create confusion. For consistency of application over wide areas, code law is a necessity.

So many elements are at work in explaining differences in legal systems—language, geography, problems of centralization, nature of political systems and their bases of authority. Innis was particularly interested in the 'language' angle and the problem of demands of law on words. […] [With an] appeal to principles (which are abstract) [there is a] great need for a more or less static language[104] and one of great precision and fine shades of meaning—a necessity of a strong bureaucratic administration with its emphasis on unchanging rules. All the strength of centralized control [is found] here and Roman law is an admirable precision instrument [but it]

---

103 It is not clear what "Lipsay's essay" refers to.
104 Here Easterbrook jots down what appears to be "Ullman." It is likely he is referencing Stephen Ullman, *Words and Their Use* (New York, NY: Philosophical Library, 1951).

lacks the flexibility of customary oral law of the common-law tradition [in which] the interpretation of the letter [of the law] and its spirit lies with each case and its reliance on individual judicial decisions. [Common law is] a more democratic law, with great scope for change, for freedom of enquiry, and undoubtedly this is important in such areas as science and economics. But [common law has] weaknesses too in its greater vagueness, [implying] a less certain instrument of centralized control [making it] difficult, apart from favorable situations, to check absolutist tendencies of strong pressure groups—i.e., [its] lack of executive power.

In Roman law, politics dominates law and uses it. In common law, law and lawyers dominate politics, and their preoccupation with specific cases makes for a loss of continuity and a lack of awareness of problems of duration or time.[105] The immediate 'problem' [in common-law countries] is the thing, to be solved as it is met,[106] with little room for theoretical speculation. In the case of economics, [...] [most] take a problem with no need to consider the theoretical apparatus necessary to attack on it. [As for] theory, the search for principles, there is little room for this. Innis was greatly impressed with the ability of lawyers to master facts in a short period of time, then move on to the next case.

On p. 60 [in *Changing Concepts of Time*, Innis wrote the following:] "Traditions of procedure in common law countries emphasizing the oral tradition in the court and in Parliament imply a background unsympathetic to the social sciences with their emphasis on the written tradition." But [here also he recognized the] problem of lack of depth in law which goes with quick shifts from one case to another.

Social sciences show a very different weakness—an inability to shift quickly from one problem to another, but greater mastery of complex problems. [They entail] a long and tedious process of enquiry, which is very different from procedures of courts. Lawyers are obsessed with the facts, the social scientist with fine abstractions.

Common-law hierarchies run counter to military and ecclesiastical hierarchies but in its tone and method [they are] very close to hierarchies of business and the connections between business and law are very close. Their outlook is much the same [in terms of their] preoccupation with problems, with the present, and impatience with theory or abstract principle. [...] The problem of continuity is neglected by both. [...] [Innis] regards it as one of the functions of social science to offset the effects of the obsession of common law with the present fact and its impatience with concepts and the abstract principle.[107]

---

105   Easterbrook writes and underlines the word "Business" in the margin alongside this paragraph.
106   The editor has replaced Easterbrook's "solve as we meet it" with "to be solved as it is met [...]."
107   At the end of this paragraph, Easterbrook types "III p. 61" indicating that the subsequent paragraph addresses pp. 61–5 in *Changing Concepts of Time*.

Innis's comment on divine right notions [...] [on pp. 62–3 in *Changing Concepts of Time*, concerns the] strength of these in the English Crown and later Parliament. [This] produced a reaction in the divine right of the United States [...] and the divine right of its union as opposed to the divine right of states (also a problem in Canada, i.e., the divine right of provinces vs. that of Ottawa) and the central place of law in politics as set out in the written constitution. [...] [This is] reflected in the importance of U.S. Supreme Court decisions in economic and social reform issues—issues in which legal aspects, although only one aspect, are taken as the primary facts. The fact, the case, the problem. [...] [The] difficulty is to find the principle which provides some coherence and continuity to the decision-making process.

[As for Innis's] reflections on U.S. imperialism, he associates it with the decline of common law and the emphasis on written law. Roman law is linked with a concern with territorial control, expansion over space. [Innis recognizes here a] reliance on political solutions although not without misgivings, including signs of control over communications exerted through political machinery, e.g., witch-hunts.[108] Common law is associated in England with the slow rise of freedom of expression in any sphere. Roman Law in the United States [instead is] identified with increased centralization and this control is a characteristic of countries in which common law found no place. [There is a] problem of cause and effect [in Innis's observations]. There is a correlation here, but contrasts in law systems symbolize rather than explain recent trends in U.S. politics. [Innis is pointing to the] problem of administration over great space without centralization and without reliance on the written form. Where dangers are great, it is not unreasonable to expect a closer approach to attitudes he associates with Roman law and its search for a solution to the problem of duration [...] [through] balance [...] [toward instead] a one-sided concern with the politics of space. Control of communications is closely tied in with the sanctions problem. It is not difficult to see reasons for the increased strength of Roman Law conceptions in the United States, but Innis is more concerned with the implications of the shift [and his recognition that] only very favorably situated areas can afford the common-law system with its weakness in executive power.

So there are two ways of looking at the problem: (a) why the penetration of Roman law, its growing strength on the North American continent, and (b) the consequences of this penetration. Innis focuses on the second. He notes its dangers, and an awareness of these dangers is itself important in helping people to understand themselves. In turning to Canada he pushes the same notions farther.

---

108 Easterbrook is referencing Innis's disdain for the anti-communist "witch-hunts" of the day.

U.S. imperialism has provoked a counter-imperialism here and at least a nascent nationalism. [This has involved and facilitated an] increasing bureaucratization of economics and politics, and the decline of common-law values. [...] [For Innis this led to his] historical pessimism or, rather, skepticism since he believed to the end that increasing knowledge of the forces that shape our thoughts and thinking processes is itself an antidote, or at least a hope that we will achieve clear vision in time.[109]

---

109 Along the margin, Easterbrook writes the following: "Great complexity & uncertainty → rules—clear cut & unchanging—conformity—Essentially a problem of bureaucracy, administration—life & flexibility in face of processes which call for uniformity & the status quo."

January 6, 1953: *Ways of thinking and developments in law*

In the first class of the new year, Easterbrook discusses the paper Innis was to have presented as the newly elected president of the American Economic Association. At its annual meeting in December 1952, Easterbrook participated in the panel honoring Innis during which his unfinished work was read. Easterbrook (who helped prepare the paper for publication in the *American Economic Review*) made Innis's draft available to students. Easterbrook points out that Innis's interest in communications began with his research on "trade routes regarding the exchange of staples, that is, trade routes of commerce (space)," which he later developed through his work on "trade routes of culture or the exchange of ideas and information." Easterbrook elaborates that in both Innis's staples and communications research he was interested in "values and problems [that were] much the same, [...] [namely the] freedom of the individual in his exchange or use of the intellect on the one hand [...] [and the] stability requirements of power structures on the other." Here he references Innis's analysis of the "aggressive individualism" that characterized the activities of the Northwest Company alongside its need for stability. The inability to reconcile these during the fur trade resulted in its failure to manage this problem (a problem, Easterbrook points out, that was fundamentally the same control vs. freedom problem Innis examined when he assessed the Greek city-state). A central question Innis posed was how to preserve values associated with individual freedom given "the survival needs of the political structure within which such values are preserved or destroyed." Easterbrook goes on to address the class as follows:

There is nothing new about this problem. Havelock attacks it from a different slant in his *Crucifixion of Intellectual Man*, and Cochrane's *Christianity and Classical Culture* centers on it. What Innis did that distinguishes his work from others was to place the communications problem squarely in the center of the picture [...] [as he gave] the study of communications a strongly historical bent formerly lacking and in doing this he greatly enlarged the area of inquiry both in terms of space and in time. Toward the end, he was working toward considering more directly the implications of his long-range studies for the study of economics of the present day and that is what his unfinished presidential address was about. [In it, he discussed] [...] what disequilibrium in communications has to do with the study of business disturbance;[110] the

---

110   For clarity, the editor has corrected this sentence in which Easterbrook wrote the following: "just what disequilibrium in the communications has to do with the study of business disturbance."

almost overriding importance of nationalism in economic writings; and the question of what produces economists.

Why do economists think the way they do?[111] Why the great rate of advance in economic thought in some areas, while its extreme backwardness in others? Do the most powerful nations produce the best economists? Why the great differences in economic approach in Roman and common-law countries? What he was trying to do was to help economists to understand themselves [...] [and why] their tools [...] [have a] very limited applicability in many instances [...] and [why it is] time that this was grasped. We understand that cultures via the study of communications and economics are culturally conditioned. If nothing else, this direction of thought should produce a more sophisticated economics. [Innis had] no quarrel with the use of highly abstract tools of advanced economic analysis but felt it rather important that the tool users know what they are doing [...] [i.e.,] the forces shaping their thought. Of course, such reflections are relevant far beyond the area of economics. And if nothing else, his writings have made many social scientists uncomfortable—not the way to popularity, but good medicine.

One aspect of Innis's work which marks it off from a good deal of thought in economic history in the United States is the absence of any break with European traditions, of turning his back on the old world. Much of our economic history in Canada is simply an extension of the economic history of Europe. And in terms of both economic and cultural pulls, it was perfectly natural for him to look to the old world in a way quite foreign to the approach of his [American] brethren across the border. This led to a worldview rather than one marked off by a single national boundary. Canadian economic history is international to a degree much greater than that of most economic histories—a fact which itself makes for difficulties in communications with those absorbed in the problems of single nations. [This is part of] the meaning of his stress on political economy rather than economics.

Last day we went over a few general points from *Empire and Communications* on the Roman Empire, beginning with the republic of the 5th and 4th centuries, the strength of the oral tradition, and the strength of deliberative assemblies.[112] This was reflected in law, [specifically] the absence of written law. The importance of trade led to the development of a commercial law of great flexibility. Although there was recourse to the written document in intercourse with aliens—the use of treaties in the law of the provinces—the oral tradition was at first strong in civil law pertaining to Roman citizens.

---

111 Innis's guiding question, which he first encountered as an undergraduate in a philosophy course at McMaster University, was "Why do we attend to the things to which we attend?"
112 Several paragraphs in what follows repeat what Easterbrook discussed previously.

It was when he turned to Rome that Innis began to emphasize the factor of law in history. Without doing much with this theme at this point (to be left until we get round to his essay in *Changing Concepts of Time*), you might note that in his work common law, broadly speaking as compared with Roman law, is taken as the more flexible legal form, less formal, less dogmatic, and less absolute in its approach to legal questions. [This can be seen by] its stress on interpretation according to the facts of the case rather than to abiding principles formulated in advance, greater scope for continuous (as distinct from revolutionary or radical change), and less reliance on tradition and authority or on prestige factors. Obviously, for him, his values are closely associated with this oral tradition and his preference clearly is here. Roman law, on the other hand, appeals to principles formulated in advance, [it is] universal and lasting, [and it is] authoritarian and relatively unchangeable. In essence [Innis underlines] a contrast between written and unwritten law (a contrast he points out even more sharply in his references to written [U.S.] and unwritten constitutions [U.K.])—the one with its greater scope for individual freedom [Britain], the other written with its emphasis on the supremacy of the law over the individual [the United States].

The contrast needs qualification, as the distinction is not as clear and sharp as this, as he knew, but it will do as a starting point. [There are] no pure [or ideal] types anyway in reality although [they are] useful for conceptual purposes—but more on this later. One minor point [to make at this stage is that there is] some confusion possible regarding the terms civil and common law.[113] Civil sometimes has reference to the whole Roman legal system. Under Roman law, [civil law] originally referred to local law (i.e., for Roman citizens) as distinct from the law pertaining to their intercourse with aliens. Now, however, civil law usually refers to the body of private law developed from the Roman law in states where the legal system is substantially Roman.

Some of this comes up in Lord Macmillan's *Two Ways of Thinking*[114]—a beautiful little essay on this general theme—as he generalizes on the basis of the same distinction that Innis has drawn. On p. 8, Macmillan writes that "the fundamental distinction between the methods of two of the greatest products the world has ever seen, the civil (code) Law and Common (case) Law" begins with Justinian's Institutes published in 533 A.D. These appeal to certain fundamental principles from which the whole law could be deduced—the conception of order, logic and reason in the regulation by law of human affairs (p. 10). Roman law continued via this conception to rule by reason long after her authority had been destroyed.

---

113 In parentheses, here Easterbrook comments that he "looked over some of the essays handed in last year and this not uncommon" indicating, again, that his presentation of *Innis 4b* directly reflected what Innis taught.
114 Lord Macmillan, *Two Ways of Thinking* (Cambridge, UK: Cambridge University Press, 1934).

Contrast this with England. Civil law was never the law of England. [Given its] dislike of things of Rome, the native growth [of its legal system], [...] [and its law's growth] out of practice, it never developed as a complete system. [In England, law was] the work not of professors or philosophers, but of practitioners [...] [and their] reliance on precedent: "what did we do last time?", not "what would be right this time?" [English law emphasized an] appeal to experience vs. fixed theory or principle or abstract reasoning—the logical method as empirical method. Code law vs. case law—proceed from principles to instances in the one [code law]; the other way round in the other.

[There is] some questioning of the hardening of precedent as producing rigidity in common law, but the appeal to facts which are never quite the same leaves room for novelty, change, twisting and turning, that is, flexibility in spite of this reliance on precedent. Macmillan shows the relationship of these two ways of thinking, inductive and deductive, to the approach to questions of religion and man's view of God. The search for infallible principles in religion on the Continent and in Scotland was a marked contrast with the course pursued in England regarding the Church of England which he quotes as the least dogmatic of all churches.[115]

In philosophy and economics the same distinction is drawn. Adam Smith, a Scot, applied deductive, fundamental principles of human nature as the starting point for deducing economic principles, although [his work was] saved from an extreme position by his acquaintance with men of commerce.

One way of thinking stresses tradition, the status quo, [and it is] conservative. The other is attracted by change vs. tradition (progress vs. stability again). This is reflected in politics—reliance on predetermined principles vs. reliance on experience. On p. 36 [Macmillan provides] interesting reflections on the French Revolution [as an example of] logic pushed to the extreme [in contrast with his] reflection that the Englishmen never recognized a revolution when he sees one. On p. 43 [he writes,] "A written constitution compels the revolutionary to face the logic of his policy; an unwritten constitution enables him to avoid it." Common law and continuity vs. upset [enabled] stability [to be] achieved via receptivity to change vs. a strenuous resistance to it. [There is a] question of how much choice [there is] in these matters as ways of thought conducive to change seem to me to be associated with areas [i.e., places and times] in which the security of the larger framework is not seriously threatened. With growing uncertainty there follows the process of hardening, [as with] the growing strength of the written tradition and what is sometimes called the process of bureaucratization which Innis would call a monopoly of the media of communication. Obviously, he had in mind monopoly

---

115 Ibid., 27.

and competition on the cultural as well as well as the economic level when he studied legal and religious systems, and we know where his heart was.

One or two other points on law that emerge from *Empire and Communications*: As some of you know two main problems emerged following the death of the ideal of the city-state (roughly in the 4th-century B.C.). Man was no longer seen as just a unit or fraction of the self-governing city but man seen now (a) as an individual—alone. [At this time] new conceptions appear on the rights of man as an individual and of the equality of all men. [...] Man alone as a conception led to a greater stress on religious or spiritual values than the Greek was inclined to give. And (b) man [was conceptualized] as a member of a much larger unity than the city, that is, the universe. And law and jurisprudence reflected both these changes in outlook.

This was seen in the revision of the law of Rome—originally a law of the city for a very restricted body of citizens. With the growth of Roman power and with problems concerning the place of the individual in the larger structure, there emerged the new conception of natural law—the rights of man as natural rights and in the nature of things, according to reason. [This was] a very marked shift away from the religious and ceremonial aspect of law and from the Greek's interest in ethics and the question of "what is good." Now [it became] a practical question of the rights of individuals in a world state—the state as the creature of the law, enforcing the rights of man, [and ideally constituting] a restraint, the only one, on the naked use of force.

We find in Cicero a conception of the true law—one rooted in reason, eternal and unchangeable, binding at all times on all peoples. [According to him,] justice stemmed from God and the nature of things with all men subject to one law and equal before the law. This raised questions of mutual rights and mutual obligations which all states must recognize if they are to endure. The argument emerged that a common agreement about rights and responsibilities was the only alternative to rule by force. Authority [now was to be] based on law and justified on moral grounds as the law of God (Cicero wrote *Republic* and *The Laws* about the middle of the 1st-century B.C.).

This conception of jurisprudence was developed in the 2nd and 3rd centuries after Christ. In the 3rd century, the constructive period of the Roman jurist came to an end and the era of codification begins culminating in Justinian's 'Institutes' which appear in the 6th century. It was a system of law designed as the instrument for a highly centralized system of authority. Its emphasis was upon the authority of the state—the great source of authority for most of Western Europe in a later period. [It emphasized] a higher law than the legislation of any particular state—a law unchangeable and divine, of universal applicability and rooted in reason.[116]

---

116 Here, in parentheses, Easterbrook adds a reference: A.A. Visiliev, *Justin the First* (Cambridge, MA: Harvard University Press, 1950).

Yet well before this codification, there were signs of the development of conflict which the laws were [crafted to] solve. As early as the 3rd century, with growing political decadence in the west, signs of an increasingly sharp division between things of the world and of the spirit emerged. [This involved a] loss of faith in the state as high points in men's moral perfection; a growing independence of religious institutions; obedience to Caesar and to God no longer the same; and Christianity stressed the divided jurisdiction of Church and state. Before Christianity morality and religion were centered in the state, symbolized in the monarch who appears as both secular authority and divine ruler. Now [there emerged a] division between things temporal and things spiritual, and western Europe was to face over long centuries this conflict of Church and State. And law itself was to reflect this growing cleavage. This was very clear in the medieval world, but [we should take] a closer look at Rome and, more particularly, the Byzantine empire before we move on.

Before turning to Byzantium, I want to refer briefly to a paper Innis read in Paris in 1951, titled "The Concept of Monopoly and Civilisation."[117]

---

117 As this paper was not yet published, in pencil Easterbrook informed students that he "will put it with other papers on Innis (2 or 3 copies of it)", adding that it is "useful regarding his notion of monopoly and for the perspective it gives of his treatment of its problem [indecipherable word or words] history." At this juncture, Easterbrook's lectures jump from January 6 to 20 with no indication of notes prepared for January 13.

January 20, 1953: *Conditions enabling the Byzantine empire*

As the lecture notes for January 13 appear to be missing and because Easterbrook previously told students that the subject of Byzantium would be pursued, fortunately his notes for the 20th begin with what are likely these additional points. Before reproducing these below, given that Easterbrook said he would reference Innis's then unpublished paper, "The Concept of Monopoly and Civilization," for the reader's information the following is an excerpt from its opening paragraphs. Originally a presentation Innis made at le Collège de France in Paris in the summer of 1951, Innis addresses Byzantine methods of balancing the temporal and spatial aspects of its empire involving military, religious, and artistic capabilities:

"In confining my comments to political organization, I shall restrict my attention to two dimensions—on the one hand the length of time over which the organization persists and on the other hand the territorial space brought within its control. It will be obvious in the case of the second consideration that organization will be dependent to an important extent on communications in a broad sense—roads, vehicles of transmission, especially horses, postal organization, and the like for carrying out orders. It will be less obvious that effective communication will be dependent on the diffusion of a knowledge of writing or in turn a knowledge of an alphabet through which orders may be disseminated among a large number of subjects.

A discussion of the other dimensions of a political organization, namely, duration, raises numerous problems. Examples of organizations which have persisted over a long period such as the Roman, late Roman, and Byzantine empires suggest that attention must have been given not only to the administration of territorial space but also to ways and means by which survival was achieved. Obvious devices involved with the problem of duration were the organization of force, notably in defence and the encouragement of industry and trade essential for the support of defence. Force in itself implies a hierarchical arrangement but also an arrangement which permits the rapid advancement of ability to the top. Every soldier must carry a marshal's baton in his knapsack."[118]

---

118 Innis, "The Concept of Monopoly and Civilization," 85–6. Easterbrook was as an Associate Editor for this edition and was primarily responsible for the paper's publication.

Below, Easterbrook proceeds to tell students that while Innis treated Greece as an ideal-type *culture*, he regarded Byzantium to have been an ideal *empire*. Conceptually, for Innis, empires constitute the largest and, at least from a long-term political-economic perspective, most important examples of organizational media. His lecture continues with a lengthy recounting of Innis on Byzantium's success, likely in anticipation of comparing it to Innis's concerns regarding the modern American empire.

Examples of organizations that have persisted over long periods suggest that attention must have been given not only to the administration of territorial space but also to ways and means by which survival was achieved. Reliance on force raises the questions of its limitations, [especially given] the enormous demands it makes on the resources of the country protected. The Byzantine army seemed to have met the problem by the extraordinarily effective use of available resources and the necessary continued use of force meant the presence of a continued effective demand for ability at higher levels in the army, as bureaucracy goes stale unless under continued pressure. But at best, this raises problems of continuity in terms of succession and the inherent tendency to growing rigidity present in the bureaucratic form. Only in exceptional instances can reliance on force solve the problem of continuity. The limitations of force in this direction may be overcome by reliance on religion and its concern with control over time as implicit in its concern with immortality and eternity.

In the Byzantine empire, religion was effectively linked with force. The architecture of Constantinople reflects the glorification of the state and prestige of religion. Imperial ceremony was joined to religious ritual. Sculpture and painting reflected the demands of both religion and the state—not an easy balance to maintain since the conservative character of religious belief renders it less adaptable to the demands of force and the attraction of able leaders may result in a religious hierarchy which may embarrass if not threaten the state.

Innis's concern with monopoly and the problems posed by monopoly is very apparent in this paper. He reviews the situation in Babylon and Egypt from this point of view, [most particularly concerning their] enormous powers of duration. This power was present in the difficulties that Sumerian culture presented to conquerors such as the Assyrians and the Persians. In Egypt, a king-priest balance was upset following the decline of political organization and the absolute powers of the king, a bias which left Egypt open to invasion from other empires.

Rome, on the other hand, failed to find an adequate support in religion. To the east in Constantinople, however, a balance of control over monopolies of time and monopolies of space explained the success evident in the duration of the Byzantine empire.

Following the collapse of the Western Roman empire, in the face of invasion, loss of control over territorial space was followed by the rise of control over time in the west. A religious monopoly was built up through dependence on a limited body of scriptural writings on a relatively permanent medium, that is, parchment. [This was] an immensely powerful ecclesiastical organization, strong in duration of time but weak in its political control of space. Its monopoly invited competition from the new medium paper. [This facilitated] the revival of Greek learning with its destructive effects on the monopoly of Latin as a language [involving] cheap paper, the rise of the vernacular in literature, and the spread of literacy with its implications for monopoly. Differences in languages were emphasized as important in the determination of national boundaries. This divisiveness was enhanced [in the modern West] with the application of mass production in printing, which in the emphasis on freedom of the press has given rise to new monopolies in which problems of duration are neglected.[119]

[...]
(a) Roman bureaucracy.
(b) the traditions of classical Greece with their strong individualism.
(c) the spiritual ideas of the Oriental east—Christianity and Oriental religion.

It is important to realize that this was a delusional age [involving] political breakdown and the search for an escape from uncertainty [and that these conditions were] favorable to mystery religions and their rituals. [This was] apparent in the rise of the Persian (Iranian) cult Mithraism, with its pomp and ceremony, its sense of fellowship and discipline. The flood, the ark, the adoration and the shepherds, Heaven and Hell, sacrificial atonement, the last judgment, resurrection, sanctification of Sundays and December 25, all appeal to the masses with its emphasis on the afterlife. [It was] an alternative to their superstition and to the speculations of the educated. [Mithraism was] very strong in the army but it gave way before a greater rival. Christianity, with its obscure beginnings in Palestine, encouraged mysticisms, gave hope, and had attractions in its elaborate rituals, rich symbols, and its appeal to charity as a life principle. [Christianity also had much] scope for the influence of Greek philosophy with its intellectual content helped by legends, saints, and miracles.[120]

---

119 At this point some of Easterbrook's notes appear to be missing, including a page that links the end of this paragraph with what follows, beginning with "(a) Roman bureaucracy."
120 On the margin Easterbrook writes, "blend."

The fusion of these three elements provided a balance between individualism and the needs of political stability: a combination of Oriental authority held in check by Roman bureaucracy and its trained executive and supported by Greek democracy. This achieved what one writer refers to as "that elusive constancy of things which the twentieth century has set itself to recapture."[121] This was achieved in Byzantium via a joint rendering to Caesar and to God of each of these things.

Success in achieving this balance meant the establishment of a single bulwark against the peoples of Asia which threatened the whole civilization of the Medieval world. To this success the modern world owes the preservation of the wisdom of the ancients.

I cannot go into Byzantine history here, but a few points:

It is necessary to go back to Diocletian and his reforms 284–305 A.D. He placed the army under the control of the government, achieved uniformity in legislation, and divided the Empire into two Empires—east and west. Probably the most important [reform was that he] utilized an Oriental conception of the King as Divine—the Emperor as demi-God, descended from God, [a King that] persecuted Christians. [As a result of] their abdication, civil wars, and Constantine [...] [becoming] the sole Emperor, [...] [Constantine] took up Diocletian's administrative system and continued efforts to deify the position of the Emperor. [When he] committed himself to Christianity after his struggle for Emperorship, Christians were a minority, about one-fifth of the population, but [Christianity was] [...] the strongest religion and was given full legal recognition in the Edict of Milan in 313 A.D. The Church was seen as a State Church, the Emperor as its Chairman, and the grateful Church did not object [as it] had its defender in a dangerous world. The Church-State conflict seemed to be at an end.

---

121 The author is Robert Byron who is referencing the artistic tradition of Constantinople as perfected in the paintings of El Greco. Robert Byron, *The Byzantine Achievement, an Historical Perspective, A.D. 330–1453* (New York, NY: Knopf, 1929), 34.

January 27, 1953: *Byzantium: history of an ideal-type empire*

Easterbrook continues his previous lecture by summarizing Innis's analysis of Byzantine civilization. The detail provided below likely reflects Easterbrook's recognition of the importance of this empire for Innis as a model of duration and vibrancy entailing its variously balanced attributes and capacities.

Establishment of Constantinople. As the natural meeting place of Europe and Asia [it was a] magnificent location from almost any point of view. [It was] well located against attack from enemies of the Empire. [It had] both a strong army and strong navy necessary to [engage in an] effective attack. [...] [It was also in a] central location on the world's major trade routes [resulting in] much mixing of cultures and races throughout its history.

Constantinople became the Second Rome (although Latin Rome would never accept it as such), where Greek, Roman, and Church East met and mixed. [It became a] center of learning where Greek cultural elements were backed by Roman military traditions and the law of Rome.

It was Constantine who effectively linked imperial with religious power [through the] divine right of the emperor as the unquestioned center of authority, political and religious, protecting the Church and using it to his ends.

Western Rome went under in the 5th century before the barbarians, the Visigoths, and later the Huns. Constantinople [also was] under attack but this was diverted to the west. Later, the Ostrogoths tried again, but luck and circumstance left Constantinople more or less intact as Rome, old Rome, fell apart. Following A.D. 476, Constantinople became the new political center of the Roman Empire as the barbarians were in control of the West (southern Spain, Italy, and Eastern Africa) while the Byzantine Empire retained control of much of the Balkan Pan, Asia Minor, Syria, and Egypt.

This political separation was eventually followed by religious separation.[122] The cleavage slowly widened between the Papacy and the Eastern Church as the latter was closely associated with greater political power. [It undertook a] slow development of independence from West Rome but at the price of domination by the state. Yet it was a state that benefitted enormously from the sacred character of emperorship. Through Christianity, Greek individualism was curbed and Roman

---

122 Penciled in the margin beside this sentence, Easterbrook writes the following: "not unchecked—periods of reconciliation, drawing together."

bureaucracy was modified. These in combination gave it an extremely strong despotism, strong in defense and in religious unity.

The next great name following Constantine was Justinian (nephew of Justin I), 527–65 A.D. [He faced] many problems, including Persian, Bulgarian and Slav attacks, and the opposition of those who would restore the old unity based in the West. However, Justinian established peace with the Papacy and managed to preserve and combine the imperial idea of old Rome and the Christian idea in a more or less balanced concern with space and time. [He exercised] absolute rule but one tempered by law. [Under his leadership, the empire] reconquered much of Africa and Italy and southern Spain, [as well as] islands of the Western Mediterranean, and the Mediterranean again became a Roman lake. Greater difficulties [were experienced] in the east—Persians troublesome, also Huns and Slavs, but an elaborate system of fortifications held the lines to the east. His greatest reform involved the Institutes and other compilations of law which gave the emperor power based on the absolute authority of an immutable, unchanging law, while the Church, in its stress on social justice, lessened the hardness of old Roman law. A period of great cultural and artistic advance ensued, [as demonstrated by] architecture and sculpture. A balance between the traditions of old Rome and the Church East [was attained] but [it became an] oversized empire. At the end of his reign, [Justinian was] financially broke and the solution of difficulties with the Papacy proved to be only temporary.

Chaos ensued for a half-century following his death and a solution [...] [was pursued by] strengthening its oriental despotism. In the 7th century, under savage attack from Persia and the even more dangerous Arabs, Islam (which rose in this century) spread over the whole Mediterranean world but was thrown back at Constantinople in A.D. 673. The sharp break with Rome occurred at this time. Greek replaced Latin as the official language and came to dominate both written and spoken forms. The Byzantine Church broke with Rome, and an Empire emerged in which no distinction was drawn between national and religious feeling. [There was] now complete independence [...] [from the] West [and Constantinople became] the great bastion of the civilized world against the Arabs who attacked again in A.D. 712 and A.D. 717–18. Its success against these was a victory more significant than Charles Martel's against the Arabs at Poitiers in A.D. 732.

But the 8th century was a dark one, torn by religious controversy. Byzantium was under heavy attack on all sides—it lost most of Italy, Crete, and Sicily to the Arabs—and Constantinople was besieged by Bulgarians who came very close [to seizing Adrianople] in A.D. 813.

The great years under the Macedonian dynasty—A.D. 867–1057—were years of remarkable recovery [in which the empire's] internal unity was restored. [It had re-emerged as] a strong Oriental Empire now at the peak of its greatness. [The Byzantines were the] champions of Hellenism and the orthodox faith. Constantinople—the great and unquestioned center of European civilization—regained its mastery of the Mediterranean and later regained control of the Balkan peninsula and southern Italy. [...] [It became] the strongest power in Asia as well, [involving a] great extension of its religious influence [through its] missionaries [leading to the] conversion of Russians. [By the] 10th century, Russia [had become] a Christian nation modeled on Byzantine civilization with Kiev the great religious center. [Constantinople again exercised] enormous influence over the whole civilized world. Its infallible emperorship was secular and divine. The Church was an instrument of expansion. It had a powerful and efficient army, a fine navy, and enormous wealth. Through its mercantile activity it monopolized the wealth of the known world, and its intellectual advances were just as great.

In the 11th century, signs of the end of this splendor [emerged due to] (a) the rise of feudal centers of authority, and of religious feudalism based on landed property (monasteries) and the increasing power of the Patriarch of Constantinople. [These developments led to an] increasing friction with the emperor and with the Papacy of Rome.

(b) The First Crusade in 1096 A.D. [...] covered Constantinople as much as it did the Holy Land and this increased friction between East and West [...]. Greeks now were heretics to the Latin. [For the Byzantine empire this marked the] beginning of its retreat and loss of territories, and as Venice became independent [it experienced] losses in the Balkan area and [...] a new period [of ascendancy] for the Turks of Asia followed.

Yet as late as the 12th century [the empire was] still enormously wealthy. It is estimated that the Byzantines had two-thirds of wealth of the world [and it enjoyed] a period of renewed intellectual and artistic advances. But its wealth [...] [also was] an invitation to attack [...] [as, for instance,] the fourth Crusade backed by the Papacy and the ambitions of a rising Venice which was out to capture the Empire's trade. In 1203, Crusaders finally took the city [Constantinople] and pillaged it the following year. The year 1204 seemed to be the end for it—books and works of art collected over nine centuries were dispersed and mostly destroyed. Culturally, [there have been] few tragedies in history to equal this. The end of Constantinople as the eastern bulwark of Christendom, that is, in terms of a highly centralized organization, opened the way for later Turkish conquests. Venetians and Latin princes divided the spoils of Empire.

There followed in the 13th century a short period of Latin control. Latin feudal land lordship [was based] more on the model of western Europe. The Venetians took over the bulk of the Empire's trade, but the Latin grasp was weak and in 1261 the Greeks took control again. [Constantinople was] a pale shadow of the old power, but a short-lived recovery followed. However, with civil wars, and social and religious disunity, commerce was lost to the Venetians and Genoese [and its] economic base was gone [as there was a] renewal of attacks from the East and no help whatever from the indifferent West. [The empire met its] final end as a political force in 1453 [when the Ottoman army conquered Constantinople], yet in these last years [there arose] a great artistic Renaissance. It was then the end of a centuries-old defense against barbarism in which Constantinople stood alone much of the time, but it left an enormous cultural impact—in Islam itself, in the Slavic east, and in the West. Her cultural hold on the Oriental world was never broken to this day—in Russia, Eastern Europe, [and among the] Turks, Greeks, Serbs, and Bulgarians. [The Byzantine empire was an extraordinary example of the] persistent power of a culture, [as demonstrated by its influence on] Spain, France, and England [and as likely will be the case] even centuries from now [...] long after its economic or material basis is gone.

A glance at the state and its rule of law: It was an absolute autocracy checked politically only by the fundamental laws of the Roman people involving the deep-rooted feeling that [state authority is rooted in the] power of delegation by the people to the Emperor. The Emperor was the source of all law, yet the law was something above him. Justinian's law was Roman law. The Isaurian (A.D. 717–867) Emperors introduced civil law principles in the law and humanized it. The Macedonian period [of the empire] (A.D. 867–1081 A.D.) tried to return to Justinian law, but much of the Church ethic remained.

So, the Byzantine state [was itself a] symbol of authority [and this involved the] worship of the state and the Emperor as its head and symbol. [Its power entailed] controlling a Church—a religion in which religious and secular elements mingled. There was no scope for discussion or controversy in the political arena but much room remained for differences in religion, which they took with great seriousness.

This attitude to things spiritual was of prime importance in the question of duration and long-lived stability. The attitude of people was an intensely religious one as life in this world [was understood to be relatively] unimportant and eternity was the big question and questions concerning eternity were vastly more significant than those of this world. So religious questions were of vital importance, and the Emperor was so closely identified with the Church that he frequently ran into religious controversies. The Church itself followed the early Church model, that is, it copied the organization of the secular state (i.e., strict control from top to bottom), and it left the last word with the Emperor. This worked reasonably well [as there was] not much interference by the Emperor in Church affairs. In the 5th century, [...] for instance, heresy was a crime against the State and punished by it, particularly where this constituted a political danger (as it usually was).

Much of Byzantium's powers of endurance must be sought in its religious mystical patriotism [in which] the infallibility of divine leadership was a great positive force. There was no apathy here—[the Byzantines were] champions of Christianity [engaged in] a world mission. The divine Emperor was confronted with this intense religious feeling of the people and his power was further circumscribed by an administrative bureaucracy with its rules and its trained executive, and by the continued vitality of Roman law and the concept of uniformity of justice for all. He had great power yet it was not an arbitrary power, and this great power was needed in a highly dangerous world, full of enemies, lacking in allies.[123]

Since the people took their religion so seriously, often minor points of difference in interpretation could have serious political consequences.

(a) That concerning the two views of Christ, whether of One Nature, or Two Indivisible Natures, whether of single divine nature, or of two, the human and the divine. The first obscured the humanity of Christ and questioned the position of Mary. This was a problem for two centuries which weakened the state as long as it lasted. There are no differences so bitter and irreconciled as religious ones—religious war is a frightful thing.

(b) The Iconoclastic controversy [among imperial and Church authorities beginning in the 8th century constituted] a Puritan movement to destroy all graven images. It died out only in the 9th century and was a source for a time of great strains and tensions within the imperial structure.

These examples illustrate the enormous part that religious feeling played in the life of the people. Religion was vastly more important than politics, yet the divinity of the Emperor, God's representative, was not in question and solidarity persisted in spite of such strains. This element of sanction, of unquestioned acceptance of leadership as a right and a problem, is the great element of continuity that wielders of power are prone to overlook.[124]

---

123 In the margin Easterbrook adds, "When later royal absolutism came back (Louis XIV—no such checks on arbitrary rule)."

124 In parentheses at the end of this sentence Easterbrook adds, "Timasheff on law—the element of coercion, the element of sanction of what is 'right' both there in any enduring legal form."

In this crucial area of religion, the biggest unsolved problem was the relations of the Church with Papacy. There was jealousy of the old for the new capital, and when Rome ceased to be the political center it still claimed primacy. Rome never allowed Constantinople even second place. Toward the end of the 6th century, the Patriarch took on the title of worldwide leadership [and it was] a break reinforced by language barriers as the Latin West came to face the Greek East. Internal squabbles in the Byzantine Empire only embittered relations (Byzantine 'solutions' had to take into account problems in the East of its empire and these frequently were not acceptable to Rome).

Up to the 7th century, the Papacy had acknowledged overlordship of the Empire. In the 8th century, it dropped this allegiance and looked to the Franks of western Europe. The crowning of Charlemagne [on December 25, A.D. 800] was a blow from which Constantinople never recovered as reconciliation was out of the question. In the religious sphere, Rome at no time dropped its claims to world power status and the Fourth Crusade destroyed the last chance of reunion.

Two different conceptions of Christian organization and authority emerged—Papal infallibility vs. Constantinople's clinging to the democratic ideals of early Christians and its refusal to accede to absolute Rome's demand for absolute submission. In the East, there was greater tolerance and flexibility. The power of the Byzantine Church was based on the rich rituals that enhanced the majesty of the Emperor, its close ties with the people, and its refusal to accept foreign domination, built up a national sentiment and its theology was sufficiently free so as not to stifle intellectual activity.

Backing this power and stability—in administration and faith (administration [involving and supported by its] army and navy [...]) —was her great economic strength. Fundamentally, Constantinople was a Greek city-state thriving on its trade. It was a magnificent commercial city, with trade at its peak in the 9th and 10th centuries. [Furthermore, it was] a closely regulated economy, [in terms of] prices, wages, hours, standards of consumption, and the level of profits through its machinery for state intervention and control in the guilds or royal monopolies as with silk manufactures. This was a system of regulation that lasted as long as the empire did.[125] It had a solid economic base for a bureaucratic economy existing in a world of enormous and pressing uncertainties as it was never free from the threat of attack, and [there was a] feeling widespread over long centuries that onslaughts would eventually break down the defenses of the Empire. This same uncertainty

---

125 In the margin and connected to the end of this sentence using pencil, Easterbrook writes the following: "Yet control not watertight [...]. Freedom of both advance—very important regarding military conquests."

may help to account for the deeply religious sense of the people [...] [as reflected in their concerns regarding] immortality and their preparation for eternity by subjection of the flesh, and by contemplation (monasteries and convents were crowded in this theocratic empire).

Well, [the fall of Constantinople in] 1453 [constituted] the wiping out of a great civilization—one which left a great legacy in arts and learning. [...] [It had been a] great stronghold for 1,100 years of learning and light in a very dark world, combining the administrative skill and stability of Rome, the spiritual feeling of the East, and the liveliness and aesthetic feeling of the Greeks.

[Constantinople did] not merely play a passive role as the custodian of past learning or the preserving of the treasures of the ancient world to be revived in the Western Renaissance in Classical literature and thought. It was an active force in the civilized world of its time and [we would live in] a very different world today if Byzantine had gone under before the Persians, Hungarians, or Arabs. It saved Hellenistic culture, and [...] by a practical machinery of government imposed on the highly individualistic peoples of a city-state, it also saved, intact, the great codification of Roman Life (as in Roman law as it was perfected between A.D. 450 and 564) to be revived in the 11th century. [This was] the great link between the ancient world and the modern [as law is] the first essential of stability in any empire, and this along with its religious impulses served to balance the short-sighted rationalism of the Greeks.

Byzantium left no great literary works, yet it built great libraries, and it subsidized education [resulting in a] great divergence between the written and spoken tongue. The vernacular had a life of its own, and the Church never lost contact with the common language of the people. [This was] important for its organic unity.

The reasons for its decline [included the] Black Death—Constantinople lost eight-ninths of its population [over the course of] eight attacks from 1347 to 1431.

It was an empire strong in such material considerations as economics and military power. [...] [These capabilities involved or were] based on compromises between the imperial bureaucracy with its administration of a great area on the bases of papyrus and an ecclesiastical hierarchy with its use of parchment and its concern with time. It had a realistic awareness of the importance of political power, but also of its limitations and the dangers of a one-sided concern with the problems of the moment, one of our afflictions today. The Keynesians tell us that failure to cope with the short-run means no long-run. [But we] could argue that our failure to take into consideration long-run elements of permanence is a guarantee of an unstable and very brief short-run. This represents much of the difference between the thinking of John Maynard Keynes and Joseph Schumpeter [...] [as we] cannot assume that the long-run will look after itself, and if the pressure is so great that we must concentrate exclusively on the short-run the game is up anyway. Innis's concern was that in the state of communications is to be found the Keynesian's attitudes toward time and its faith in the ability of the political machinery to keep things rolling—both biases of a paper civilization.

Continuing with this birds-eye view of *Empire and Communications*, later developments are more easily traced in his sections on parchment, paper, and the printing press.

February 3, 1953: *Implications of media—Byzantium to the 20th century*

Easterbrook begins by reviewing what had been discussed concerning the Byzantine empire. Using *Empire and Communications*, he follows this by addressing Innis on subsequent historical developments involving writing and printing. In the latter part of the lecture, he probes questions concerning nationalism and monopolies of knowledge, and relates Innis's interest in communications with capital investments, news, and advertising. As he concludes, Easterbrook addresses Innis's thoughts regarding values and the capacity of civilization to survive.

Finished up pretty much with Byzantium last day. [To review what was discussed,] periods of retreat were marked by consolidation along the lines of greater despotism and greater separation from the Latin West. Its greatest years were from the mid-9th to mid-11th century when western European struggled with the problems of restoring a shattered unity. The empire's biggest problems [...] [involved its] internal unity and cohesion in the religious sphere [as it was] important that [there be] no clear line between national feeling and religious sentiments. The Church and the Empire were one in the people's minds, and their refusal to accept foreign domination from the West or farther east [also was important].

The empire's economic strength backed this political duration. [Constantinople was] a city-state accumulating its capital via trade, a trade harnessed along with industry to the needs of the state.

Too commonly [Constantinople has been] regarded as playing a passive role; that of the great repository and preserver of ancient learning and science. [But it had] a strong impact on all nations which came into touch with it. It left no great literary works, although there is not full agreement on this, yet [it built] great libraries, [and it] subsidized education [enabling] the vernacular to have had a life of its own [thus facilitating a] great divergence between the written and spoken tongue.

<u>Notes regarding western Europe—Empire and Communications and The Bias of Communication.</u>[126]

---

126 Beneath this heading, by hand Easterbrook adds the following: "(1) Many points are raised [by Innis]. Any one of which could be basis of a course in itself. (2) China, Mohammedanism, India. (3) *Empire and Communications* (135–6): Constantine 'emphasized a strong centralised authority and joined a powerful ecclesiastical interest to a military bureaucracy [...]. Christianity became a religion of conquerors' [...]."

[According to Innis's] reflections on the Byzantine empire (in *Empire*, p. 139), it developed on the basis of a compromise between organizations reflecting the bias of different media: that of papyrus in the development of an imperial bureaucracy in relation to a vast area, and that of parchment in the development of an ecclesiastical hierarchy in relation to time.

With the spread of Mohammedanism—[and with the] decline of papyrus exports from Egypt—[the Roman empire] disappeared from Europe in the 8th century.

In contrast with papyrus, which was produced in a restricted area under centralized control to meet the demands of a centralized bureaucratic administration, and which was largely limited by its fragile character to water navigation, parchment [instead was] the product of a widely scattered agricultural economy suited to the demands of a decentralized administration and to land transportation, rough as it was. [Parchment suited this] continental character and for Innis the continent lent itself to bureaucratic organization.[127]

Another illustration of the tendency for each medium of communication to create monopolies of knowledge to the point where breakdown occurs—[a breakdown that is] internal and [that implies an existing] weakness before aliens [make incursions] on the fringes—[can be found in the case of the Holy Roman empire, which involved the] rise of a new monopoly based on parchment, and its breakdown following the introduction of paper.

Regarding the age of parchment, the spread of monasteries covered a great area in the West by the end of the 7th century. Mohammedanism was defeated in the West in 732. With the rise of the French Empire of Charlemagne—crowned emperor by the Pope in 800—reading and writing was a highly skilled craft. But [it implied a] political weakness, as reflected in the Teutonic practice of equal division among heirs, [resulting in an] empire split into national and intendent kingdoms.[128]

The attacks of Norsemen and Magyars [on the French empire] included separatist tendencies as local groups coalesced in defense.

In the 9th century, 886 marked the defeat of the Danes at Paris. A new kingdom of France then emerges in which conflict of Church and state has a long history involving drastic measures [taken by the latter] to weaken secular authority, aided by parchment in support of a powerful ecclesiastical organization with a monopoly of knowledge ([including a system of monastical] education).

---

127 In this paragraph, Easterbrook directly reproduced what Innis wrote and, accordingly, references Innis, *Empire and Communications*, 140.
128 In the margin, Easterbrook writes what appears to be the following: "9th to 15th centuries—fully destroyed by presses."

The development of paper in China took place about 105 A.D. using rags (linen made by regrading flax fibers) and the use of a brush (Confucius say, a picture is worth a thousand words as Life has demonstrated). [This enabled the] rise there of a government bureaucracy based on paper. [One result was the development of a] gulf between the governing and the lower classes which created a vacuum into which spread the Buddhism of India took place. In its spread to China, it found a useful medium of communication in paper and the development of block-printing [and a] reliance on a simple script which was understood widely and facilitated imperial control over wide areas—in short, control over space—although a difficulty with the continuity of control was seen in China's inability to solve dynastic problems. Regarding China as a case study in space control—[...] [especially its] duration aspects—I do not feel competent to generalize [on, for example, its] frequent loss of control to such invaders as the Mongols. [Instead, we] must treat it here as one area in which very little can be said [although it] would be an ideal case study given its centralized bureaucracy based on paper offset by a simple script and a tenacious language. Some interesting recent writings on the time problems of Chinese empires [have been published] but I have not digested them sufficiently to see their implications clearly—a study in itself. This is a highly complex area that is much less static than a superficial examination of its history would suggest.

Paper was introduced into Eastern Europe in the first half of the 8th century with paper production by the Mohammedans at Baghdad. The influence [of paper's use] was felt in Constantinople in its later days, particularly after the final separation of the Churches of East and West in 1054.

Paper manufacturing appears in the West late in the 13th century (about 1275). [Initially, paper was] important in [facilitating its] commercial expansion (Usher's *History of Mediterranean Banking*[129] [addresses the] oral tradition and the rise of written instruments in bills of exchange and insurance documents, at first only as records whose legality [...] was based on the word of witnesses and others). With the fall of Baghdad to the Mongols in about the middle of the 13th century, the spread of paper and its production and use in Italy was particularly marked after 1300. It spread from there to France and Flanders.

Paper manufacturing was a skilled monopoly, a product of cities [...] [that had particular] market factors and a cheap supply of rags. [Its production and use] weakened the control of monasteries of rural districts [and, in relation to this, it

---

[129] Easterbrook is referencing Abbot Payson Usher, *The Early History of Deposit Banking in Mediterranean Europe* (Cambridge, MA: Harvard University Press, 1943).

facilitated the] appearance of cathedrals and universities in the cities as the new centers of learning.

Innis has little to say on another area well worth exploring but again one in which I can say very little—i.e., the impact of <u>Muslim</u> civilization on Western Europe, particularly via Spain and Italy [involving their] vast libraries, particularly in Spain.[130] Its influence was widely felt, the more so when they lost their grip on Spain in the 13th century. Jews were active intermediaries between this civilization and that of Western Europe [due to their interpretative role enabling the] translation of Arabic works on a large scale into Latin, for example, some of the works of Aristotle. This was followed by the accommodation of Aristotelian teaching to biblical doctrine adapted to Christian teaching as those became available to the West. This process was aided following the fall of Constantinople in their <u>translation</u> directly <u>from the Greek</u>.

Latin as emphasized in monastery and the church lent itself to a monopoly of knowledge in priestly hands and widened the gap between the written and the oral tradition. [It was a] learned language in a highly complex script. [As such, it] left a gap between the vernacular everyday speech and that of the written instrument. Translation of the gospel was forbidden, although this was overcome to some degree by memorization and some translation in spite of prohibitions regarding translation into the vulgar tongue of the people. Charlemagne supported vernacular literature which had been translated orally and it was difficult with the use of paper to check the spread of heretical writings.

The Church was aware of the problems and the rise of the Dominicans and Franciscans helped to bridge the gap between the older monasticism and the vernacular (13th century).

In a section in *Empire* on <u>Roman Law</u> (pp. 159–65) [...] [Innis addressed] developments in relation to trade and commerce and the interests of urban centers. But more importantly [Roman law was] used by emperors to hold the Papacy in check and [...] [in turn] canon law was developed by the Church.

Roman law strengthened the position of monarchy in France [furthering the] great prestige of the legal profession with its close ties with the University of Paris and the strength of French lawyers—a powerful profession acting in support of the king. Their prestige was used in support of the rule of the emperor, weakening the position of the Papacy and the written tradition. In the state, law took grip in the bureaucratic administration of the kingdom and accentuated the conflict of king and Church. Law as the right arm of the state posed great if not new problems for the Papacy.

---

130 Easterbrook writes "Cordoba" above this sentence, likely referencing its library containing four hundred thousand volumes.

Different developments took place in England regarding the oral tradition and common law rooted in local customs. [It was an] unwritten [...] customary law out of which grew the jury system and parliamentary organizations. England thus escaped the influence of law as a professional monopoly [and it developed] much looser notions of property and property rights [and the law was more] subject to reinterpretation as conditions changed. [This enabled] greater flexibility for the growth of trade and of political discussion. The strength of the vernacular was opposed to the dominance of Latin in religion, and the Bible was translated into vernaculars by 1382.

[On pp.] 165–6 [in *Empire and Communications*, Innis provides a] summary regarding a [Christian] civilization dominated by parchment as a medium [and that] developed its monopoly of knowledge through monasticism. The Church's monopoly position was weakened by the introduction and spread of paper, but collapse was averted by its reorganization and counterattack, e.g., the Inquisition and preaching in the vernacular. Paper supported the growth of trade, cities, and education beyond the control of monasteries. [...] The strength of literacy in the vernacular was reflected in the spread of heresy, and literature supported by court patronage aided the vernacular and such writings and those of Dante, Giovanni Boccaccio, and our friend Chaucer.

It is at this point that Innis turns to a question he was writing about at the end—the rise of nationalism and its relationship with changes in communications. Nationalism (or better [put, a] national feeling) [...] as we know about it today was a late development, centuries after the rise of the state—possibly as late as the 18th century. Anyway, this national feeling could be exploited by the king against the Church as national or state particularism disrupted the universalism of the ecclesiastical organization. [It was] used by French kings vs. the supremacy of the Church, as English kings had used it against French cultural and religious influence.

France, [as Innis writes in *Empire and Communication* on p.] 167, provided for a time, before internal conflict became too sharp, an example of "a fusion between a monopoly of knowledge developed by ecclesiastical organization with emphasis on parchment and a rural monasticism, and a monopoly of knowledge developed by political organization with emphasis on paper and urban industry and trade [which] gave power and influence to the French Empire." Probably balance is better than fusion, since the element of conflict is never buried very deep [...] [although any such state of] balance is a precarious one.[131]

---

131 In the margin Easterbrook writes, "16th–17th centuries."

Innis makes scattered comments on the general significance of paper. [It became] cheap and conducive to the spread of writing, particularly with the rise of printing, and block-printing in books became widespread early in the 15th century (as early as 1409).[132]

[Innis also provides] references here and there to the oral tradition in India. It had virtues but was weak in terms of space control over large areas. India was subject to invasions which brought with them Buddhism and writing [which facilitated] a spiritual unity [but it was] weak in [terms of its] political bureaucracy.

There was a precarious balance in India [...] between the oral (religion) and the written (paper and space) [...] [This contributed to its] weak space control. Contrast this with China ([with its] written [tradition], [use of] paper, [and control over] space). [...] There, paper spread to break the [ecclesiastical] time monopoly and emphasize space and political bureaucracy.[133]

In chapter 6—"Paper and the printing press"—Innis gets into the modern era. The strength of guilds of copyists and makers of manuscripts in France, with its centralized control, led to escape in areas that were less subject of a monopoly of communication. Germany was one such area, where feudal divisions made central control out of the question. The development of printing there took place in smaller establishments. This was followed by the spread of printing techniques in Italy, the Low countries, and to England (e.g., William Caxton's publication of English works such as Chaucer).

By 1500, presses were established in the larger centers of Europe. [Evidence that these] gave strength to the vernacular is apparent in the work not only of Chaucer, but of Machiavelli and Rabelais also. The age of the printing press had begun.

French state policies, by encouraging the production of paper ([an example of] good mercantilism [as it encouraged a] home industry) [...] [but also by] curbing its use, favored a large export trade in paper which was used in areas [...] [that were relatively] free of censorship. The Netherlands and Switzerland capitalized on these large supplies of cheap paper used by a comparatively free press.

---

132 Here, Easterbrook references Lewis Mumford, *Technics and Civilisation* (New York, NY: Harcourt, Brace & Company, 1934). He also writes the following: "the quill pen, agricultural age, paleotechnic—the iron pen—eotechnic [phase] and the later plastic product, the new technology or neotechnical age in which we live—uses each as a symbol of shifts in history of technology and civilisation—but a long way still from mass production or the impact of industrialism with its overhead costs and its expansive drive."

133 "Omit" is written in the margin of this paragraph but, as Easterbrook did not cross it out, the editor has retained it.

This spread of printing went along with a great expansion in news services [and this constituted] a tremendous aid to finance and the rise of exchanges in which communication is the heart.¹³⁴

In England, printing was suppressed but Tudor absolutisms hastened the Renaissance and the Reformation. Henry VIII aided scholars and abolished monasteries. Political writings were restricted but [this led to] an emphasis on literary works and drama, and Shakespeare was one of the beneficiaries. His genius in part was a matter of good timing as he wrote before the full effects of printing were felt.

[Use of the vernacular emerged alongside] the place of the printed work.¹³⁵ At first printing strengthened written traditions [...] [due to printers'] stress on manuscripts, but in the 16th century it had encouraged a rapid growth of writing in its vernacular.¹³⁶

By the end of the 16th century, (i) a monopoly of knowledge had been erected on the basis of parchment being overwhelmed.¹³⁷ [What subsequently took form was the] foundational beginnings of a new monopoly based on paper and the emergence of separate political jurisdictions ([or] kingdoms, [and divisions such as] Lutheran and Anglican) in which church was dominated by state. In France, early in the 16th century, the French Church was separated from Rome through the Concordat of 1516. Also, (ii) the vernacular by this time had become the basis of literature in European countries. Strong divisive tendencies emerged based on the vernaculars and the tradition of the scriptures gave these texts a sacred appeal. These aided the rise of sects and greater demands for toleration. The emergence of Calvinism accompanied these changes. This divisiveness was reflected in the rise of the spirit of nationalism¹³⁸ (Kohn¹³⁹) and with it the dangers of misunderstandings among nations.

[Given the] greater freedom in Holland and England, they replaced France and Germany as centers of learning. Germany went under in the religious wars of the 17th century (1618–48) and the absolutism of France checked new trends there. In England, curbs on freedom of the press were evaded to some extent by the immense output of pamphlets and new books. Parliament itself continued its

---

134 In the margin Easterbrook adds, "industrial revolution, 1540–1640."
135 Here Easterbrook cites Innis, *Empire and Communications*, 183.
136 Easterbrook links the printed vernacular with nationalism by penciling an arrow from the word "vernacular" to "nationalism."
137 The editor has modified "had been overwhelmed" to "being overwhelmed."
138 Under the word "nationalism" Easterbrook writes, "national tongues heard" and "no common language."
139 Easterbrook likely is referencing Hans Cohen, *The Idea of Nationalism: A Study in Its Origins and Background* (New York, NY: Collier Books, 1944).

suppression of political controversy, but new letters evaded censorship. Advertising emerged in the 17th century as a new source of revenue and the rise of a controversial literature in the area of religion led to a greater interest in science. Discoveries in geography, astronomy, the circulation of the blood, and so on, led to a new interest in facts and action. The work of Hobbes and Locke later illustrated the new strength of a vernacular prose in literature and reflected the increasing belief in reason and experience, and the legal supremacy of Parliament in 1689 reflected the feelings of the time in England. [Parliamentary supremacy enabled England to] escape from the *monopoly of written* (dead) forms [of knowledge] in the unwritten constitution. The emphasis on flexibility and tolerance also were important in the introduction of new techniques of communication in finance and commerce. Private and public finance reflected the change and they were basic to the rise of bourses and exchange for the handling of international trade. Daily news sheets begin to be read widely in England at the beginning of the 18th century, and in 1774 the end of copyright monopolies under common law saw the reading public benefit from large numbers of cheap reprints of important works. An almost insatiable demand for reading material of any sort was built up. In spite of difficulties in discussing politics, advertising and the appeal of war news aided newspapers, and pamphlets and novels filled the gap where newspapers were restricted because of taxation and the fear of libel suits. Literary activity was an outlet so long as political repression continued.[140] This had important consequences for the colonies.

Swamped by book imports from England and Holland, newspapers [in the American colonies] became the great medium of domestic interest. Printers in a strong political position were able to throw off attempts at control (the Stamp Act of 1765 showed their strength) [and they had an] important [influence] on the Bill of Rights, and it was aided further[141] by the development of advertising.

Innis argues that, in part, the American Revolution was a product of differences in the development of printing in the mother country and the colonies. The attempts by Parliament to dominate newspapers,[142] and the use of force in that direction, strengthened opposition in the colonies to Parliament's claims of supremacy and the <u>written constitution</u> was in part a defense against Parliament's encroachments. And religious tendencies antagonistic to episcopalianism added strength to this resistance.

---

140 Here, Easterbrook instructs himself to "touch on this regarding newspapers."
141 The editor has changed the word "greater" to "further."
142 Editor changed "attempts of Parlt. domination of newspapers" to "attempts by Parliament to dominate newspapers."

Innis's remarks on France illustrate the limitations of a preoccupation with political solutions based on force. Severe checks on the paper industry led to not only large exports of paper to such centers as Geneva but [...] [they influenced] French thinkers as well, whose works were published elsewhere and whose influence could not be escaped by France itself. Resistance to attempts to limit publishing were met by evasion and, in spite of all attempts to the contrary, the new influence of advances in thought in the physical sciences and in speculative writing proved impossible to check. Renewed attempts at suppression hastened the French revolution. Nevertheless, the policy of restricting free publication for a time meant a balance of Church and state which enabled France to extend her empire for a time to North America, even though this strenuous attempt at balance in the end was a failure.

A great turning point in the history of communications [took place] with the extension of the industrial revolution to the area of communications.[143] Powerful machinery was applied to paper production, [specifically] steam power and advertising. [These impelled an] enormous output of paper, [yielding] new pressures which could not be resisted. Power [was pursued through the use of] [...] paper and printing—problems which are with us yet again—[and Innis's] main illustration was *The Times* of London. Mass circulation newspapers and their political power [...] hastened the end of restrictions on publication. The Crimean war and the Franco-Prussian war were a big help for circulation. Mass production was extended to what we would call the dime novel—cheap paperback novels and reproductions.

The drive for newspaper expansion was even greater in the United States. Swamped by English Competition in novels and literature in general, newspapers there became the great medium of manufacturing. The fast press and the importance of domestic political issues gave the newspaper a central place in public reading. A new impulse [...] [emerged with the] use of wood pulp in place of rags. This was felt in the 1870s and further included the impact of industrialism regarding the need for great supplies of raw material, power, and faster transportation. The power of the newspapers was seen in their political ability to influence regulatory action in the fields of prices and tariffs.

In closing *Empire and Communications*, Innis concludes with a few general observations on the impact of mechanization via the newspaper in the field of communications:

---

143 In this sentence the editor has substituted "A great turning point" for "A great height of land was attained [...]."

(i) [he addresses] the emergence of concentrations of power in this area.
(ii) [mechanization's] influence on words regarding a simpler spelling and this included [the heightened] strength of the vernacular.
(iii) a growing gap between literary and scholarly work of any standard and the general reading [ability] of those mainly influenced by newspapers. This was a gap filled by textbooks, Book of the Month Clubs, best sellers, and sensational literature.
(iv) growing political instability in the sensationalism of the newspaper and its ability of build-up mass feelings, as seen in foreign policy.
(v) Innis also included [some discussion regarding the consequences of mechanization on] economic instability, [including the] deepening of depressions—how come?[144] [He also addressed the] one-sided emphasis on expansion, participation of markets, and on change without regard to the strains imposed by change on economic structures marked by the increasingly heavy fixed costs of large-scale industrialism. News could heighten the optimism of expansion and the reaction in periods of depression. This is an argument on which I would like to have your comments. There are two aspects to it. (a) Technological—the growing inflexibility that characterizes large-scale production, not only in communications, but also in industrial and other areas in which the large unit with its huge advertising expenditures displays a cumulative power to grow larger. (b) Psychological—the pressure of the present and the loss of foresight [involving a] sensationalism that exaggerates the cyclical swings, the ups and downs of activity. Industrialism is a long-range problem that cannot be handled from a short-range point of view. It is difficult to know how far to push this aspect of communications.

The situation is somewhat different in Europe [where there is the] greater strength of the book and [there are] smaller markets regarding language and legal differences. [As such, there is] less scope for large-scale advertising and dangerous political influence on a weaker press. [However, in Europe, the direct] political use of newspapers by the state is more common.

It is argued that differences in the influence and place of the newspaper in various countries have heightened misunderstanding. In the United States, the strong newspaper and the weak book. In Europe, [Innis observed] the reverse: the weak newspaper and the stronger tradition of the book. What of Innis viewing the war of 1914–18 as one between the newspaper and the book—i.e., as symbols

---

144 In the margin, Easterbrook writes "unexplained" likely indicating that he thought this had not been adequately explained by Innis.

of different ways of looking at things?[145] What to make of this? [There are] great misunderstandings regarding the U.S. press by [analysts in] countries in which statements in the press are to be taken as indications of state policy. A political press [as in Europe] vs. a free press [as in the United States],[146] and these must be read very differently. Misunderstanding is to be expected [and their] relevance to international frictions are not difficult to see. But to gauge the importance of such differences in the place of communications is very difficult. Nazi propaganda was not a new technique in Germany as the newspaper had long been used with effect to sway public opinion, to arouse or lessen animosities as one turns on a tap—manipulative in the political area rather than in the economic. The situation is reversed in the United States. Failure to see the newspaper in this light was a weakness of the enemies of Germany, just as in Germany [there was the] inability to see intelligibility in the English and U.S. newspaper which led them to the wrong conclusions, if, say, Belgium […] [was to be] attacked.

The same point of view is expressed by Innis in relation to radio. The Second World War was viewed in the large as a clash between the newspaper and radio. The power of the mechanized word, seen in the rise of the Nazis, […] [was experienced] later in the English-speaking world in Churchill and Roosevelt. The use of communications to sway whole masses of people—the emotional response (Mead[147]), then the information to strengthen that response. Russia is aided by its language [which makes it] difficult to propagandize Russia.

Another point worth thinking about—again, this is highly speculative—are correlations between (i) the sudden rise of printing and religious wars of the 17th century and (ii) sudden new developments in communications and the equally savage barbarism of the 20th century. I should emphasize that Innis was not [postulating] a one-sided explanation in terms of the effects of technology of communications, but [rather] a raising of questions that are of supreme importance to us today. But to show a correlation to be a spurious one, it is necessary to show how there is no question that changes in this area may be productive to extreme disequilibrium [and that such changes] may threaten established positions with strength enough to meet, with force, the attacks on their position […]. [Rapid and widely applied developments in communication] may be productive of misunderstandings to a point where resort to force appears to be the only way out. This view at least

---

145 Above the words "newspaper and the book" Easterbrook writes "shorthand" (likely indicating this dichotomy to be an oversimplification).

146 Above "political press" Easterbrook writes "manipulative" and above "free press" he writes "informative."

147 Easterbrook may have been referencing Margaret Mead, "Public Opinion Mechanisms Among Primitive Peoples," *Public Opinion Quarterly* 1, no. 3 (July 1937): 5–16.

challenges more orthodox interpretations and invites comparisons with them. It was not set down by Innis as the last word, but it is likely to change or modify positions [regarding, for example, a technology's or medium's neutral implications or associations with 'progress'] which have been taken for granted out of force of habit. Communications are <u>inseparable from people's ways of life</u> and drastic changes here may be so upsetting as to evoke primitive behavior, the substitution of thought for action, not uncommon when symbols lose their meaning and new symbols are difficult to find. Suicidal tendencies are not uncommon among primitive tribes when sudden technological shifts threaten their culture and the meaning it has for them.[148]

Closely linked in modern history have been two tendencies greatly influenced by communication changes. <u>Nationalism</u> on the one hand and monopolies of knowledge on the other. [Regarding] the latter, whether the state or a religion provoke reactions, [...] these give birth to new monopoles of knowledge. The growth of nationalism in Germany and Italy, and the centralization of control (state and religious), evoked their reaction in communism, a Western invention that crystallized the revolutionary literature of the west. Nationalisms use monopolies of knowledge to achieve their ends, or the matter might be put the other way—together, they produce communications systems that are best described as manipulative, and it is difficult to see where this will end.

<u>Nationalism as a byproduct of communications</u> has run directly counter to industrialization and technologies which would overcome boundaries and feelings if unimpeded in their effects. This itself is productive of disequilibrium. The expansive powers of industrial production have been sharply limited by the tendency of communications to erect barriers to the best and widespread use of such powers.[149]

The ease with which the alphabet could be adapted to large-scale machine industry facilitated the spread of literacy, advertising, and trade and via the newspaper to [further modern society's] space bias.

<u>One problem</u> raised right at the end which he had hardly begun to explore [...] involved the possibilities of radio as checking <u>the bias of paper</u>. It is not clear whether radio reinforces the old bias and <u>helps to check it</u>.[150] If we think of <u>form</u>, is there really much change, apart from greater possibilities for the state to emphasize time factors—e.g., in the cultural stress of the B.B.C. [British Broadcasting Corporation] and to a lesser degree the C.B.C. [Canadian Broadcasting

---

148   Although Easterbrook writes "omit" in the margin alongside the next three paragraphs, given that they are of substantive interest (and he did not cross them out) the editor has retained them.
149   Easterbrook types below this paragraph, "p. 212 *et sequ* to finish this." He almost certainly is referencing the final six pages of Innis, *Empire and Communications*.
150   Above the words "old bias and helps to check it" Easterbrook writes "too close."

Corporation]? [This orientation might imply] a greater self-consciousness concerning the dangers as well as the possibilities of new media. The C.B.C., under heavy pressure regarding the proximity of the United States and the limited Canadian market, is likely to give way before pressure of a spatial sort. Perhaps this is one reason why Innis was so interested in the strengthening of cultural ties with Europe as an offset to this pressure. [It is] no answer to say that a people get what it deserves, at least not until a full range of alternatives are present. If it is simply a choice between Groucho Marx and Bob Hope, how much choice is this? [Are there] no other values than this to be exploited? A look at the listener of the B.B.C. would suggest that [potentially] there are many doors opened to the public, and if the material is well presented, it is very far from certain that Hope could hold his own. There are other values than commodity values and somehow they must be brought home. To deny them is to close down alternatives and to increase the monopoly of space. So radio has its possibilities <u>as a check</u>, but there is no certainty that it can so act if organized space pressures have things their own way. [Innis would have] no argument against a <u>balanced diet</u> of Hope and Arnold Toynbee, but it is disastrous to have no choice in the matter.[151] It is difficult to foretell the impact of new developments but the past has much to teach us in this respect.[152]

One other point he raised which he had no time to get far with [...] [involved the] matter of common law and Roman law in relation to communications and nationalism.[153] Concerning U.S.-Canadian relations, the only defenses in this country [Canada] appear to be (i) a strenuous effort to recapture the vitality of

---

151 In referencing the need to balance Toynbee with comedians, Easterbrook was referencing more than Toynbee's influence on Innis's concerns regarding civilizational collapse. Also, and more significantly, Toynbee's advocacy of high standards for a liberal education was echoed by Innis. For example, Innis viewed the C.B.C., the National Film Board, and other such organizations as potentially crucial mediators of reflective thinking capacities.

152 In the margin, linked by pencil to his references to radio, Easterbrook asks if radio constitutes an "extension of [the] written form or [does it have a] close appeal to [the] oral tradition?"

153 At this point, several sentences are crossed out. Beside these is a margin note—"touch on this shortly"—indicating that they were addressed at some point during the lecture, perhaps referencing Easterbrook's subsequent (and, to repeat, crossed out) notes, which are as follows: "[Innis in *Empire and Communications* on p.] 212 [states that] 'the effects of printing on nationalisms have been conspicuous in common-law countries. Greater flexibility here was important to trade expansion and to freedom of the press. [There was also] greater <u>decentralization</u> [...] [in the powers of] state and church, greater emphasis on democratic control was accompanied by greater freedom of press from state and ecclesiastical control, and this greater freedom in written communications produced a monopoly position in the book and paper industries which greatly sharpened the impact of mechanization in communications systems and in stressing vernaculars' reinforced nationalism and the divisive influences of language."

the oral tradition regarding the creative aspects of discussion and free inquiry—an effort, in other words, to counteract the narrowing influence of <u>mechanized communications</u> with its profound and fatal bias; and (ii) an equally strenuous effort to bolster cultural values which in sum are rooted in European traditions or ways of life in which mechanized modes of conduct have their offsets in the concern with values which cannot be measured or evaluated in the marketplace—things of the mind and spirit on which no dollar sign can be put. Failing this, mechanization takes command to an even greater degree, instability piles on instability, and cultural suicide appears to be inevitable. Innis was aware that he was going against the current and his pessimism appears to be soundly based, particularly when so-called learned gentlemen can write the fatuous sort of review that appears in the last issue of the *Canadian Historical Review* [revealing that its author had] no awareness of what Innis was getting at nor the technique he was applying.[154] [There are] some notes [by Innis] on his unfinished paper regarding law and economics which I shall touch on at a later point.

So much for *Empire and Communications*. Next, we will take a closer look at the newspaper in economic development.

---

154 See p. XLVI n. 101 above.

February 10, 1953: *A brief comment on Innis's methodology*

As the notes for February 10 are very brief and given the length of the previous lecture (thus the possibility that it was continued on this date), Easterbrook may have prepared what follows to conclude what he had previously presented.

We turned to a look at *Empire and Communications* [in our previous class]. Innis was breaking new paths here. It was an exploratory work with many loose ends, raising questions that could be answered only tentatively. His later work was based on this, [...] filling in the outline set out here with no claim that a later product would closely resemble the structure being worked out here. A closer look at the history of China and India, for example, might call for modification or reinterpretation of the views outlined here and [I have] no quarrel with this [as Innis provided] an open invitation for experts in such fields to look at things from this point of view and their criticism was to be expected. Such staples as papyrus, parchment, and paper, and the technologies of their production and use were the starting points of inquiry. The control of communications based on each are associated with very different cultural arrangements, but [there is] no simple cause and effect relationship [...] [and there are] many ways of viewing the process as a whole. The important thing is that experts in[155] different areas find common grounds for discussion and that this is the advantage of communications studies. [Although it is] a better means of breaking down scholarly monopolies of knowledge, it is difficult to find a sign that [a greater] interest in communications will link together the humanities, the social and the natural sciences, or at least make these mutually intelligible and interesting.

It's amazing how many bright people there are outside the area of economics. Many of them are repelled by its reputation as a dismal science, its apparent materialism. [...] Yet the study of economics itself is a useful corrective since sooner or later it must meet the test of reality for speculative thinking which can become very woolly at the edges unless cross-checked at intervals by reference to the material fact. [...] The use of such 'hard items' as basic resources and technologies [...] as starting points is hard on those who go in for the building of elaborate structures of speculation, but even though [this may be] a check on the imagination, it is scarcely a curb on the use of intelligence.

---

155 The editor has replaced "workers over" with "experts in [...]."

February 17, 1953: *The press, time, economics, and Innis's unfinished paper*

Most of what follows is Easterbrook's review of Innis on the history of press freedoms, political journalism, press economics, advertising, and the price system. Easterbrook finishes with some discussion concerning Innis's end-of-life interests through the lens of his unfinished paper for the American Economic Association.

Not reproduced below is Easterbrook informing students that Karl Deutsch will visit to discuss his "work in communications at M.I.T." Misfiled pages indicate that Deutsch attended the next class (February 24) and then, again, the first class in March. This might explain why no lecture notes can be found for either week. Nevertheless, Easterbrook concludes *Innis 4b* in the final pages of what follows.

The introduction of paper [...] [enabled] a revolution secondary only to the rise of the alphabet and writing. [As Innis writes in] chapter 6 of *Empire and Communications*, the press was well-established in Europe by 1500. The beginning of the great age of the printing press had destroyed earlier monopolies by 1600. [Its use enabled the] rise of Holland and England as centers of learning in which the vernacular was dominant. New interests in science, biology, geography, and astronomy [developed involving] appeals to reason and experience vs. established authority. The greatest economic advance and the greatest interest in economic problems [took place] where [there was the] greatest access [...] [to ideas and opportunities] challenging tradition and authority. [The question that Innis pursued in his final paper] "what produces economists?" recognized economics as a science that emerged first in such areas. The situation in the American colonies was of great interest [to him as there the] earlier dominance of the newspaper [was one of] the reasons why a newspaper civilization, with its sacred cow, the freedom of the press, emerged. Innis also was interested in <u>the consequences of its dominance</u>.[156]

Now, turning to the <u>press</u> and <u>its role in communications</u>, see the Preface and chapter 1 in Innis's *Political in the Modern State*, and in *Bias*, "The English Publishing Trade in the Eighteenth Century" (also see Fred S. Siebert, *Freedom of the Press in England, 1476–1776*).

---

156 The preceding two sentences have been altered by the editor. Originally, Easterbrook (somewhat cryptically) wrote them as follows: "Situation in American colonies of great interest—earlier dominance of newspaper the reasons <u>why and the consequences of such dominance</u>—a newspaper civilisation—with its sacred cow, the freedom of the press."

On this continent [North America], the free press is a symbol of human liberty over a wide range of activities. It is taken as the basis of freedom of discussion in the areas of political democracy and religious toleration. The struggle for a free press was fought out in England of the 16th and 18th centuries [and involved] great changes in communications with the most profound consequences for human liberties in politics and society. A review of these changes, centering on the struggle for liberty of expression in every sphere in these centuries, will serve as a background for Innis's views on the place of the press in the nineteenth and particularly the 20th century.

In England this was a slow and painful process, with many setbacks. [It has been] an experiment which only recently has entered a new phase. Looking back to strategic developments in the 16th century, [there proceeded] a very rapid growth of government controls affecting speech, and a great variety of devices used to dam up or channel information. [Controlling speech and information was] comparatively easier before the rise of printing, but the new technology came to raise problems for ruling authorities which they struggled to solve over [the course of] three centuries. Control devices ranged from the Star Chamber under Elizabeth, to the law of seditious libel applied liberally, to taxation and state subsidies of the 18th century.

Controls were very strict under Elizabeth (1558–1603) and Charles II (1660–85) and during the Protectorate—Cromwell (1653–9)—[and then became] somewhat more relaxed during the Commonwealth and again in the late 17th century. The Tudors assumed arbitrary authority and did not worry about constitutional rights, while the Stuarts looked to the divine right of kings. The main argument in every instance was that stability of government and the peace of the realm made strict control of communications a necessity.[157]

Although there is some argument about the timing of the introduction of printing in England and about the initiator, William Caxton generally gets the credit regarding setting up the first press at Westminster in 1476.[158] He did this

---

157 In pencil underneath "control of communications a necessity" Easterbrook asks, "an argument now?" The next paragraph is crossed out, as it mostly repeats what is contained in those preceding it. One exception reads as follows: "The press an integrated part of the entire social organism affecting and being affected by the society of which it is a part—decline of government controls of press in late 18th century parallels the growth of enterprise and an increase in democratic processes [and these] cannot be seen apart from [their] social and political context." Here he cites Innis, "The Press, a Neglected Factor in the Economic History of the Twentieth Century," in *Changing Concepts of Time*, 77–108.
158 In the margin, Easterbrook writes the following: "(1) 16th–17th century—a critical period—(2) freedom of press as symbol of changing climate—one slowly moving to parliamentary democracy and religious [word indecipherable]—(3) background for Innis views on press of 19th and 20th centuries—points that of [indecipherable words]."

on his own initiative and at first faced no censorship or control by an ecclesiastical or secular authority. Others came in and in the 1520s over 30 printers and booksellers were busy in the trade. However, their growing influence occasioned alarm and led to regulation. The Tudors from Henry VIII (1509–47) followed a policy of strict control and this continued over the whole 16th century [...] [during which there was] no room for dissenting opinions and the Crown was the only power capable of checking these. [There was] very little opposition, and 'liberty' only was experienced momentarily by British subjects during this century.[159] It was a troubled century. The old nobility was hard hit, the clergy was made dependent on the crown, dynasties were wiped out, sects were persecuted, and opinions were punished as treason. [As a consequence, England became a] nation ready for peace from internal turmoil at almost any price. The squabble of the York and Lancaster houses was not forgotten, and Henry VIII was seen as the best hope of rescue from anarchy. Even the middle classes were willing to put up with arbitrary rule as a civil war was to be avoided at all costs [...] [and the] breathing space [required] to repair their fortunes was needed. Domestic tranquility [was to be secured] at any cost [...], and Henry and Elizabeth were able to identify themselves with such [a need for] peace and with the new spirit of national feeling which appeared with the decline of feudalism. And, in spite of a new interest in political affairs that came with education and the printed word in the vernacular, the Crown held the printers in line who would have satisfied such an interest. Anyway, [there was] no toleration, and dissent was crushed [as the monarchy was] aware of the dangers of rational inquiry.

Through Orders in Council and Star Chamber decrees, and in defiance of the Magna Carta, control over the press was unlimited. Elizabeth completed what Henry began and over the century no serious problems arose from political or religious discussion. The Privy Council was the instrument of the crown. Its proceedings opposed individuals [...] [engaged in] 'seditious or unfitting words,' evil opinions, unseemly words [...] [that questioned] the rules laid down by proclamations (or ordinances). [...] The royal proclamation was the main implement used to control printing. It was highly effective.

Special privileges were afforded to 'good' printers and, later, monopolies were used as devices of control, but these were dangerous in that those who were excluded [in effect were] encouraged to work on prohibited books and established secret presses in spite of prosecution.

---

159 The editor has changed "'liberty' of British subjects of small moment over this centuries" to "'liberty' only was experienced momentarily by British subjects during this century."

It is only toward the end of the 16th century that signs of an effective opposition appear—printers for economic reasons, Puritans for religious reasons, and here and there, a member of parliament for political reasons. Religious non-conformists who were unable to appeal to the public slowly grew strong enough to exert sufficient pressure to weaken Elizabeth's elaborate system of control. A member of Parliament, Peter Wentworth, actually dared to deliver an address on 'liberty of speech,' and, although he died in prison, his speech was not without effect (late 1570s or early 1580s).

The Stuarts[160]—James I, 1603, and Charles I, 1625—[were engaged in a] clear-cut struggle between the Crown and those who would limit its powers. The Tudors had accepted their powers as beyond question. James sought a constitutional theory to establish his position—the notion of divine right, supremacy of king over the law, the Church, and Parliament. Authority was sacred, flowing directly from the office of King. [His emphasis was on] unity, not balance. No distinction was made between church and state, religion and politics. It was heresy to question the ecclesiastical powers of the Crown, and sedition to question the established government of the church—[England was] a church-state. The Crown supported the Church of England but there was widespread fear of their Roman Catholic sympathies and many Protestants deserted to the Puritan ranks. Puritanism was dangerous since it sought to destroy the unity of ecclesiastical-state government, and it had trouble with Catholics too since they [the Puritans] sought to separate the Church and state. The Crown was determined to uphold the unity of the state and the uniformity of religion at all costs. Prosecutions of political offenders took place for their religious non-conformity [as the need for] uniformity meant persecution. But resistance was strong and, in the first half of the 17th century, increased freedom was given not because of any quaint notion of the virtues of freedom, but because [the Crown had] no choice.

Freedom demands found their focus in Parliament and were fought around religious questions as their primary issues, but Parliament itself was equally interested in <u>suppressing discussion</u> which questioned its demands for power. Parliament insisted on its own rights of discussion of all issues while it denied the same rights to others. This involved a heavy reliance on legal weapons. To publish libelous or seditious materials was a criminal action. The Crown relied heavily on the Star Chamber for the suppression of political discussion and carried this to such extreme that this organ of the Crown, with its freedom from

---

160 Preceding this paragraph is a sub-heading that reads, "<u>The Stuarts</u>: p. 107." Although it is not clear what work Easterbrook is referencing, most likely he is citing Innis, *Political Economy in the Modern State*.

the restraint of common-law precedent, was overthrown in 1641. Its penalties against pamphleteers were so drastic (ears, nose cut off, etc.) as to provoke reaction. Martyrs raised public sympathy and brought toleration and freedom of the press a step nearer. Finally, [Parliament] realized that there was no alternative to permitting freedom of opinion.

However, the printing trade achieved freedom from regulation only very slowly. It took tremendous pressure—religious, political, and [other forms that were related to] trade—to force Parliament to create its system of control in 1640 out of what was left of Elizabeth's and the Stuarts's control techniques—techniques which included patents of monopoly, trade regulations, church regulations, and a rigorous licensing system. The granting of monopolies aroused intense opposition from master printers who had been excluded. Escape from licensing was achieved through single news sheets, ballads, and almanacs. Leakages were impossible to check (e.g., forbidden matter could be included in a dedication or introduction). The sheer weight on examiners regarding the volume of material and the danger of missing dangerous passages made such control difficult.

Backing the push to freedom was the growth of a powerful commercial class and its interest in public affairs. A news-hungry public backed them up. This was a period of conflict and a wide interest in international as well as domestic affairs. News sheets from abroad were difficult to control, particularly those from Holland. Attempts at regulation only produced more martyrs. And where pamphlets were checked, a loophole was found in the production of a flood of news ballads. The big problem was how to entrust anyone with the 'official' news necessary to counteract rumors [in order] to guide public opinion. The Stuarts never solved this question, nor did the leaders of the commonwealth.

Over the twenty years of the Long Parliament [1640–60] much experiment [took place]—from freedom of the press to very strict regulation. It never discovered a satisfactory formula. But there was no question of growing demands for liberty of opinion with such leaders as John Milton and Henry Robinson. "Areopagitica: A Speech of Mr. John Milton for the Liberty of Unlicensed Printing to the Parliament of England," 1644, did not have much effect at the time but its influence grew with the fame of its author [despite] some drawbacks in that he himself served as an official licenser and censor of newsbooks. [Milton was] more interested in intellectual liberty than of freedom of the press as for him Roman Catholic literature and day-to-day journalism went beyond the pale. But there were others, [Richard] Overton and John Lilburne [for example] were seeking religious toleration and political democracy. Lilburne was a Leveller and the petition of the Levellers to Parliament on freedom of the press in 1649 was the most explicit statement of the importance of and need for freedom of the press:

As for any prejudice to Government thereby, if Government be just in its Constitution, and equal in its distributions, it will be good, if not absolutely necessary for them, to hear all voices and judgements, which they can never do, but by giving freedom to the Press; and in case any abuse [of] their authority by scandalous Pamphlets, they will never want able Advocates to vindicate their innocency. And therefore all things being duly weighted, to refer all Books and Pamphlets to the judgment, discretion, or affection of Licensers, or to put the least restraint upon the Press, seems altogether inconsistent with the good of the Commonwealth, and expressly opposite and dangerous to the liberties of the people, and to be carefully avoided, as any other exorbitancy or prejudice in Government.[161]

More and more, appeals by ruling groups for support of the populace, the middle and lower classes, on political and religious issues were becoming the order of the day.

The licensing system had collapsed in 1640, and the result was a flood of newsbooks dealing with all matters and the demand was insatiable. Parliament slowly set up a new machinery of regulation that could no longer ignore the state of public opinion. [This still involved] censoring, but it was unable to check criticism of Parliament itself. The biggest news event of all was the treason and execution of the king in 1649—a gift to new vendors (like Edward's resignation [in 1936]). Following this, the army took control. With Cromwell as Lord Protector, for a decade strenuous control measures were taken involving the question not of suppressing information but of determining how it was to be doled out and by whom. [At this stage, it was] really too early for freedom of the press [as there was] inexperience [...] [among] the channels of information in providing information and of the public in digesting an uncontrolled flood of information and comment. And still there was not much toleration by anyone of divergent views, yet in the Puritan Revolution period there appear the seeds of later doctrines of religious toleration, political democracy, and real liberty of the press. Parliament was a more responsive organ in the end than any absolute monarchy could be. [Only when it was] less able to grant monopoly patents, and resort to law courts [to restrict information], another step forward [could be taken].

With the Restoration in 1641, the later Stuarts, having learned their lesson, leaned more heavily on Parliament and talked less of the royal prerogative. Control devices were still utilized—licensing, printing patents and copyrights, and the use of orders in council. The printers of the later Stuart period were still far from free as the courts and Parliament were still frightened of the dangers inherent in uncontrolled channels of communication. They objected to publicity although the

---

161 Easterbrook writes "201" at the beginning of this quotation to reference a page in Fred S. Seibert, *Freedom of the Press in England, 1476–1776* (Urbana: University of Illinois Press, 1952).

suppression of Parliamentary news became more and more difficult to effectuate [despite the fact that the] law of treason with its death penalty [was imposed] in several instances regarding treasonable publications. [There was thus] a real and present threat to freedom of expression over [most of the] 17th century. The law of seditious libel was another method of restraining the press. It was developed and applied by common-law courts in later part of this century. It became the best way of handling attacks on the government as sedition could be implied to mean anything damaging to the government. The truth of the allegations was not regarded as important, rather the intent, whether or not malicious. Within Parliament an increasing interest in the freedom of speech of its members emerged even while checking such freedom outside Parliament. This inconsistency became more apparent as time went on and the public burning of seditious material tended to backfire (like Boston censorship). Yet the fear of taking the country into its confidence continued.

An important element [in this history was] the presence of political groups within Parliament striving to gain ascendancy through public support. [...] So long as a strong minority encouraged circulation of such items as Parliamentary news, suppression became almost impossible. Coffeehouse discussions, newsletters, pamphlets, and newspapers were encouraged by such factions and, by end of the century, the House of Commons permitted such liberties as the official publication of its votes on important issues.

In 1688, the Revolution brought in William and Mary and the ending of all claims by the Crown of control over the press. Parliament now alone was supreme in this area. And for a quarter century (to 1714, the end of Queen Anne's reign almost) a great deal of freedom [emerged] for publishers of domestic news.[162] Old regulations had become ineffective and [authorities were] slow in devising new ones. [One result was the] end of monopolies and licensing for the time being. But still there were restraints regarding the law of seditious libel and the House of Lords still refused the publication of its votes [...] and in process a new system of regulation through taxation was being worked out. This was the great 18th-century device of control of communications devices and techniques. Still generally held by political leaders [was the belief] that the stability of government as well as their continuance in office called for some control of communication media. But direct control was out [of the question] in the face of the growing belief in freedom of expression in the area of politics.

---

162 In the margin Easterbrook adds the following: "Crown had relinquished all claims to control to content and communications—Parliament in a state of indecision."

Printers themselves were interested in control in the interest of order in the printing trade. [They faced the] dangers of chaos as their established possessions were threatened by freedom of entry into the printing trade. The government's solution was a revenue tax on printed matters. There were two purposes: [...] income for foreign wars and an effective means of regulation. The Stamp tax of 1712 hit at newspapers and pamphlets which depended for their sale on cheapness and sensationalism.[163] Printers were unhappy about it [...] [due to its implications for the] suppression of news and increase in costs. Larger printed books were exempted, as were religious and school books and trade papers. By hitting at newspapers' circulation the tax also was a blow to advertising because of the effects of increased prices on circulation. A special tax on advertisements [constituted] a further handicap [...] [as were] heavy duties on imported paper. These taxes killed a sizeable number of newspapers but the remainders found ways of avoiding tax. Joseph Addison and Jonathan Swift had various and caustic remarks to make concerning the tax (for example, in Addison's *Spectator*). Swift wrote to Stella [Esther Johnson] (in his *Journals*), "Do you know that all Grub-street is dead and gone last week?" This was an exaggeration, but the effects of the taxes were important nevertheless. However, there were various loopholes. In many instances, the tax on advertising was almost impossible to collect and the discovery that a larger number of sheets meant a substantial reduction of tax led to weeklies of more than six pages. The tax also encouraged the growth of the provincial press (country publications).

Later stamp acts over the 18th century were instituted more for revenue purposes. The Seven Years war led to an act of Parliament regarding a stamp tax in the American colonies of a penny per sheet, a two-shilling tax on advertisements, etc., in 1765.[164] It was repealed in 1766.

The main advantage of taxation as a control device was that it made profits difficult, and it increased the need of government subsidies and political bribes. [...] These were very useful [...] [means of] subsidization [that in effect constituted] a control device in the face of the obvious fact that tenure in office was no longer a matter of royal favor but of the public support of at least the more literate and educated elements of society. The new theories of government of John Locke were having their effect, yet public support depended on the information, arguments, and opinions that reached the eyes and ears of the leading groups in the nation.[165] The problem was to communicate a favorable picture of a political group or to achieve support for an announced policy. Political writing now was a marketable commodity.

---

163 The number "310" appears at the end of this sentence—presumably, a page reference in Siebert.
164 The number "321" added to Easterbrook's notes after "etc." likely is a page reference in Siebert.
165 Here, Easterbrook types "328"—likely another a page reference in Siebert.

Leading literary figures of the early 18th century were aided [as they were] bribed by political leaders as effective shapers of public opinion. The use of their talents went to the highest bidder, although many did have scruples. Political journalism and politically sponsored journalism were a big factor in the literary and political history of the 18th century (Daniel Defoe, Jonathan Swift, Joseph Addison, Richard Steele, Henry Fielding, Tobias Smollett, and Samuel Johnson). Political writings [for some were] the way to financial security. Addison's support of the needs of his party (a Whig) was well-known. [In return, writers received] preferments and pensions. Swift, [for example, was] a Tory. The more reputable stayed with the party of his political convictions [...] [although,] later in the century, the Literary figure gave way to the political journalist, as under Walpole. Literary men, with the spread of literacy, became less dependent on political support and [many] abandoned it to become newspaper writers and editors. With these, the government-subsidized press came into its own. With the establishment of government and opposition presses, the newspaper became more and more an effective instrument in political warfare. A good example of this [...] [took place during] the South Sea Bubble scandal in 1721. [It was a] financial mess [with the] government a target, and the opposition press had lots of ammunition. The *London Journal* ran a big campaign to unseat the government, and the Whigs were forced to buy it off. Much of the subsidization [took place in] secret, particularly under Walpole as part of his plan for political control of communications (he bought off opposition presses or these were prosecuted in courts and subsidized those who were favorable to his government [such as] those who used the material he gave them). [Through these methods, Walpole] assured his ministry a favorable press and a long time in office (fell in 1742). This scandal regarding secret subsidies put an end to the practice. New devices, such as political posts and preferments [emerged instead]. By 1760, the newspaper had come to be almost solely dependent on subscriptions, copy sales, and advertising, plus [...] government support could be gained in indirect ways. Direct subsidies returned later in the 18th century, but [it was] never [again] the factor it had been. The stamp taxes were still a heavy handicap, and another way out than government support lay in increased advertising and the pressure in that direction became very great. This led to rise of *The Times* in 1785 and *Morning Post* of 1772.[166]

One of the most significant changes in the 18th century was the access of reporters to Parliament (to both Houses) and permission to report proceedings by

---

166 The number "345" is included at end of this sentence which, again, likely is a page reference in Siebert.

the end of the century. This was an achievement brought about by the representative character of the House of Commons and the need for the support of the electorate.

> (a) Power of the press: Big London dailies were able to exert pressure against restraints, and an increased stress on party policies increased the necessity of a favorable press. Early in the century, there was a great fear of displeasing Parliament by referencing Parliamentary debates and penalties were issued for so doing—fines, jail, and so on for 'mistakes,' that is, printing of debates in error. Some loopholes existed as in monthly magazines omitting names and letting the people guess. Such publications as the *London Magazine* and the *Gentleman's Magazine* were under heavy pressure to publish such news [...] [concerning] important trials and so on, and in the interests of circulation they took increasing risks.
>
> (b) Intensity of competition: In the second half of the 18th century, competition between dailies and triweeklies became increasingly intense and the thirst of the public for reports on the proceedings of Parliament somehow had to be assuaged.

By the 1770s, the publishers were solidly united against arbitrary restrictions on their freedom, not only [on their] reporting but also their exerting of influence in so doing. It was in this decade that newspaper publishers united to force Parliament into abandoning arbitrary restrictions. Their political influence was just beginning to be realized, [becoming] a great and new source of power. Parliament acted from now on only against misrepresentations, not against reporting itself, and misrepresentation could be avoided only by giving full freedom to reporters. Parliament now acted in full public view, and the move to a responsible representative assembly was greatly accelerated.

So, the 18th century was a highly significant century in the history of human freedom—the so-called age of the enlightenment, of the triumph of 'reason' over authority, of the wearing down of old established systems of control. John Locke and his political theories emerging out of the Revolution of 1688 were important in changing the attitude of the government to the press and a free press no longer was a bad thing. Over the century, partisan[167] persecutions, and attacks for treason or sedition, were greatly weakened. The common-law courts recognized the right of Parliament to determine cases which related to breach of privilege, that is, of Parliamentary privileges, but common-law lawyers argued that the question of

---

167 Editor has changed "part" to "partisan."

whether a privilege existed should be decided by the courts. This was not fully accepted by the House of Commons until the 19th century, but it gave ground steadily on this question of its privileges over the later 18th century. Shifting interpretations [unfolded concerning] [...] such questions as the personal libel of a member, reflections on Parliament, or the government in general, the King or his ministers. The personal reputation of members was jealously guarded—their dignity was sacred, but difficult to keep sacred. The newspaper publishers became the big target but a dangerous one. Seditious libel, [understood] as anything pertaining to criticism of the government, ran more and more counter to common-law decisions and interpretations that reflected the principles of freedom of expression. New concepts of the constitutional relations between the government and its subjects were reflected in court decisions. The corrupt Parliament of George III (1760 *et seq*) was easily attacked and publishers aided the opposition seeking to reduce the powers of the Crown. The public became more and more excited via the press by prosecutions that touched on the liberty of free expression.

By the end of the 18th century, the battle for freedom of the press was, in effect, won, even though some minor but irritating curbs still existed. The principle or theory of liberty of the press, regarding [the public's] enlightenment, and the provision of information to the whole nation on any subject, [had been] established. The 19th century saw it put fully into practice.

An article that you might look into with profit is his [Innis's] "Newspaper in Economic Development" (in *The Tasks of Economic History*[168]) published in December 1942.[169] [Some of its more salient points include the following:]

(1) [his] note on advertising—p. 1.[170]
(2) Mark Twain—p. 2.[171]

---

168 Easterbrook is referencing Innis, "The Newspaper in Economic Development," *The Journal of Economic History, The Tasks of Economic History* 2, no. S1 (December 1942): 1–33.

169 Easterbrook is citing Ibid. In pencil, he also references it as the first chapter in Innis, *Political Economy in the Modern State*, 1–34.

170 This page reference is from Ibid. Here, from pp. 1–2, Innis writes the following: "Studies of advertising are exposed even more than studies of the press to the bias of the subject and they tend to advertise advertising: to show that it is very good or very bad. Publications on the press are an indication of the importance of advertising the press, in showing what a powerful influence such a paper or such an editor or such a publisher has had on the community. Histories of newspapers and biographies of journalists are all too frequently obvious forms of advertising. The modern newspaper dominated by advertising creates an atmosphere which makes a study extremely difficult and hazardous."

171 On Twain, Innis wrote: "I can perhaps run the risk of violating Mark Twain's dictum that we have freedom of the press and freedom of speech and the good sense not to use either of them.

(3) The growing power of the printer in increasing the possibilities of change of those in control of government—becoming a positive force long before [the press was] fully free.
(4) 1814—John Walter and *The Times* used the power press, using steam, and [this marked] the beginnings of the mass production of paper.
(5) [Innis] carries the story regarding freedom of the press to its climax in 19th-century England—the principle had to be made a working principle in the face of restrictive taxation [policies and were] still important enough to force evasion and the search for loopholes.
(6) Free development of the Press in the United States and the early rise in the importance of advertising had its repercussions in the mother country. The penny press of the United States led to the adoption in London of the practice of [selling copies for a] low price to build big circulations and to a widening interest in advertising revenues and sensationalism. Back of this was the pressure of overhead costs as the industrialization of the newspaper field continued.
(7) U.S. papers achieved political influence more easily in a society lacking a clearly marked class structure, and exploited rivalries of growing metropolitan centers.
(8) Introduction of the telegraph in the 1840s [constituted] another technological revolution, particularly regarding war news. Stereotyping was introduced in 1861 via plates of whole pages—the roll press and so on. Such developments were much more spectacular in the United States [...] [given its] freer [access to new] technology. In the 1880s and 1890s, sulfite and mechanical pulp displaced rags, and linotype appeared by 1890.
(9) Displacement of the printer [i.e., control of the press] by the publisher in England in the second half of the 19th century. Problems of ownership [then emerged] regarding large-scale production.[172]
(10) Economic consequences of monopoly accorded[173] by the press by the Bill of Rights. [The Bill] gave newspapers a defense against industrialism centered in the paper industry. Power [among publishers was held] in terms of their control of paper production [...] [and access to] continuing supplies and in terms of tariffs (newsprint became tariff-free in

---

I cannot pretend to have walked unscathed in the crossfire of overdrawn, exaggerated claims regarding the press, and of overdrawn and exaggerated attacks on suppression, brutality, overstatement and misrepresentation." Ibid., 2.
172 In the margin next to this point Easterbrook wrote, "omit."
173 Editor has changed "accord" to "accorded."

1913). And in England, the big publishers, Beaverbrook, Northcliffe, and Rothermere, acquired timber limits and mills in Newfoundland and Canada.

(11) [Innis also provides his] reflections on the freedom of the price system and the spread [...] [of the press, advertising, and] of literacy. Literacy meant a wider market, more readers, and an incentive on the part of the press to encourage compulsory education. At the same time, not always the highest levels of literacy were appealed to [...] as a bigger reading public emerged but not necessarily a better-read public. [Innis is addressing the] <u>problem of content and form again</u>—[and for him] the <u>form's the thing</u>.

(12) Much [is here also] on the relations between publishers and politicians [...] and the dangers for both. Newspapers lose favor wherever they are too obviously or closely the mouthpiece of politicians [...] [and they] lose prestige where they are dominated by governments. This occurred in England and there were consequences where newspapers on their part sought to shape political events without due weight to the responsibilities they were assuming, and yet the pressure on newspapers is very great [...] to build up circulations and maintain them. [...] [It became] necessary to stress what has news appeal. [...] [As such, the newspaper] may be a positive force in producing instability [...] [and an] increasingly effective news organization may vastly sharpen the effects of changes in producing greater sensitivity to change itself. [This is] not [just] a matter of accuracy of the news but also of the cumulative impact of where it is presented to catch the eye. A comparatively small, isolated event may become a matter of world-shaking importance in effects on public feelings and sentiments.[174] Profound consequences [may take place] where millions read [about such an event] and it would not take many such events and the news of them to produce highly dramatic reactions.

Some points are raised here regarding advertising that he sought to develop later in his unfinished paper [for the American Economic Association]. [For example, he addresses] the pioneering of newspapers in [...] [their use] of low prices and quick turnover with an emphasis on mass output. We take this for granted today in many fields [but this was] not the case when newspapers turned to building up mass circulation based on low prices. [As for] fixed pricing [...] [they were] pioneers in this area too. The one price system [...] made possible large-scale

---

174 Easterbrook penciled out the next sentence: "Interesting point regarding recent loss of U.S. and British plan in West Germany—headlines—in Boston papers."

advertising on a mass scale, and this meant appeals to low-income groups. Comics were a big factor in maintaining circulation and the newspaper was followed by the department store with its one price and quick sales on low markups for a variety of offerings under one roof [and its use of] lavish advertising.

With such developments, the editorial sections of the newspaper declined rapidly in influence. Success meant bigness in both newspapers and those who advertise successfully via newspapers. Oligopoly in the one area buttressed that in another area—i.e., communications, and in trade. Appeal must be made to all levels [of society] and the pictorial proved to be the most effective device of all [to do this] and the tabloid [newspaper was] a pioneer in this respect. The increased importance of advertising tended to turn journalism itself into a branch of commerce [...] [resulting in] a weakening of its influence in the area of politics. This was particularly apparent with the appearance of radio with its more effective personal appeal to a wider audience.

[Innis undertook a] comparison of relations of the press with politics and trade in England and in the United States. In England [there had been a] long preoccupation with politics as the major theme of news coverage [while the] tie-in with trade was less close in England and advanced techniques were less advanced and effective. However, the strong influence of developments in the United States has helped swing English newspapers [...] in the direction of a greater interest in advertising and a lessening emphasis on politics. In the United States, the strong position of advertising existed from the beginning and the [...] political[175] influence of the U.S. press was apparent in the success of its demands for freedom of the press.

In the United States, the impact of the newspaper on the whole economy was much greater than it was in England because of a greater of freedom from taxation, the comparative weakness of the book, and its better position with respect to libel laws than in England. [As such, there was] greater play for technological advances with its extremely uneven or lumpy type of change. This favors sudden changes, disequilibrium or instability and, along [with it, a] chain of consequences that are often difficult to analyze. Among these consequences had been the great step-up in the speed of communications and transportation [involving the] pressure for a more rapid transmission of news using telegraphs and railways, postal systems, and cables. Speed was the big word—over a wide market both geographically and in terms of income levels—and this emphasis has been significant for the rate of change in the whole economy.

---

175 Editor has changed "politics" to "political."

There is not much question that the newspaper was an enormously potent force in building up a mass market, itself an essential [component] of advanced industrialism. In terms of literacy, the fixed low price and emphasis on wide circulation and rapid turnover played a central part in the development or rise of big units of production and distribution [...] [and their] pressuring for more rapid communications in related areas such as telegraph and transportation. This has been an example of <u>free innovation</u> in areas of advanced technology and the whole rate and course of economic change or growth in the United States would have been very different without it [...].[176] So the newspaper's influences pervaded and in good part shaped every highly significant area of national life, and this went without challenge until the radio emerged. The newspaper greatly facilitated the <u>spread of the price system</u> via its widening of markets, its emphasis on small coins, and its reaching down to the lowest income levels ([the department store] Woolworth is not conceivable without it). [Also important were] the <u>pressures it generated</u> to further expansion [...] [employing] such items as comics, of course, which have the virtue of tapping all income levels even though comics do not mean the same thing to different grades or groups of readers.[177]

Innis argues that we would learn much that is useful[178] from the study of cyclical and secular change via the study of communications—regarding <u>secular</u>

---

176 Here, in parentheses, Easterbrook references Shepard B. Clough—likely, *The Rise and Fall of Civilization* (New York, NY: McGraw-Hill, 1951)—and writes the following: "strategic factors in U.S. economic development—ideology, immigration, borrowings regarding techniques—nothing on communications."

177 In the margin of this paragraph, Easterbrook adds the following: "3 points → (1) pressure for change—regarding mass market (2) pervasive aspect—no part of life untouched (3) part in society & cyclical change." In parentheses at the end of the paragraph, Easterbrook added, "McLuhan and content regarding comics." Likely, this is a reference to Marshall McLuhan, *The Mechanical Bride* (New York, NY: Vanguard Press, 1951). Curiously, in 1979, McLuhan claimed that he first became aware of Innis's communications work when Innis put this book on the reading list for *Innis 4b*. However, his awareness of Innis surely predates this since, for one thing, Easterbrook introduced them to one another in 1948. More puzzling is that none of the reading lists found in the archives concerning Innis and *Innis 4b* include *The Mechanical Bride* while the readings that Easterbrook initially assigned did not include it either. However, in his lecture of October 14, Easterbrook told students that "Survival rests in the end on sanction and sanction is a problem of communication which itself calls for greater enlightenment as to the culture which we take for granted. That is why McLuhan's *Mechanical Bride* should be *added* to this readings list [as it] takes advertising seriously" (emphasis added). This indicates that prior to Easterbrook listing it, the book was not part of Innis's course. Having said this, despite the absence of evidence, it is possible that Easterbrook shared chapters of McLuhan's book with Innis prior to its publication and that these were referenced in earlier iterations of *Innis 4b*. Marshall McLuhan, "The Fecund Interval," in Havelock, *Harold A. Innis*, 10.

178 The editor has changed "of use" with "much that is useful."

shifts in technologies of communications and their consequences (1890s to 1929) and regarding the mass production of wood pulp and the use of linotype and its industrial impact [...] [As for] cycles, [he also emphasizes the] influence of large advertising expenditures in boom times, sharp declines in depressions, [and their impact in] accentuating these swings. For Innis, the velocity of the circulation of newspapers was not unrelated to the velocity of the circulation of goods, [nor to] notions regarding liquidity preferences, [i.e.,] consumers' likes and dislikes for money vs. goods. Communications studies are also important in the study of the rise and influence of metropolitan centers.

According to Innis, "It may be that Veblen's classification between the pecuniary and the industrial becomes less sharp with an appreciation of the economic role of the newspaper."[179]

As for Thorstein Veblen, he greatly influenced Innis and yet posed difficult problems for him—the dichotomy of the engineer and the price system [involving] forces and obstacles to change and production held in check by financial considerations. This was useful in Innis's Canadian economic history—technology [in Canada was] the dynamic [...] [while] pricing factors were treated apart [...] [and there were] restrictions on free technology.[180] [...] Veblen never resolved this dichotomy, that is, he never treated technology and pricing as interacting elements within a system. Nor did the Innis of Canadian economic history. Innis found his solution in the study of communication which embrace both [...] [technology and pricing and he] treated them in [terms of] an integrated whole of technology, pricing, and institutions.[181] Communication pervades all three as illustrated by the history of the press. [...] [For Innis, this was an] ideal case of free technology and pricing working [themselves] out in an institutional complex that embraced all sectors of economies and societies.[182]

Meaning [or why is this important]? A study of communications may provide a technique [that is] useful in both the financial and commodity fields via the influences operating in both areas—velocities [and] preferences. [Innis sought to develop] a common technique that does not juxtapose these and treat them in the sense of a dichotomy but as elements subject to an analysis that embraces both. I think this realization made him turn more directly to communications and away

---

179 Innis, "The Newspaper in Economic Development," 32.
180 "Free technology" refers to a technology or technique available for use and developed without direct cost.
181 Editor has changed "tech. pricing institutions" to "technology, pricing, and institutions."
182 The next paragraph was crossed out but is included as the editor deems it to be germane.

from the study of staples in terms of a sharp division between technology and pricing of the sort we find in Veblen's *The Engineers and the Price System*.[183]

Another notion important to economics is the tendency in interest theory to regard time as a straight line. Yet technological factors make this questionable[184] [...] [as they may] mean uneven rates which give time itself different dimensions at different times—time as "a series of curves depending in part on technological advances."[185] Time becomes a variable in its meaning and implications—e.g., the distinction between long and short-term securities narrows greatly with increases in the speed of communications and such time distinctions cannot be ignored. Marshall's distinction between the short and long run needs reconsideration from this point of view. Innis helps to clarify some of his time concepts, [...] [including] the meaning of time as an interval which changes in meaning and significance in good part according to the rate and character of technology, [especially in terms of] changes in the pervasive area of communications. Thought along these lines—i.e., the meaning of the time dimension to the social scientist and particularly the economist—would help counteract a preoccupation with the spatial concept based on the extent of the market or the area of control. [...] ["The Newspaper in Economic Development" thus is a] very useful essay, and some of this [is further] developed in his incomplete paper. Now a word on this.[186]

[Innis called it] "The Decline in the Efficiency of Instruments Essential in Equilibrium," but his alternative titles were "Bias in Economics" and "The Menace of Absolutism in Time."[187]

[In his introduction, Innis references] quaint notions of Canadians as interpreters between the United States and the United Kingdom, "as though anyone could interpret for individuals who betray such unmistakable evidence of lunacy."[188] [As Innis recognized, there is a] need for sense of humor among social scientists, especially Canadians.

[This paper was] read [by Chester Wright for Innis] at the American Economic Association's meeting in December 1952. It is an attack on North American economists because of their concern with specifically national problems, particularly those of a legislative sort, [...] [and this] makes for increased specialization

---

183 Easterbrook writes in parentheses at the bottom of this paragraph, "chapter regarding history of press—[indecipherable word]." This likely is referencing Innis's "The Press, a Neglected Factor in the Economic History of the Twentieth Century," in *Changing Concepts of Time*.
184 Easterbrook types "33" here, citing this page of "The Newspaper in Economic Development."
185 Ibid.
186 In the margin Easterbrook writes "Time as variable."
187 Below this Easterbrook wrote, "very tough paper."
188 Innis, "The Decline in the Efficiency of Instruments Essential in Equilibrium," 16.

and tight little monopolies of knowledge within the area of economic study. Innis obviously looked to economic history to help break these down.

For Innis, the task of economic history is to extend the <u>universal applicability</u> of economic theory, not by the revision of theory but instead by strengthening a <u>central core</u> of interest. [This is an] <u>old question</u> regarding the universality of economic thinking or economic principles derived from the study of a problem in a particular environment. It is doubtful that the same tools can be used for the study of primitive societies and those of advanced industrialism, even though the basic ingredients of land, labor, and capital are there. [...] [These] don't mean the same thing in different environments. [As Innis writes,] "The economic historian must test the tools of economic analysis by applying them to a broad canvas and by suggesting their possibilities and limitations when applied to other language or cultural groups."[189]

I have the feeling that the limitations far outweigh the possibilities, even taking into account recent developments in theory. Some general conceptual tools are useful when adapted to historical use—equilibrium, for example—and the use of models.

But given the state of economic studies, the attitude to economic analysis, the place held by economics in social and scientific studies, differences here reflect differences in cultural areas, systems of beliefs, and sets of values. Such differences seem to me to rule out altogether any search for general or universal laws that may be expected to operate in any sort of environment, or they operate so broadly that consideration of them does not take us very far (e.g., supply and demand).

Fundamentally [this is] a problem in communications [...] which shape our way of looking at things. We have looked at the contrast between <u>common</u> and <u>Roman law</u> as a communications problem, and the differences here are highly significant to the way we look at economic problems. The distinctions between legal systems also operate in the field of economics. Roman law economists, in spite of the influence of the classical tradition in England, rarely attempt to treat economic cases or problems apart from consideration of the whole structure in which economic life goes on. [There are] no pure economists [...] [and there is] no isolation of the economic element. Innis mentions the interesting example of Vilfredo Pareto—first class economics but quite as much a sociologist. Schumpeter's work is interesting on this point too. He developed an analytical system but it is impossible to grasp without close reference to his sociology and his writings on political science. [...] [Also note] Marx writing in the European tradition, and his economics was a branch of his sociology. The German Historical school will be known to you through your work in the history of economic thought. It is interesting

189 Ibid., 17–18.

in that on this continent in the last decade or so there has been a great swing to what might be called the Roman Law way of looking at things—the abstract, the universal in terms of the structuring of situations. Talcott Parsons is a leader in this movement [and it is a movement that is] a long way from the economics of common-law economists of the Classical and neo-classical schools and the econometrics of the present.

If you think of Classical economics for a moment (omitting Smith since he was a Scot and Roman law influences were great in his work), you'll recall that David Ricardo was interested in specific problems and the working out of techniques of analysis directed at their solution. [For example, the] position of the landlord, the definition of economic rent, and the problem of distributive shares [...] [were each] a practical problem or case and Ricardo was a very practical person. Malthus had specific problems in mind, [...] [as did] John Stuart Mill, and Marshall's interest was in partial equilibrium. Marshall looked to the European Gustav Cassel for general equilibria notions. The same attitude [can be found] in American Economic Association meetings [...] [which emphasize] the practical problem and techniques for handling it—taxation, fiscal policy, monopoly. A search for principles is not absent, but a pragmatic bent [is its] very strength. The problem's the thing, and this is to be handled in its economic context only—political scientists and sociologists can look after other aspects.

I mentioned Innis's distinction the other day between the approach of common-law lawyers and social scientists—the case or problem on the one hand, the principle or abstract theory on the other. <u>Economics</u>, because of its much closer tie-in with business, private and public, has tended to reflect the common-law outlook of these areas [and it] has never fitted comfortably into the social sciences in the English-speaking world. Common-law economists speak much [the same] as common-law lawyers and find little difficulty in tying in with business. In some universities, economics is part of the business school.[190] Their impatience with history and their problems approach have made for a cleavage between economic theory and economic history on this continent which has no parallel in Europe. Some attempts are being made to apply theoretical models to history (e.g., Walt Rostow), but it is of doubtful value. Statisticians can go historical, as with the National Bureau [of Statistics], and Simon Kuznets writes on the study of growth over time, but again [their focus is] <u>the problem and [it is] a very curious kind of history</u> at best.

---

190 Easterbrook draws a line here to his margin note, "elaborate," and continues with the following: "economics as branch of bureaucratic school education."

This distinction between the two ways of looking at the facts of the case and the search for principles (and an interest in general theory) are far from clear-cut. There has been a great strengthening of European influences in the social sciences on this continent in the past few years, and Roman law traditions are much stronger than they used to be. Nevertheless, it remains sharp enough to cause great difficulties in the social sciences [as demonstrated by] misunderstandings, broken communications, and splinter groups. The Economic History Association is a splinter group of the American Economic Association and this complicates[191] the problem of understanding as between Europe and America.

The danger of the problems approach is that it emphasizes national problems and increases divisiveness among national groups based on language. Statistics come in for much attention in this regard. [...] [Innis] closely identified it with national problems and with the interests of the strongest element in a language group. [According to Innis,]

> Progress has been defined as that kind of effort that can be measured in statistics. Statistics tend to take the heart out of mathematics.[192] They are collected with relation to specific distinctive problems of states with different constitutions, federal and unitary. They are suppressed and distorted for military purposes and their value depends much on the literacy of the populations concerned. [...] Statistical calculations which become a basis of national policy have implications for statistics compiled later in relation to the effects of the policy and make comparisons with other nations more difficult. Nature copies art. [...] An obsession with statistics determined by national boundaries increases the dangers of frictions of political entities.[193]

Statistics, a kind of language, are an aspect of communications which reflects the importance of national boundaries. It emphasizes the particular rather than the general [...] [and Innis] contrasts statistics with mathematics with its universal applications [...] Statistics reflect specific problems of quite different areas of administration or control and [are typically] used in the interests of these. [As Innis puts it, quoting Oscar Wilde,] "Nature copies art." Statistics is like the hourglass feminine figure that may be molded or compressed according to the ends in view.[194] This is not far from the time or duration problem [...] [that interested] Innis [...] [as statistics] make for discontinuity—for preoccupation with the moment, for lack of consideration for aspects of human existence which transcend

---

191 Editor has changed "and to complicate" to "and this complicates."
192 Easterbrook draws a line at the end of this sentence toward a penciled note referencing "[John] Nef & 16th & 17th centuries [...]."
193 Innis, "The Decline in the Efficiency of Instruments Essential in Equilibrium," 18–19.
194 Here Easterbrook adds two words that are mostly illegible, although the first appears to be "stability."

national boundaries. [The use of statistics] increases divergencies that are already <u>great</u> because of language differences.

Again, statistics reflect the character of the state. They can be used as an instrument of control and suppression. [...] The centralized state seems to him to be closely associated with late or soft capitalism [...] [as with the] socialized [state in] Australia, or the extreme case of Russia [...] [where, as a] late state [it has an] extreme reliance [...] [on the] power of the state, and statistics so used enhance national differences. Mathematics brings men together in common understanding, like music (unless this is nationalized too). Statistics separates them, the greater as state power using statistics is greater.[195]

These reflections on statistics have puzzled many and will continue to do so unless they are closely identified with the area of communications. [For Innis, statistics are] a language which may be quite as much a differentiating factor as differences in speech or the written word. Again, the stress is on symbolic usage [...] [and it] suggests differences in understanding between areas where it is put to different uses—the problems approach vs. the search for general principles as in Maths, and so we are back to the common and Roman law dichotomy again. The question of the moment or the search for the enduring principles—short-range vs. long-range thinking—the forethinker as distinct from the man of action, that is, concern with the problem of the moment.

But there are serious problems of communication with common-law countries as well as between these and others. Innis uses a quote from Lord Bryce who suggests that where law lies within the domain of economic interest, the more its rules tend to apply generally and judges look to economic theories[196] for rules, but where human emotions enter, freedom of the individual, and so on, divergencies appear.[197] Other than for the considerations present, the relevance of this quote is far from clear at first reading. A tenth reading suggests that economics itself

---

195 On the margin of this paragraph Easterbrook writes "<u>Generalisation.</u>"

196 Easterbrook wrote "economies" but, given what Innis writes in the article addressed, the editor has changed this to "economic theories."

197 The quote by Bryce that Easterbrook is referring to is as follows: "The more any department of law lies within the domain of economic interest the more do the rules that belong to it tend to become the same in all countries, for in the domain of economic interest Reason and Science have full play. But the more the element of the human condition enters any department of law, as for instance that which deals with the relations of husband and wife, or of parent and child, or that which defines the freedom of the individual as against the State the greater becomes the probability that existing divergencies between the law of different countries may in that department continue, or even that new divergencies may appear." Quoted in Henry John Randall, *The Creative Centuries: A Study in Historical Development* (London, UK: Longmans Green, 1947), 234 n. 2.

cannot be dissociated from human values and emotions, but [rather it] reflects them to a point where <u>economic theory</u> itself changes with <u>changing attitudes</u> of, say, the relation of the individual to the state.[198]

This has dangers for law in common-law countries where judicial decisions in the economic realm are so common. It is dangerous for both law and economics. The judge looks to precedent, but in the economic sphere this involves a lag between the pressures for change and judicial decisions which look to what happened last time. The following is a tough quote [from Innis]: "We may well ask for how far economics has become an indication of the lag between case law and public opinion and how far legislation is a result of the efforts of economists to hasten changes in case law."[199] Chew on that for a while, and some have shown that they have very grand teeth. A concrete case might help such as Roosevelt's reform measures. These economic reforms faced legislative obstacles. [...] Economic pressures were exerted to change the law in response to a public opinion that was impatient with the conservative characteristics of legal decisions. This makes for misunderstandings between lawyers and economists that are apparent where economists act as witnesses. The communications problem emerges again, this time within a common-law area as each looks to the other for guidance—the judge for economic principles which stay put and the economists for judicial decisions which allow scope for change. The character of economic life is important in the shaping of attitudes toward the common law.[200]

Economics with a spatial bias [thus is] lacking the <u>time awareness</u>. Innis is closely identified with public opinion and the pressure for change and the use of law to hasten change, yet law must stress continuity, must look to precedent or principle. [...] Law's conservative influence is an irritation for economists who are unaware of the importance of measures in which the continuity factor cannot be ignored. A lag is inevitable where there are different ways of looking at the time problem. And misunderstandings are inevitable if such differences are not grasped or understood.

The <u>character of economic life</u> [therefore is] important in shaping attitudes toward the common law and such attitudes reflect the state of communications. Speedy and accurate communications enhance the rate of change, call for more rapid institutional adjustments, and lead to highly developed and complex

---

198 In the margin Easterbrook writes, "This not much help in judicial decisions in which economic problems are raised."
199 Innis, "The Decline in the Efficiency of Instruments Essential in Equilibrium," p. 20.
200 Below this paragraph Easterbrook writes in pencil the following: "dangers to law—it's read for continuity when subject is economic pressures."

economic organization [...] [and this is] particularly important in commerce with its reliance on effective information. This itself may be a stabilizing force in that it makes for greater uniformity over wider areas and weakens regional or local monopolies. Tendencies to revolution [thus] may be checked by improved information channels, but the very rate of change itself is important to the way economists think and important in affecting their attitudes to law. Pressure for greater flexibility [thus takes place] in the face of greater pressures for change.[201]

One point Innis makes which is not all clear [...] [concerns] the effect of an expanding press and better communications in lessening the possibility of revolutionary change. It is not easy to reconcile this with the general lack of stability [...] [that Innis associated with a] mechanized press. To the degree that local monopolies are weakened, information quickly and widely spread, and greater uniformity should result. Whether or not revolutionary change is reduced must rest with the strength of obstacles, including law, to rapid change. The bias of economics toward spatial concerns is enhanced, and the lag between law and economics tends to increase in the same ratio. My own impression is that Roman law notions are even now being induced in economics through the pressure of the other social sciences, including economic history, and that with increasing bureaucratization itself a product of greater uniformity via communications, the lag Innis refers to may decrease as time goes on with both economics and law reflecting Roman law influences to a greater degree. Whether or not this will tend toward stagnation is very difficult to say, but that it means less rapid change seems to be most probable.

[Innis also] turns to a few reflections on Canadian economic history, [specifically,] pulp and paper and its place in trade and in the pricing system. [This is a] great area [of study] for [understanding the] unrestrained expansion [...] of the American Constitution, control over public opinion, and favorable resource and market factors. What of the consequences? The rise of monopolies was offset by other monopolies. [...] The biggest impact [...] [was] on information ... and Innis returns to the theme of mass market formations [...] [involving] small coinage and huge turnovers [and their] effects on the velocity of circulation, both domestic and international, as the newspaper has pressured improvements regarding [telegraph and telephone] cables. Advertising has been part of this development, [along with] the rise of great department stores, and [increasing] pressure for industries able to produce in mass quantities. Newspapers tended to concentrate on industries

---

201 Easterbrook places an asterisk at the end of this paragraph that guides his attention to a margin note that states the following: "[D]istinction between main argument & generalization of argument not made, or at any rate, not brought out, i.e., rate of change in communications = preoccupation with print—some consideration in commerce & information improved by an expanded commerce in which communications [are] central."

able to deliver the goods produced by mass production industries—i.e., <u>pressure to bigness in economic organization stemmed from changes in communications</u>. Opposition [or competition has emerged] to elements which tend to narrow the market [...] [resulting in a] reaching out to new areas of demand, particularly the feminine element with its control of the purse, something the car and <u>beer</u> industries have known for some time. The relevance of his reference to the Castles [...] [involves this] appeal to the feminine element. [...] [It is] curious that his last written communications [found at the end of his paper] should refer to dance—the catering to feminine tastes. [...] Now no more.

Where was this taking him? It is not easy to say [...], but there is not much question that his main concern was <u>with the bias in economics induced by the state of communications</u>. I am certain that the American Economic Association was saved a good wallop or two by his inability to complete the paper—the spatial bias of economics; its case method; its preoccupation with the short-run; its failure to understand the forces that shaped the preconceptions and the interests of economists; [and] economics as an aspect of communications, to be understood and improved as a discipline through a better understanding of itself. The theme should be familiar—*one way to freedom is to understand the forces which would enslave us.* [...] [This, Innis believed, is] the beginning of wisdom—everything else is futile without it.²⁰²

At this point, Easterbrook says : "And that's about it." He then addresses the final exam and finishes the course by telling students the following :

Obliged to you for the cooperation you have shown—not an easy year for any of us—but if you once latch on to the problems Innis was concerned with, you'll probably never be the same again.

---

202 Below this paragraph Easterbrook writes, "T of G [...] & McLuhan *Mechanical Bride*." "T of G" likely is shorthand for H.L. Mencken, *Treatise on the Gods* (New York, NY: Knopf, 1930).

Appendix I

Course documents

The following documents were located in files 8, 10 and 11 in box 014, Accession B1979-0039, University of Toronto Archives.

SUMMER VACATION READING LIST FOR STUDENTS ENTERING FOURTH-YEAR IN ECONOMIC THEORY AND ECONOMIC HISTORY*

Students entering the fourth year of Commerce and Finance or Political Science and Economics have to choose two courses from a list of options, particulars of which will be found in the *Calendar* of the Faculty of Arts. The choice made will be subject to the approval of the Supervisor of Studies.

Economic Theory and Economic History are compulsory for all students, and Political Science is compulsory for students in Political Science and Economics. Great advantage is to be obtained from reading during the summer vacation, and the following books are suggested:

Economic Theory

Roll, Erich: *A History of Economic Thought*
Cannan, Edwin: *A Review of Economic Theory*
Chamberlin, Edward: *Theory of Monopolistic Composition*
Knight, F.H.: *Risk, Uncertainty and Profit*
Marshall, Alfred: *Principles of Economics*

Myrdal, G.: *Population*
Smith, Adam: *Wealth of Nations* (Modern Library Edition, Edited by Cannan)
Timlin, M.: *Does Canada Need More People?*
Harrod, F.F.: *John Meynard Keynes*
Poigou, A.C.: *Memorials of Alfred Marshall*
Sitgler, George F.: *The Theory of Price*

Economic History

Adams, Brooks: *The Law of Civilization*
Arnold, Matthew: *Literature and Dogma*
Benedict, Ruth: *Patterns of Culture*
Burckhardt, Jacob: *Force and Freedom*
Butler, R.: *Origin of Printing in Europe*
Carter, T.F.: *The Invention of Printing*
Cassirer, Ernst: *An Essay on Man*
Childe, V. Gordon: *Man Makes Himself*
Cochrane, C.N.: *Christianity and Classical Culture*
Collingwood, R.G.: *Idea of History*
Dickinson, G.L.: *Greek View of Life*
Ehrenberg, Richard: *Capital and Finance in the Age of Renaissance*
Goodspeed, R.J: *New Chapters in New Testament Study*
Guerard, A.L.: *Literature and Society*
Innis, H.A.: *Political Economy in the Modern State*
Jaeger, W.: *Paideia*
Knight, F.H. & Merriam, T.W.: *Economic Order and Religion*
Leavis, Q.D.: *Fiction and the Reading Public*
Liddell Hart, B.H.: *The Revolution in Warfare*
Lin Yu Tang: *Press and Public Opinion in China*
Morison, S.: *The English Newspaper*
Mahan, A.T.: *The Influence of Sea Power on History*
Maine, H.S.: *Ancient Law*
Mencken, H.L.: *Treatise on the Gods*
Oman, C.W.L.: *A History of War in the Middle Ages*
Petrie, W.M.F.: *The Revolution of Civilization*
Randall, H.: *Creative Centuries*
Rashdall, H.: *Universities*
Ridgeway, W.: *Origin and Influence of the Thoroughbred Horse*
Scott, F.: *Architecture of Humanism*

Sorokin, P.A.: *Social Mobility*
Teggart, F.J.: *Processes of History*
Timasheff, N.S.: *Introduction to the Sociology of Law*
Troeltsche, E.: *Social Teaching of the Christian Church*
Ullman, B.L.: *Ancient Writing*
Usher, A.P.: *History of Mechanical Inventions*
Wollner, A.C.: *Languages in History and Politics*
Wallas, G: *Art of Thought*

* In addition to Harold Innis possible other author(s) and the precise date of this list are unknown.

Fourth-year reading list in Economic History**

Department of Political Economy

Arnold, Mathew: *Literature and Dogma*
Cochrane, C.N.: *Christianity and Classical Culture*
Dickinson, G.L.: *Greek View of Life*
Innis, H.A.: *Political Economy in the Modern State*
Innis, H.A.: *Minerva's Owl*
Innis, H.A.: *Empire and Communications*
Innis, H.A.: *The Press*
Innis, H.A.: *Great Britain, The United States and Canada*
Jaeger, W.: *Paideia*
Kroeber, A.L.: *Configuration of Culture Growth*
Mahan, A.T.: *The Influence of Sea Power on History*
Maine, H.A.: *Ancient Law*
Menchen, H.L.: *Treatise on the Gods*
Morell, P.: *Poisons, Potions and Profits*
Oman, C.W.L.: *A History of War in the Middle Ages*
Randall, H.: *Creative Centuries*
Rashdall, H., et al.: *The Universities of Europe in the Middle Ages*
Ridgeway, W.: *Origin and Influence of the Thoroughbred Horse*
Sorokin, P.A.: *Social Mobility*
Troeltsche, E.: *Social Teaching of the Christian Church*
Woolner, A.C.: *Languages in History and Politics*

** List likely prepared by Harold Innis in 1950.

Reading List for Economics 4b***

Department of Political Economy

Boase, T.S.R.: *Reading and Listening*
Cochrane, C.N.: *Christianity and Classical Culture*
Dickinson, G.L.: *Greek View of Life*
Gowers, E.: *Plain Words*
Havelock, E.A.: *Crucifixion in Intellectual Man*
Innis, H.A.: *Political Economy in the Modern State* (pp. vii to xvii, 1 to 55, 256–70)
Innis, H.A.: *Bias of Communication*
Innis, H.A.: *Empire and Communications*
Innis, H.A.: *The Press, a Neglected Factor in the Economic History of the 20th Century* (Oxford University Press, 1949)
Innis, H.A.: *Strategy of Culture*
Innis, H.A.: *Great Britain, The United States and Canada*
Jaeger, W.: *Paideia*
Kroeber, A.L.: *Configuration of Culture Growth*
Lambert, Constance: *Music Ho!* (Penguin)
Mahan, A.T.: *The Influence of Sea Power on History*
Maine, H.A.: *Ancient Law*
Newton, E.: *European Painting and Sculpture*
Oman, C.W.L.: *A History of War in the Middle Ages*
Pevsner, N.: *An Outline of Architecture* (Penguin)
Randall, H.: *Creative Centuries*
Rashdall, H., et al.: *The Universities of Europe in the Middle Ages*
Richards, I.A.: *Mencius on the Mind*
Ridgeway, W.: *Origin and Influence of the Thoroughbred Horse*
Sorokin, P.A.: *Social Mobility*
Troeltsche, E.: *Social Teaching of the Christian Church*
Woolner, A.C.: *Languages in History and Politics*

*** List likely prepared by Harold Innis in 1951.

First Essay Topic****

Economics 4b—Economic History
　　Contrast the demands of Roman Law and of Common Law on Words with special reference to

1. Innis: Technology as a cause of changing attitudes toward time
　　(To be published by University of Toronto Press around October 15)
2. Innis: Roman Law in the British Empire
3. Gowers: *Plain Words*

　　Date Due: December 1, 1952.

**** Assignment prepared by Tom Easterbrook in 1952 using questions written Harold Innis in 1951.

FINAL EXAMINATION QUESTIONS (1951)*****

University of Toronto
Faculty of Arts
Annual Examinations, 1951
Fourth Year—Honor
Economics 4b—Economic History
Examiners—The Staff in Economics
Candidates will answer FOUR questions.

1. Discuss the conditions under which institutions become concerned with problems of duration or time.
2. Discuss the role of the oral tradition in Western civilization.
3. Indicate the problems of language incidental to a shift from a written to a printing tradition.
4. Describe the significance of paper to communication particularly in a contrast between China and the West.
5. Trace the implications of technology to communication in the United States and Great Britain in the 19th century.
6. Discuss the problems of control of information under conditions of imperfect competition with special reference to Canada.
7. Indicate the limitations of an emphasis on communications to a study of civilization.

***** Exam questions written by Harold Innis in 1951.

Final Examination Questions (1953)******

University of Toronto
Department of Political Economy
Annual Examinations, 1953
Economic History
Examiners—The Staff in Economics
Candidates will answer FOUR questions.

1. Discuss the significance of technology to the characteristics of society with special reference to a single medium of communication.
2. "Greek civilization was a reflection of the power of the spoken word." Comment.
3. What devices were developed in the Byzantine Empire in the interests of duration and how far were they successful?
4. Outline Dr. Innis's treatment of the role of law in history and expand your answer with particular reference to one of the following: (i) the demands of law on words, (ii) the relations of law and politics, (iii) the significance of law to innovation or change.
5. Write a short essay on the role of the newspaper in economic development.
6. Discuss the effectiveness of the concept of monopoly in the study of communications.
7. What is meant by "the mechanization of communications." What are its implications for the place of the university in the modern world?
8. Comment on the historical and contemporary role of advertising as a force in the communications field.
9. What relevance has the Innisian approach to communications for the study of economics?
10. Discuss any one of the following in the light of your study of communication problems: (i) nationalism, (ii) freedom of the press, (iii) sanction, (iv) entropy, (v) propaganda.

****** Exam questions written by Tom Easterbrook in 1953.

APPENDIX II

Innis's final paper: Harold Innis, "The Decline in the Efficiency of Instruments Essential in Equilibrium"

from the *American Economic Review*
Vol. 43 No. 1 (1953), 16–22

Copyright American Economic Association, reprinted with permission of the *American Economic Review*.

THE DECLINE IN THE EFFICIENCY OF INSTRUMENTS ESSENTIAL IN EQUILIBRIUM[1]

Note: The untimely death of Professor Harold A. Innis on November 8, 1952 deprived this Association of the presidential address that he was to have delivered at the December 1952 meetings—an address which all acquainted with him or his work knew would be not only humorous and filled with incisive comments but intensely thought-provoking. However, we do have a preliminary draft of the first portion of his intended address. It should be remembered that the portion printed here was written when he was extremely weak and often in much pain. No doubt it would have been extensively revised and more closely knit together had he survived to complete it. This fragment, though very typical of the author, is essentially introductory in character. It barely reaches the point where he begins to develop his real subject and does not make clear the main thesis he had intended to expound. Fortunately, however, during the summer, he had discussed his proposed address at considerable length with his oldest son, Donald Innis, who has kindly prepared the brief summary included here, covering the main points which his father had intended to develop.

CHESTER W. WRIGHT

When my friend Bob Coats as federal statistician became president of the American Statistical Association under circumstances similar to my own in relation to this Association, he compared himself to James VI of Scotland who became, as you remember, James I of England; and he drew interesting parallels between the interventions from the north to the south in the two cases. I am too aware of the ultimate fate of the Stuarts, in particular of Charles I, the son of James, to wish to press this comparison further. But I must begin this paper with remarks which may be helpful to you in explaining its contents. A social scientist in Canada can only survive by virtue of a sense of humor. (Stephen Leacock was a logical result.) He can scarcely fail to be amused by the goings on in this country and by the antics of Great Britain, or fail to be disturbed by a realization that he can do nothing about it. Occasionally he is described in after-dinner speeches as an interpreter between the two countries as though anyone could interpret for individuals who betray such unmistakable evidence of lunacy. In a sense, perhaps, a realization that he lives in such a large insane asylum may be an indication of sanity, but it is unavoidable that he should have serious doubts about his own sanity. My old friend the late Professor Robert McQueen used to write from Winnipeg, half in earnest half in jest, "I'm depressed and fear I'm becoming known as a luncheon speaker. Can't you do something to get me an honest job?" For these reasons the

[1] Alternative titles on the manuscript are: "The Bias of Economics" and "The Menace of Absolutism in Time."

social scientist must do his best to maintain a sense of humor or a sense of balance, and if he appears on occasion to strain for effects I hope he will be forgiven. It is dangerous to appear humorous at the expense of one's elders or, as the Anglican prayer book has it, "one's betters" and I hope that anything I have said will be accepted in the proper spirit. We can at least say that we have a properly developed inferiority complex and know our places.

My appointment is a tribute to the toleration of the social sciences—a recognition of the capacity of a subject to overlook regions and nationalities and bifurcations within the social sciences even to the lowest stratum of the economic historian. An expression of this tolerance has not been achieved without recognition of the importance of political devices in checking the disastrous effects of a majority vote with concentration on the election of representatives from densely populated areas. I know that someone will be muttering that majorities also have rights, and it may be that when that awful day of judgment arrives when someone writes a doctor's thesis on the presidential addresses of this Association, as has been done for the American Historical Association, the claims of majorities will be justified.

The limitations of tolerance have of course been evident. Candid observers have expressed regrets at the relative neglect of problems of economic theory or of universal problems and the increasing prominence of sessions concerned with specifically American problems—indeed specifically American legislation. Groups with specialized interests have hived off from the Association, including a group in which I have a special interest, namely economic history, and have set up their own side shows outside the main tent; or they have seen the space outside crowded and have preferred to carve out places for themselves within the main tent and form what a predecessor of mine has called splinter groups. The climax has perhaps been reached with the selection of a president from one such group. The responsibility of the president for the general programme makes him aware of the difficulties he has created, partly through the warnings of his predecessors and partly through his own experience. In other words I am in the position of the man who was about to be hung; when he was asked whether he had anything to say, he replied "This will certainly teach me a lesson."

Having learned my lesson, I must begin by pleading for a general emphasis on a universal approach and by insisting as an economist that economic history is primarily concerned with the task of extending the universal applicability of economic theory and of strengthening a central core of interest. In the words of Plato the task of all knowledge is to discover "the limits and proportions of things." The economic historian must test the tools of economic analysis by applying them to a broad canvas and by suggesting their possibilities and limitations when applied to other language or cultural groups. How far, for example, are we justified in asking students from other societies essentially agricultural—let us say the Chinese—to conform to the tests applied in doctorate examinations primarily reflecting the characteristics of a system which has grown up in relation to an industrial society? The problem of semantics alone compels resort to the devices of the parrot in reliance on memory. Graham Wallas as a result of his wide experience with Indian students has reminded us that the English language has only slight emotional associations for them, that examinations emphasize only phrases and words of books and that training in English for the Indian civil service probably produced results similar to the results in the Chinese civil service.[2]

Within the West itself the problem of communication is scarcely less acute. In European countries more profoundly influenced by canon law and Roman law the social sciences develop along different lines than in Anglo-Saxon common law countries. Talcott Parsons has suggested possible common ground but it may be questioned whether he recognized sufficiently the contrast between the work of Pantaleoni (and his emphasis on mathematical economics and in turn his influence on Pareto) and that of common law economists. The impact of Pareto's training in engineering and in science was evident in a concern with the mathematical approach to the social sciences. In turn Pareto was compelled to write a sociology to accompany his rational approach—a phenomenon with little precedent in the Anglo-Saxon world.

The problem of the application of theory becomes even more serious. The significance of language as a differentiating factor in Europe has probably increased with the telephone and radio. In turn statistics will vary in their significance as national groups, based to an important extent on language, tend to concentrate on the range of statistics which show their pre-eminence in various lines, particularly those which emphasize the largest elements or those increasing most rapidly in their societies. Progress has been defined as that kind of effort that can be measured in statistics. Statistics tend to take the heart out of mathematics. They are collected with relation to specific distinctive problems of states with different constitutions, federal and unitary. They are suppressed and distorted for military purposes and their value depends much on the literacy of the populations concerned. The significance of Keynesian economics to administrative systems limits possibilities of comparison. Statistical calculations which become a basis of national policy have implications for statistics compiled later in relation to the effects of the policy and make comparisons with other nations more

[2] *The Art of Thought* (London, 1926), p. 254.

difficult. Nature copies art. Monetary manipulations and tariff adjustments reflect and intensify the significance of vernaculars, particularly as effected by journalism and the radio and have their implications for statistics. We are familiar with the efforts of Colin Clark to overcome these difficulties but we can scarcely be unaware of the limitations of his work. An obsession with statistics determined by national boundaries increases the dangers of frictions of political entities.

The significance of statistics will vary with attitudes toward the state. A census may be conducted for military purposes, and the scriptural injunctions against enumeration are not without foundation; or for purposes of more adequate distribution of tax and other burdens, including railway rates. In the patriarchal traditions of Roman law the state has been regarded as an instrument of oppression and the proposals of Marx and Lenin assumed a withering of this concept of the state and substitution of the worker for the bourgeoisie. The rapidity of the spread of capitalism reflects the character of the state. In Sweden and in Australia the industrial revolution was comparatively late with the result that a soft capitalism was accompanied by nationalization, co-operative movements and labour governments. In Russia the state as an instrument of power was used conspicuously to overcome the difficulties of the frontier, notably in building the trans-Siberian railway, and much the same might be said of Canada in extending railways to the Pacific.

If we narrow our concern to countries in which common law plays an important rôle we are by no means free of difficulties. The concept of possession in common law and in German law essential to the expansion of commerce and of economics in contrast with the concept of absolute ownership in Roman law is by no means a guarantee of uniformity. Bryce remarked that

> The more any department of law lies within the domain of economic interest, the more do the rules that belong to it tend to become the same in all countries, for in the domain of economic interest Reason and Science have full play. But the more the element of human emotion enters any department of law, as for instance that which deals with the relations of husband and wife, or of parent and child, or that which defines the freedom of the individual as against the State, the greater becomes the probability that existing divergences between the laws of different countries may in that department continue, or even that new divergences may appear.[3]

Sir Frederick Pollock has pointed to the bias of the common law toward competition in that it must draw its resources from contentions between competitors. The character and frequency of disputes are important elements determining the profits of the legal profession. But Holmes

[3] Bryce, *Studies in History and Jurisprudence*, Vol. I, p. 123.

has stated that a constitution "is not intended to embody a particular economic theory whether of paternalism and its organic relation of the citizen to the state, or of *laissez-faire*." Pollock complained that case law had been largely modified by doctrines in favour among economists and publicists and that "judges ought to be very careful about committing themselves to fashionable economic theories."[4] Failure to protect themselves was almost certain in his opinion to involve mistakes to be remedied by legislative amendment which is sure to be unsatisfactory. We may well ask how far economics has become an indication of the lag between case law and public opinion and how far legislation is a result of the efforts of economists to hasten changes in case law. Certainly the enormous expansion of legislation reflects an unhappy relationship between economics and law. Many of you will be familiar with the problem of an economist who appears as a witness and who makes statements in a written brief which are regarded by lawyers as concessions to the enemy. In turn economists acting as arbitrators become annoyed with the tactics of lawyers and favour the appearance of concessions as an indication of truth.

Changes in attitudes toward common law vary as between different countries and within the same country as between different periods, and will depend to an important extent on differences in the character of economic life particularly as reflected in the division of labour and in trade. These in turn will vary with the effectiveness with which information can be made available regarding commodities to be exchanged. Highly developed media of communication will become evident in the emergence of organized exchanges but the effects of inaccurate and inadequate information will be apparent in outbursts such as the South Sea Bubble and the various phenomena described by Arthur H. Cole and Charles Mackay and such as appeared in real estate booms in the cities of this continent, especially in Western Canada, and in gold rushes.

As information was handled more efficiently dangers of fanatical outbreaks became less acute. Quetelet in 1835 commented on the influence of an expanding press in checking tendencies toward revolution. It had "singulièrement contribué à faciliter la réaction et par suite à rendre les grandes révolutions à peu près impossibles; elle presente cet avantage immense qu'elle ne permet pas aux forces de s'accummuler d'une manière effrayante, et que la réaction se manifeste presque aussitôt après l'action, quelquefois même avant que l'action ait eu le temps de se propager."[5] The invention of the telegraph and its

---

[4] Pollock, *Genius of the Common Law*, p. 108.
[5] A. Quetelet, *Sur L'Homme* (Paris, 1835), Vol. I, p. 290.

rapid extension in continental land areas and in submarine cables enormously enhanced the availability and the accuracy of information for the purposes of trade. It fostered demands for the equalization of accessibility. Newspapers in Chicago, especially the *Chicago Tribune*, protested vigorously in the early 'sixties against the exploitation by New York interests of the difference in time between the two cities. Western papers were compelled to pay high rates for market reports controlled by New York interests in the Associated Press of that day. The regional monopoly was gradually weakened in the latter half of the nineteenth century and came to an end finally with the formation of the Associated Press.

By this time my bias will have begun to wear thin and in fairness I should indicate its character in so far as my limitations permit. I have been primarily interested in the economic history of Canada and in particular factors which explain its peculiarities, especially the successive importance of staple raw materials to mention fur, fish, lumber, wheat, minerals and pulp and paper. I am concerned in this presidential address with the problems inherent in the pulp and paper industry as related to the production of information for purposes of trade and the efficiency of the price system. The industry occupies a peculiar position in that it is protected by the Bill of Rights in the American Constitution and by its possibilities of control over public opinion. Possible checks through the development of legislation in raw material producing regions, for example the provinces of Canada, have been offset by vertical integration in which large American newspapers control their own industrial operations in Canada.

The effects of the enormous expansion in the production of raw material following improvements in technology in the use of wood were evident in the sharp decline in prices of newsprint in the later part of the 19th century and in the expansion in the production of information by newspapers. The monopoly of the Associated Press evident chiefly in the control of morning and Republican newspapers was offset by the development of the Hearst Press and the International News Service and by the development of the cheap press concerned primarily with evening papers by the Scripps, McRae, Howard interests in the United Press. The impact on information can be suggested in one or two illustrations. Lowering of the price of the newspaper was dependent in part on the denominations of money used in various cities. In Chicago and in St. Louis the mint was persuaded to distribute quantities of pennies and department stores co-operated by advertising goods for odd amounts and thus hastening the use of small denominations. In San Francisco on the other hand Scripps papers were handicapped by customs continued from the gold rush period which implied refusal to recognize small denominations. In the Yukon Territory as late as 1926 coins smaller than 25 cents were regarded with disfavour. The drive for cheaper information regarding prices, especially in department stores, had important implications for the currency structure and for velocity of circulation. The broad implications of prices of newsprint for the distribution of information in large cities were paralleled by developments on a wider field. During the second world war high cable rates to Australia were reduced by subsidy and the position of Australia in the information field greatly strengthened whereas the high rates to Spain were said to play an important rôle in keeping Franco out of the war.

An increase in the circulation of newspapers and a policy of low fixed prices designed to facilitate increased circulation were paralleled by the increasing importance of advertising as a source of revenue and the necessity of developing policies to attract advertising. The newspapers played an important rôle in the building up of the great department stores as distributing organizations and also in changes in the methods of production. In England for example the *Daily Mail*[6] found itself faced with the problem of finding industries with a productive capacity adequate to the demands of purchasers created by advertising. Drapers as advertisers were limited by their capacities to supply particular articles. In a systematic search for industries with relatively inexhaustible capacities of production the *Daily Mail* concentrated on the building industry and on a system of advertising developed beyond the immediate possibilities of the paper itself. The Ideal Home Exhibition was organized to supplement the newspaper. The newspaper is concerned in a search for mass production industries to meet its advertising requirements. Its position leads it to take a critical attitude towards trusts[7] as narrowing the market or towards the domination of government by powerful groups. Edward W. Bok concentrated his attention on the position of women as purchasers. He was said to have changed the physical appearance of domestic furniture, eliminated the parlor from domestic architecture and persuaded the Castles to introduce more and better dances.[8]

* * * * *

HAROLD INNIS

Appendix III

Tom Easterbrook, "Harold Adams Innis 1894–1952"

from the *American Economic Review*

Vol. 43 No. 1 (1953), 8–12

Copyright American Economic Association, reprinted with permission of the *American Economic Review*.

II

Arthur H. Cole observed recently that economic historians who achieve the presidency of this Association are much more than economic historians. Harold Innis like Edwin Gay was a man of wide interests and stimulating mind. His influence extends far beyond his writings and it would be unjust to him to stop with his written words. The following observations are based quite as much on conversations with him as on his published work; it is hoped that in this way some of the virtues of the oral tradition which he esteemed so highly may be preserved even though the written form win in the end.

It was perhaps inevitable that from the beginning Dr. Innis should attack the problems of history on a broad front. Writing as a Canadian economic historian he was constantly faced with the fact that in Canadian development the strategic decisions, the shaping influences, had always to be sought outside the country's political boundaries. Study of an economy so vulnerable to external forces made the writing of a national economic history out of the question. And there is the fact, too, that this history is marked by the absence of any break with European traditions, of alienation or turning back on the old world. Much of Canada's economic history is simply an extension of European economic history; only over the past century has it become an extension of the economic history of the United States.

Study of this "international" economy of Canada led him early in his work to the conclusion that ranking in importance and closely associated with economic influences and pulls were cultural influences and pulls, and his interest in cultural relations is apparent long before he turned from "staples" to "communications." In the shift of interest from pre-occupation with the trade routes of commerce to the trade routes of culture, from the exchange of staple commodities to the exchange of ideas or information, there is no suggestion of a break or loss of continuity in thought or interests.

Another element of continuity in his work is apparent in his set of values, or more loosely, his likes and dislikes. There stands out in every phase of his activity—writings, lectures, departmental administration—an intense individualism, an almost obsessive preoccupation with the virtues of unrestrained exchange (whether reference be to commodities or ideas)—the spirit of free enquiry, the give-and-take of spontaneous discussion, faith in the creative powers of the individual left alone. There is the suggestion of "ideal type" method in his writings on the aggressive commercialism of the New England fisheries and trade in the North Atlantic and in his frequent references to the oral tradition of Greece.

This attitude may be illustrated from his writings and is perhaps most clearly brought out in his dislike, even contempt, for the written tradition, his fear of the written word as frozen, final; throughout there is apparent a constant struggle to break down this finality and to weaken or destroy the inherent tendency to monopoly of communications which he firmly believed to be a fatal defect of the written form. This helps to account for the absence of final or complete statement in his publications, his impatience with orderly presentation or the continuous development of narrative, his technique of juxtaposing unlike elements as a means of seeking insights into process. He searched, probed, sought elements of strength and weakness, but nowhere gives any indication of interest in constructing a system, or a theory of historical change.

Along with this individualism went an equally intense realism. There is no lack of awareness of the weakness of small units, of maritime areas faced with the power of continents, or of the limitations of the city state. In the main his work centers on the history of bureaucracies, administrative units in control of large territories, in short, empires in which centralized control of communications has been the rule rather than the exception. How to reconcile his set of values with the survival needs of large power structures was for him one of the crucial questions to be asked of history. He first raised this question, I think, in his study of the Northwest Company, a transcontinental fur trade organization, which in its failure to achieve a balance necessary to reconciliation of the demands of enterprising individuals in the trade with the stability requirements of the organization, bowed out to a power more successful in its handling of the problem. The same question is writ large in his reflections on the values of Greece in the world of Rome, and although little of this has appeared in print, in his frequent references to the amazing survival powers of the Byzantine Empire. He raises the question again in his remarks on the United States in his recently published volume of essays, *Changing Concepts of Time*, whose subtitle might well have been "Washington, the Third Rome?"

There is no suggestion that the problems he was concerned with are new problems or again, that his use of communications studies as a means of understanding different cultures and economies is uncommon among social scientists. What he *did* do in his examination of the communications networks of empires, the means or mechanisms by which ideas, information, orders, commands, are given or exchanged, was to give the whole a strongly historical twist or bent and in doing so to greatly enlarge the area of enquiry both in space and in time.

As I have indicated, there is a close and logical connection between his recent work on communications and his earlier studies in Canadian economic history. How he came to shift from concern with trade and staples to the stability conditions of empires is one of the few questions relating to his work in which a simple explanation seems to be adequate. As he put it in conversation, he set out to adapt the work of J. M. Clark and Thorstein Veblen to his own field of historical investigation—technology and the price system—unused capacity as a factor in economic history—and developed in the process tools which he put to highly profitable use. He employed these with great effect in his studies of the fisheries, the fur and timber trades, canal and railway developments, the wheat economy of the prairies and the early industrialism of central Canada. It was when he turned to the new and more complex industrialism of hydro-electric power, pulp and paper, and new metals, that he felt the need of broadening his concepts, sharpening the old tools and devising new ones.

More immediately, it was in his study of the pulp and paper industry that he was driven to consider that primary medium of communication, the newspaper, and its place in economic development. A reading of his articles on the newsprint industry and the press will bring out, I think, the growing recognition on his part that in *all* his work *communications* had been, in fact, the unifying theme and that to continue in this direction he had no recourse but to turn to the study of history of media of communications, their timing and their impact. In short, study of communications seemed to be the most effective approach to an understanding of the larger environment of economic activity, and although he seemed to be moving a long way from matters normally the concern of economic historians, the economic element was never overlooked or forgotten.

It was not much more than a decade ago that he embarked on this new venture, and his work over this period bears witness to his prodigious labors and his almost frightening self-sacrifice. When I expressed misgivings as to the risks involved in this move into the large and complex area of communication systems which extend into every avenue of human experience, an area, moreover, in which experts of every stripe and color had established strong vested interests, his reply was that in spite of the imperfections which were certain to be present in this working in strange territories, experts might put right what was wrong, and much more important, that it was high time that localized monopolies of knowledge held by antiquarians and others were broken down.

It was perhaps inevitable that there should be misunderstandings and occasionally hostility, but there was cooperation too and a genuine and growing interest on the part of those who could help. And there were sufficient indications of awakening interest in alien quarters to make him reasonably certain, before his work was cut short, that the venture had not been in vain. I saw much of his correspondence over this past summer and can attest to this change, but I cannot help feeling that the years of the early 1940's must have been for him very lonely years.

In his later work, technology and pricing factors cease to provide the backbone of his enquiries and come to serve more and more as starting points. Major changes over history in the technology of communications are themselves culturally conditioned, and Innis' writings on law, religion and politics attest to the absence of the technological determinism with which he is sometimes charged; he was too aware of the close interrelations of technology with institutions and physical environment to fall into this trap. In his analysis of the determinants of change in communications systems and the consequences of such change in specific cases there was one test of performance which he invariably applied, namely, the degree or extent to which these changes strengthened the element of monopoly in communications networks, or conversely, weekened or destroyed obstacles to the free exchange of ideas or information. In his reflections on twentieth century industrialization of the means of communication in the United States, the arch-criminals are identified as vast monopolies of knowledge which, as he put it, threaten "a continuous, systematic, ruthless destruction of elements of permanence essential to cultural activity" (*Changing Concepts of Time*, p. 15).

The villain of the piece is bias in communications which in present-day North American culture is manifest in its fatal obsession with things of the present, its one-sided concern with the logistics of territorial control (whether this be geographic area or markets), its reliance on political action for the solution of all ills. Changes in communication, both in form and content, have led to a neglect of problems of duration, stability, a neglect which has destroyed empires in the past. In his own words:

Shifts in new media of communication have been characterized by profound disturbances, and the shift to radio has been no exception. An emphasis on continuity and time, in contrast with an emphasis on space, demands a concern with bureaucracy, planning, and collectivism. Without experience in meeting these demands, and appeal is made to organized force as an instrument of continuity. . . . Lack of experience with problems of continuity and empire threatens the Western world with uncertainty and war" (*The Bias of Communication*, pp. 188-89).

The tragedy of Innis is the abrupt halt to work in process by one at the height of his powers. The loss is the greater because of the author's attitude toward the written tradition, an attitude which makes prospects for completion of his edifice of thought by others exceedingly dim. Those familiar with his writings need no introduction to his method—the amassing, sifting of evidence, the intuitive flash with connection between fact and conclusion seldom clear, finally the process of working back, establishing the connection so that others may see, communicating more effectively with those who care to read. The brevity of this phase of increasing intelligibility may lessen the immediate impact of his thought and writings, but I doubt that it will reduce the force of impact in the long run, however long run be defined.

There is one aspect of his later thought which should be stressed, and that is the tendency to turn more directly to consideration of the interrelations of economic and cultural elements. There are clear indications in his more recent writings, including the unfinished paper that follows, and in conversations with him over the past year, of increasing concentration on the implications of changes in communications for economic thought and policy; questions concerning the consequences of disequilibrium in the communications area for the study of business disturbance, the strength of nationalism in economic writings ("What produces economists?"), bring out very clearly the direction in which he was proceeding at the end.

Looking back on the course he pursued so steadily, I find it difficult to escape the conclusion that some such road as that he followed is the road all economic historians will follow, if they go far enough.

W. T. EASTERBROOK

University of Toronto

APPENDIX IV

Tom Easterbrook, "Innis and Economics"

from *The Canadian Journal of Economics and Political Science* Vol. 19 No. 3 (1953), 291–303

Reprinted with permission. Copyright © Canadian Political Science Association 1953.

INNIS AND ECONOMICS[*]

W. T. EASTERBROOK
University of Toronto

Over the three decades of teaching and research allotted Harold Innis, no subject concerned him more than the state of economics. He looked to economic history to enrich and broaden economic thought, and he sought to explain fashions in economics and to make economists intelligible to themselves. Although Veblen's influence left its mark on his work, Innis remained throughout a disciple of Adam Smith and no name appears more frequently in his observations on economics past and present. His plea was, as he put it, for "a general emphasis on a universal approach" and in his unfinished paper he writes, "The economic historian must test the tools of economic analysis by applying them to a broad canvas and by suggesting their possibilities and limitations when applied to other language or cultural groups."[1]

Apart from this search for perspective in economic thought there were other elements of continuity in Innis's thinking which give his life's work a coherence and a unity whether his interest centred on Canadian economic history or the duration powers of empires. It is scarcely necessary here to refer to his dislike of concentrations of power in any form or to his uncompromising belief in the free and creative powers of the individual, attitudes which stamp his research from beginning to untimely end. In his writings on economic history, technological change, free or controlled, links past and present. In his more specific references to economics, the pricing system provides the key to his reflections on the state of the subject. Early in his work there is present the same price-technology dichotomy that is to be found throughout Veblen's writings; later Innis sought to resolve this dichotomy in his studies of communication in which he saw technology and pricing as elements interacting with politics, law, and religion in a larger network of human relationships.

If one word may be used to bring to a focus his research in economic history and his observations on the state of economics, it is *industrialism*, its antecedents, course, and consequences in economic and cultural change. It is used in the following pages to set out the principal phases in Innis's enquiries and to aid in outlining his reflections on economics in each of these phases. Examination of his writings in terms of their timing and content, of his readings over the whole period of his studies, and of available correspondence suggest a number of turning points in his explorations which mark off successive phases on the way to what was to be, I think, a philosophy of history.

The first, or Veblen phase, ends with the publication of *Problems of Staple Production in Canada*.[2] In this early phase he was concerned with the antecedents of industrialism in Canada and in his major work of this stage, *The Fur Trade in Canada*,[3] he set out the conditions for the rise of the old indus-

[*]This paper was presented at the annual meeting of the Canadian Political Association in London, June 5, 1953.
[1]"The Decline in the Efficiency of Instruments Essential in Equilibrium," *American Economic Review*, May, 1953, 17–18.
[2]Toronto, 1933.
[3]*The Fur Trade in Canada: An Introduction to Canadian Economic History* (New Haven, 1930).

trialism of coal and iron, canals and railways, wheat and tariffs. His studies at this time were marked by emphasis on the drive of technology and the efficiency of the pricing system.

The second phase begins with the article "Economic Nationalism,"[4] an article which serves as an introduction to his studies in the new industrialism of mining, pulp and paper, and hydro-electric power and his growing interest in the limitations of the pricing system and the economics of disturbance. This phase comes to a close with his *Cod Fisheries* volume,[5] a work which carried him beyond his earlier interest in staples to reflections on the problems of empires, the impact of machine industry in exposed regions, and the broader implications of technological change and marketing influences. As such it marks the end of his basic research in Canadian economic history.

In the third phase his reflections on industrialism take a new turn. Although there are suggestions of the change in his writings of the late 1930's, a glance at his reading indicates that in the summer of 1940 he turned abruptly to an intensive study of technological and pricing factors in the area of mechanized communications beginning with printing and the press. In his published work, the article "The Newspaper in Economic Development"[6] may be regarded as the first fruit of his new inquiries, and his work for the next five years or so consists mainly of explorations along lines suggested in this key article. The researches of this phase represent a strenuous attempt to apply more broadly the methods of analysis which had yielded such rich returns in his studies of Canadian problems.

The fourth and final phase was ushered in with the publication of the article "Minerva's Owl."[7] This along with his *Empire and Communications*[8] comes closest to a complete survey of his unpublished volume on the history of communications. We find him working back from the industrialization of communications to its antecedents in early empires as he had worked back in Canadian economic history to the antecedents of industrialism in Canada.

Although it is possible to mark out some such phases as these in Innis's work, there is at no point any suggestion of a break or a radical shift in his mode of approach to national or general economic history. In each phase questions emerged which called for explorations in strange territories and it is difficult to escape the thrill of the chase one experiences in tracing through these adventurous excursions in the realm of ideas. "He was,.... says Professor Brady, "in the grip of an exploratory spirit which would not let him be content with the traditional highways of economics."[9]

[4]This appeared in *Papers and Proceedings of the Canadian Political Science Association*, VI, 1934, 17–31 and in revised form in the Introduction to the volume *The Canadian Economy and Its Problems* edited by H. A. Innis and A. F. W. Plumptre (Toronto, 1934).
[5]*The Cod Fisheries: The History of an International Economy* (Toronto and New Haven, 1940).
[6]*Journal of Economic History*, vol. II, Supplement, Dec., 1942, 1–33.
[7]*Proceedings of the Royal Society of Canada*, 1947, Appendix A, Presidential Address, 83–108.
[8]Oxford, 1950.
[9]Alexander Brady, "Harold Adams Innis, 1894–1952," *Canadian Journal of Economics and Political Science*, XIX, no. 1, Feb., 1953, 92.

I

Turning back to the first phase of his explorations (1920–33), one name, from the beginning stands out in his readings—that of Veblen appears again and again throughout the 1920's, and his volumes were read and reread. This may account for one of the most revealing of Innis's publications, his "A Bibliography of Thorstein Veblen."[10] In it he sketches those influences which shaped Veblen's thought, putting heavy emphasis on his place on the frontier of the industrial revolution. "The constructive part of Veblen's work," he writes, "was essentially the elaboration of an extended argument showing the effects of the machine industry and the industrial revolution. Veblen's interest was in the state of the industrial arts which had got out of hand. . . ."[11] There is a reference to Veblen's search for laws of growth and decay and to his concern with the effects of industrialism on the preconceptions of economic science.

It is not without relevance here that Innis commented of Veblen: "It is much too early to appraise the validity of this work—certainly he attempted far too wide a field for one individual but it is the method of approach which must be stressed, and not the final conclusions."[12] And again: "His anxiety has always been to detect trends and to escape their effects."[13] [His work] stands as a monument to the importance of an unbiased approach to economics. . . ."[14] Veblen, like Adam Smith, ". . . is an individualist and like most individualists in continental countries, . . . he is in revolt against mass education and standardization."[15] Such statements will recall Innis's use of George Jean Nathan's remark that "all biography is a form of unwitting self-betrayal." Like Veblen, Innis lived through the economic strains of a new country and sought to work out their more important characteristics through studies of the impact of industrialism on a continental background.

In his method of approach, in the selection of questions he regarded as most significant, and in his emphasis on the total environment of economic thought, Veblen's influence was great beyond question. But there was, none the less, one profound difference between the two men for, unlike Veblen, Innis brought a genuinely historical bent, an emphasis on empirical or dirt research, to his work. It was through his historical studies that he lived up to his expressed hope that Veblen's attempt at synthesis might be revised and steadily improved and it was his historical insights that were to carry him into areas beyond the reach of Veblen.

In this first phase, his reflections on economics centre on the state of the subject in Canada and the contributions of research in the economic history of new countries to an economic theory developed in older countries. In his note on "The State of Economic Science in Canada" he begins with the observation that "To the cynically inclined the above title may appear to parallel the title 'Snakes in Ireland'" but, quoting Dr. O. D. Skelton, "'an era of definite promise is beginning.'"[16] On more than one occasion there is expressed the view that

[10]*Southwestern Political and Social Science Quarterly*, X, no. 1, 1929, 56–68.
[11]*Ibid.*, 64.   [12]*Ibid.*, 65.   [13]*Ibid.*, 66.
[14]*Ibid.*, 67.   [15]*Ibid.*, 66.   [16]*Commerce Journal*, 1933, 5–8.

the study of the development of new countries will have its uses in testing the validity of the principles of economic theory. "The conflict between the economics of a long and highly industrialized country such as England and the economics of the recently industrialized new and borrowing countries will become less severe as the study of cyclonics is worked out and incorporated in a general survey of the effects of the industrial revolution such as Veblen has begun and such as will be worked out and revised by later students."[17] In 1929, writing on "The Teaching of Economic History in Canada," he comments: "A new country presents certain definite problems which appear to be more or less insoluble from the standpoint of the application of economic theory as worked out in the older highly industrialized countries. Economic history consequently becomes important as a tool by which the economic theory of the old countries can be amended."[18]

In the course of little more than a decade Innis had laid the foundations for a systematic treatment of industrialism in Canada. The dynamics of growth were to be found in changing technologies applied to abundant resources.[19] He had clearly demonstrated the possibilities of the "staples approach" as a method of attack on problems of new and developing countries. He had shown mastery of one element in Veblen's dichotomy, but the other, the pricing system and its historical implications, called for further study if he was to pass beyond what might be called technological history. His reflections on pricing factors in the next phase were to take him a long step in the direction of a more adequate formulation of the relation of economic history to economic theory.

II

He made a promising beginning in this direction in his article "Economic Nationalism" (1934). New techniques applied to such resources as hydroelectric power and petroleum, the appearance of new metals and new means of transportation are seen as productive of strains or tensions between areas of the old industrialism and the new. Early industrialism was marked by a free and expansive technology and an increasingly effective pricing system; the later or more modern stage by nationalism, regionalism, and the growth of new metropolitan areas as centres of control. The consequences were apparent in the increasingly important role of the state as an agency of adjustment and in the limitations of the pricing system in the face of disturbances resulting from new technologies which strengthened divisive tendencies. It was an exploratory essay which raised issues which were to concern him over this second phase of his researches. The distinction he drew between industrial techniques making for co-operation and industrial techniques making for division was

[17]"A Bibliography of Thorstein Veblen," 67–8.
[18]*Contributions to Canadian Economics*, in University of Toronto Studies, History and Economics, II, 1929, 52.
[19]A more complete survey would include reference to the influence of J. M. Clark. In the economics of overhead costs, Innis found much of the dynamic of change in both Canadian expansion westward and the spread of industrialized communications on a world scale. See H. A. Innis, "Unused Capacity as a Factor in Canadian Economic History," *Canadian Journal of Economics and Political Science*, II, no. 1, Feb., 1936, 1–15.

similar to the distinction he drew later between communication devices which unite and communication devices which divide. In each area, industrialism and industrialization of communications, reflections on nationalism and the role of the state assume an increasingly important part in his thinking as he moves from early to late stages in their development.

In writing on "Approaches to Canadian Economic History"[20] he expresses the fear that economists' preoccupation with price statistics and their failure to take into account the unpredictable results of technological change and discoveries of new resources will rule out understanding of the historical role and functions of the pricing system and lead to neglect of the crucial role of pricing factors in economic change. Along with this growing interest in the pricing system in this phase there are signs of increasing awareness of the significance of communication techniques to modern society and to economics. His studies of modern industrialism and, in particular, of the pulp and paper industry led him to the conclusion that the newsprint industry possessed a dynamic of its own, that it exerted a pervasive influence on the climate of economic thought, and that to understand its place in economic and social change he must move beyond the well-tried staples approach. There appears in the late 1930's a shift of interest to the impact of industrialism on communications, and in this shift indications of a more adequate handling of technology and pricing. There is a faint sign of changes to come in his remark in 1936 to the Commerce students that "The increasing power of the state and its conquest of the press, the Church and the university, and of the tremendously improved system of communication . . . perhaps weighs more heavily against you than it did against us."[21]

Two years later, under the heading, "The Passing of Political Economy," he writes: "The end of the nineteenth century and the twentieth century were marked by the extension of industrialism dependent on minerals, new sources of power, physics and chemistry and mathematics. These have led to the decline in freedom of trade and the hardening of political entities in the intensity of nationalism. With these has come the end of political economy, the emergence of specialization in the social sciences, and its subordination to nationalism."[22] And he continues: "It has been argued that the disappearance of political economy is an illusion and that it will emerge from behind the clouds. But the circumstances are not propitious for another great epoch of thought. The rise of literacy and improved communication promoted the rapid growth of groups, associations and nations and reduced social scientists to a position as defenders . . . of this and that particular cause. Under the influence of modern industrialism in the printing press and cheap paper, universities have become increasingly specialized, and increasing demands for space in the curriculum have enhanced the activity of administration and promoted the growth of vested interests."[23]

These reflections on modern industrialism and the state of communications were brought to a focus in "The Penetrative Powers of the Price System."[24] He had not yet embarked on intensive work on communications but his search

[20]*Commerce Journal*, 1936, 24–30.   [21]*Ibid.*, 1936, 30.
[22]*Ibid.*, 1938, 5.   [23]*Ibid.*, 1938, 6.
[24]*Canadian Journal of Economics and Political Science*, IV, no. 3, Aug., 1938, 299–319.

for a more adequate formulation of the forces back of change, peaceful or disruptive, was moving him rapidly in this direction. There is apparent a growing awareness of the possibilities of communication studies for the treatment of change as a whole rather than change as looked at from one aspect or point of view only. There are few signs of this synthesis as yet; at some points the price system is treated almost as a thing apart, but the close relationship established between changes in the role of the price system, in techniques of communications, and in the power of such institutional elements as the state, underline the advance in his thinking which was to lead away from "the traditional highways of economics."

He writes: "The price system operated at a high state of efficiency in the occupation of the vacant spaces of the earth";[25] and he describes its part in the decline of feudalism and mercantilism and in the rise of industrial capitalism. Its drive in turn evoked the new industrialism, increased strains between areas of early and late industrialism, and the resulting instability has led to increasing intervention by the state. Its limitations today are apparent in the appearance of monetary nationalism, changing concepts of the role of government, and the interest of economists in imperfections of competition. These developments, he continues, have "reduced the value of economic theory based on Adam Smith and increased the value of economic theory adapted to nationalism."[26] Study of the historical role of the price system, its possibilities and its limitations, is looked to for a more realistic approach to the economic problems of our time.

It was at this point that he moved to new ground. Back of the pricing system, its efficiency at one time, its distortion at another, have been developments in communications which at one time increased its penetrative powers over wide areas and which now in the twentieth century have limited these powers and produced the disease of economic nationalism. The key to economic change and much of its dynamic must be sought in changes in communications, for the penetrative power of the pricing system is but one aspect of the penetrative power of systems of communication. Innis's concern with the economic history of the price system had led him directly to the communication studies of the next phase of his work. This growing awareness of the strategic place of communications in change may explain the irritation he displayed in taking Schumpeter to task for his neglect of their importance to economics. Thus, ". . . Professor Schumpeter writes, 'we pass by paper,' 'we also pass by printing' . . . The reader will forgive the reviewer who has read 1050 pages if he insists on technological advance in these industries and the effects of the 'competing down' process on economic and other literature."[27]

III

Innis was now ready for the third stage of his researches—an intensive study of technology and pricing factors in communications—using these as he had used them in Canadian economic history as spearheads for investigations which went far beyond them alone. "Communication" is, unfortunately, as Melvin

[25]*Ibid.*, 307. [26]*Ibid.*, 318.
[27]*Canadian Journal of Economics and Political Science*, VI, no. 1, Feb., 1940, 95-6.

Knight has put it, "... an omnibus label for social relationships varying from simple, direct and merely practical transmissions between persons to the shifting continuity of institutions on a world scale and throughout human time."[28] The "practical transmissions" referred to ordinarily embrace transportation factors in addition to such developments as the telegraph and the cable, the press and radio, and are in the main related to the spatial aspect of communication, the ease or difficulty with which information is exchanged between individuals or groups. It may be said, with some minor qualifications, that in Innis's work in Canadian economic history problems of communication in this spatial sense occupied a central place long before he focussed attention on the role of communications in change.[29] But a more explicit treatment of this subject awaited further researches from which emerged questions that led him to concentrate on this area of study.

For the economic historian to venture into this field there is demanded an enormous extension in the scope of his inquiries, and it is worth noting that almost half Innis's reading, as indicated by his use of the resources of the University of Toronto and other libraries, was accomplished in the years following 1940. Apart from such demands on scholarly time and energy, studies in the economic history of communications raised a problem which was to occupy a central place in the last phase of his work. In his work in Canadian economic history he had viewed technology and pricing factors as an observer of events; now, in turning to communication studies he found himself inside or part of the universe he sought to explore, subject to influences productive of bias from which there could be no escape other than through knowledge of the forces which produce bias. Although he had not been unaware of the problem, witness his early reference to the need for ascertaining trends and escaping their effects, it now becomes so central in his thinking that it provides possibly the best clue to his research of the last decade.

The early years of the forties may be regarded as a period of preparation for study of what Knight referred to as "the shifting continuity of institutions." In embarking on intensive research in the economic history of communications, Innis turned from the position he had attained as a national economic historian of high standing to one which called for ventures into strange territories, many under the control of monopolies of knowledge, dominated by experts who viewed with suspicion and worse this intrusion by an economist, and therefore a barbarian, into the backyards they occupied. Nor were his brethren inclined to applaud this strange veering off into pioneer work in an area which seemed to have little to do with economics. This change of direction gives rise to the paradox that in this new concern with communication systems he faced for a time an almost complete break-down in his communications with those who knew him best.

I have the impression that this shift to a new phase in his thinking was a vastly bigger step than he himself realized. There is apparent the intention to

[28] *American Economic Review*, March, 1953, 180.
[29] See his "Transportation as a Factor in Canadian Economic History," *Papers and Proceedings of the Canadian Political Science Association*, III, 1931, 166–84, also his "Significant Factors in Canadian Economic Development," *Canadian Historical Review*, XVIII, no. 4, Dec., 1937, 374–84.

keep communication studies within the compass of more or less traditional economic history. He writes of his ". . . concern with the use of certain tools which have proved effective in the interpretation of the economic history of Canada and the British Empire."[30] Nor does his reading suggest at the beginning any marked shift of interest to the "big" problems of empires and civilizations, stability and progress, which so occupied his attention in the last years.

Beginning in July, 1940, his readings in Canadian history gave way almost completely to the reading of works on paper and printing, journalism and the press, literature and the book trade, censorship, advertising and propaganda, and memoirs, biographies, and autobiographies which throw light on these aspects of communication. Interest in the appearance and spread of machine techniques in printing took him to studies of the press in England and the Continent, and in the United States as the area of greatest freedom of technological change. There is the growing conviction that at the heart of industrial change lie these advances in communication technology, that early developments in printing and changes allied to them were back of the extension of markets and the spread of industrialism in the old world and the new.

His first important published work in this phase was "The Newspaper in Economic Development" (1942). It consists of a review of technological advances in printing and paper making, with the power press seen as the pioneer in the development of speed in communications and transportation, exerting pressure for more rapid transmission of news by cable, postal, and express systems and more efficient transportation services. The press provided the impetus to the spread of the price system over space and vertically in terms of income categories by its penetration to lower income groups. It appealed to a wide audience of all levels of literacy and strengthened the move to compulsory education and extension of the franchise.

As the pioneer in mass production and distribution, the press, in its emphasis on volume and rapid turnover, heralded the appearance of advertising and the giant department store. Increasing concentration of power in the newspaper field encouraged a corresponding concentration in business in areas making most effective use of new developments in communications. It is suggested that in the lumpiness of technological change in communications, and the instability resulting from the sensationalism of the press and its stress on the immediate, are present valuable clues for students of the business cycle and more broadly for those interested in the dynamics of change.

Innis's observations on economics in this third phase reflect these changes in his thinking. Following brief experiments with imperfect competition and liquidity preference, he turned with more profit to observations "On the Economic Significance of Culture,"[31] wherein he sought to bring technology and pricing together in a more coherent and unified approach. He writes: "The conflict between technology and the price system described by Veblen . . . can be resolved more easily with a broader perspective."[32] Schumpeter had

---
[30]*Empire and Communications*, 5–6.
[31]*Journal of Economic History*, vol. IV, Supplement, Dec., 1944, 80–97.
[32]*Ibid.*, 83–4.

tried to narrow the gap between pricing and technology but is seen as sacrificing much in both approaches and as neglecting the political factor. Silbering was more successful in his attempt "to coordinate the political, pecuniary and technological approaches," but weakened his effort by concentration on national boundaries.

Innis sought his broader perspective through studies in communications which passed beyond political boundaries and enabled consideration of the interrelations of politics, economics, and religion in historical change. Concerning the impact on religion of changes in communications he writes: "With the rise of a vast area of public opinion, which was essential to the rapid dissemination of information, and the growth in turn of marketing organizations, the expansion of credit, and the development of nationalism, the vast structure previously centering about religion declined."[33] Commerce succeeded religion as a force for stability, but new methods of communications have strengthened division, commerce is no longer the "great stabilizer" and the results are apparent in the radically altered role of the state.

New pressures are reflected in concern with the immediate and in the break-up of the classical tradition in economics. "At one time," he writes, "we are concerned with tariffs, at another with trusts, and still another with money. As newspapers seldom find it to their interest to pursue any subject for more than three or four days, so the economist becomes weary of particular interests or senses that the public is weary of them and changes accordingly."[34] As a corrective, Innis suggests that "Economic history may provide grappling irons with which to lay hold on the fringes of economics . . . and to rescue economics from the present-mindedness which pulverizes other subjects and makes a broad approach almost impossible."[35]

The sharp contrast between the synthesis he sought and modern tendencies in economics led to increasingly pointed comments on the unhealthy state of the subject. In his review of Ronald Walker's *From Economic Theory to Policy* he writes:

Adam Smith was a distinguished representative of a century in which all knowledge was taken as a field: It was the supreme tragedy of his work that part of his contributions, namely the *Wealth of Nations*, developed around the principle of division of labour, and . . . that its application was made with devastating effects in the field of knowledge where he would have most abhorred it and where his writings stood most in contrast to it. The universe of Adam Smith was literally ground to atoms, or facts and figures, by the printing press and the calculating machine.[36]

In these years, Innis had moved from description of the state of economics to diagnosis of its condition.

The work of this phase led to an increasing interest on his part in the ability of machine-dominated cultures to survive. Growing instability and increasing reliance on force are productive of uncertainties which optimists of the nineteenth century could overlook. And since his studies of the media and techniques of communications had yielded new and valuable insight into problems centring on the character and course of historical change, it was

[33]*Ibid.*, 86–7.   [34]*Ibid.*, 92.   [35]*Ibid.*, 97.
[36]*Canadian Journal of Economics and Political Science*, X, no. 1, Feb., 1944, 107.

perhaps inevitable that he should look to the state of modern communications for light on the survival powers of Western civilization. In so doing he raised anew a problem which was at the heart of communications itself, namely the problem of understanding among peoples of different places and times.

In his article "Industrialism and Cultural Values" he speaks of ". . . the extraordinary, perhaps insuperable, difficulty of assessing the quality of a culture of which we are part or of assessing the quality of a culture of which we are not a part."[37] This "difficulty of assessment" is rooted in the bias of communications present in our own and other cultures. The clearest manifestations of this bias appear in attitudes toward time, and it was this search for clues as to the meaning of the time dimension in different cultures that led Innis to the fourth and final phase of his work. Interest in the spatial aspects of communications now gives way to concern with time concepts and the possibility of avoiding the fatal disease of bias by attainment of a balanced view of time and space as a condition of survival. The dichotomy of technology-price has given way to that of time-space and again he sought to resolve it by communication studies.

His interest at this time in the problem of understanding Russia may have been a factor in this new preoccupation with comparative history. In his "Comments on Russia" he wrote: "To be trained in political economy, a subject which has its roots in the West and which has suffered from the characteristic disease of specialization, and to realize suddenly that a vast powerful organisation built around the efforts of 180,000,000 people has arisen with little interest in this specialization is to find oneself compelled to search for possible contacts in the broader approach to its history."[38] And again: "Political economy as developed in the Western world will be compelled to broaden its range and to discuss the implications of competition between languages, religions and cultural phenomena largely neglected by it."[39]

IV

It is at this time (the mid-forties) that his readings take a new turn. The emphasis is now on the empires of the Mediterranean and, farther afield, of India and China, on law, religion, and the arts in classical and medieval cultures, on the character of communications as reflected in the alphabet and language and fashions in literature. There are increasing references to questions of power and stability, to nationalism, and to ancient and modern concepts of time. The first of his published works of this phase was the article "Minerva's Owl" of 1947, which like "The Newspaper in Economic Development" of 1942, provided the setting or outline for the following half decade. It represents a bird's-eye view of a larger work in process. *Empire and Communications* filled in some of the gaps and provided a more complete though still skeleton framework. The later sets of essays, *The Bias of Communication*[40]

---

[37]*Papers and Proceedings of the American Economic Association*, in *American Economic Review*, XLI, May, 1951, 202.
[38]*International Journal*, I, no. 1, 31. See also his "The Problem of Mutual Understanding with Russia," *Queen's Quarterly*, LIII, no. 1, 1946, pp. 92–100.
[39]"Reflections on Russia" in *Political Economy in the Modern State* (Toronto, 1946), 262.
[40]Toronto, 1951.

and *Changing Concepts of Time*[41] present the results of research arising out of problems encountered in these new explorations. In these years Innis worked back from the industrialization of communications to its antecedents and forward to its consequences for our time.

His studies of pre-industrial communications parallel in purpose and method his studies of early staples in Canadian economic history. The clay, papyrus, and parchment of the empires of the past, like the cod, beaver, and square timber of colonial North America, appear as the predecessors of industrialism and knowledge of their role and significance is looked to in both cases for light on the character and timing of the industrialism that was to emerge.

It is not difficult to discern the general pattern of change of this last phase of Innis's writings: the early stage of free and creative expansion eventually gives way before the rise of monopolies of knowledge which buttress hierarchies in state, religion, and economics; these monopolies in turn invite competition from marginal areas in which creative elements are strong; this competition is productive of disturbances as new forms of organization clash with established forms, and may be resolved only by the attainment of balance among competing forces. This solution by balance of opposing forces appears throughout his writings of this last phase wherein he juxtaposes time and space, Church and Empire, stability and change, written and oral traditions, Roman Law and Common Law, force and sanction.[42] Bias is lack of balance, it is the result of monopolies in communications representative of one point of view, and its explanation is to be found in the character of communication systems which shape attitudes and promote or destroy the possibility of understanding among peoples. The closed system rules out prospects for balance and no empire or civilization has escaped its effects.

Innis's approach "to the study of civilizations and of monopolies in relation to them" leads to conclusions which provide no optimism for the present. "Lack of interest in problems of duration in Western civilisation suggests that the bias of paper and printing has persisted in a concern with space."[43] States, divided by language, concern themselves with ". . . the enlargement of territories and the imposition of cultural uniformity . . . on [their] peoples."[44] This spatial bias of the present is productive of an emphasis on change, instability and progress, and presents ". . . graver threats to continuity than the tyranny of monopoly over time in the Middle Ages to the establishment of political organisation."[45]

These explorations of the last phase consist essentially of study of the devices by which control over space (how large an area did it cover) and time (how long did it last) has been attempted in other cultures and times—such devices as reliance on the power of the state or the sanctions of religion, architecture, and education. The problems of the present are rendered vastly more complex

[41] Toronto, 1952.
[42] There are strong suggestions of ideal type method in Innis's approach, e.g., his references to the oral tradition of Greece, the durable bureaucracy of the Byzantine Empire.
[43] *A Plea for Time.* Sesquicentennial Lectures, University of New Brunswick. (Fredericton, 1950), 8.
[45] "The Concept of Monopoly and Civilisation." A paper read at a meeting under the chairmanship of Professor Lucien Febvre, Paris, July 6, 1951.

by the impact on cultural values of industrialism in communications, by the obstacles it presents to understanding of other cultures, and by its demands for specialization in technology and thought and its emphasis on the here and now. In the United States, as the area of sharpest impact and most dangerous manifestations, the affliction of bias appears in its most advanced stages. Canadians must search for balance elsewhere and this in the face of an increasingly heavy cultural bombardment from the south.

His reflections on Keynes[46] sum up his misgivings on the present state of economics. Keynes, under the spell of the immediate and of the Common Law tradition, is contrasted with the Adam Smith and Roman Law principles and a more balanced concern with time. It is less a critique of Keynes than a summing up of the forces that made Keynes run. More instructive is his unfinished paper, unhappily entitled "The Decline in the Efficiency of Instruments Essential in Equilibrium." In the main, this is concerned with the bias exerted by present-day communications on the state of mind of economists. It assumes close acquaintance with such writings as his *A Plea for Time*, "The Bias of Communication,"[47] and *Roman Law and the British Empire*,[48] wherein he has much to say about the nature of the obstacles in the way of any universal approach to economics or the appearance of "any central core of interest." The economic historian must take into account such obstacles and make others aware of their import.

He argues that the present state of communications rules out any effective contact between different cultural groups. Within Western civilization itself, the obstacles are almost as great, and by way of illustration he points to profound differences in outlook in the social sciences of Roman and Common Law countries.[49] Law, as an aspect of communications, leaves its impress on change and on economic thought, and the difference in points of view which results is as wide as that between Adam Smith and Keynes. Similarly, modern nationalism as a by-product of the new industrialization of communications presents new and dangerous obstacles to understanding, and press and radio steadily reinforce national differences in outlook. These differences are reflected in present-day preoccupation with national statistics; concentration on national problems subject to measurement, obsession with statistics determined by national boundaries, produce new obstacles to effective communication across such boundaries, the more so since statistics reflect the character of the state. Innis then turns to a familiar theme, the strategic position of communications in economic change, and in particular, to the role of the newspaper as the pioneer in mass production and distribution. And there the paper ends.

I do not think there is any doubt as to the direction in which he was proceeding.

[46]Review: John Maynard Keynes, *Two Memoirs—Dr. Melchior: A Defeated Enemy; and My Early Beliefs*, in *Canadian Journal of Economics and Political Science*, XVI, no. 2, Feb., 1950, 107–9. Also Review Article: "Sub Specie Temporis," *Canadian Journal of Economics and Political Science*, XVII, no. 4, Nov., 1951, 553–7.
[47]*Canadian Journal of Economics and Political Science*, XV, no. 4, Nov., 1949, 457–76.
[48]Sesquicentennial Lectures, University of New Brunswick. (Fredericton, 1950.)
[49]The Common Law with its flexibility and receptivity to change, its emphasis on facts and their interpretation, favourable to the scientific tradition and to industrial development, is contrasted with Roman Law and its appeal to principles and its greater emphasis on continuity and duration.

Modern developments in communications, with their emphasis on speed of change, their contributions to instability, and their concern with the moment, explain bias in economics as reflected in the disease of specialization and the prevailing obsession with the short run. The bias of economics is that of our culture and Innis saw little evidence of any concern with its perils and less of any attempts to correct it. I have the impression that he was saved from the role of historical pessimist by the sense of humour which pervades his writings as it did his conversation, and by his awareness of the importance of humour as an element in balance and a means of distinguishing between economics and insanity. And I cannot escape the feeling that leg-pulling was not entirely absent from his writings.

I have tried to set out some of the milestones on the road followed by Innis—those which mark out the increasing range and maturity of his thought and the course of his search for what he termed "an integration of basic approaches" as an offset to the fragmentation of knowledge which destroys prospects for understanding among peoples and nations. This understanding comes only through open lines of communications and he looked to social scientists to lead the way, even though the American Economic Association lag behind, providing as it did for Innis a case study in the sickness of liberal economics.

Toward the end there were signs of yet another phase, one suggested by Innis's growing interest in philosophy and more especially the philosophy of history. In his review of Cochrane's *Christianity and Classical Culture* he wrote: "A society dominated by Augustine will produce a fundamentally different type of historian, who approaches his problem from the standpoint of change and progress, from classicism with its emphasis on cyclical change and the tendency to equilibrium. . . . His [Cochrane's] contribution to the philosophy of history is shown in the development of general concepts at the basis of progress and the adjustment of order to meet the demands of change. . . ."[50] It is doubtful if any work exerted greater influence on the general outlook of the Innis of the last days than this volume. He, too, was searching for concepts useful in "the adjustment of order to meet the demands of change," a legitimate goal for an economic historian of cultures who sought to see things as a whole in the endeavour to throw light on the economic problems of his time.

[50]"Charles Norris Cochrane, 1899–1945," *Canadian Journal of Economics and Political Science*, XII, no. 1, Feb., 1946, 97.

Appendix V

Tom Easterbrook Interview

In November 1972, Easterbrook was interviewed by Elspeth Chisholm for a CBC Radio program called "Innis of Canada: A Study of a Scholar." Only a fraction of the interview was included in the broadcast. The following is an edited transcription of the entire interview from an audio cassette held in box 03, Accession B1974–0001, University of Toronto Archives.

Tom Easterbrook (TE): I came down here [to Toronto in 1933] with no interest in history […] [but attended] a lecture or two by Innis, watched a long, lean guy loping in with his scattered notes and he proceeded, without any attention to his audience, to talk about steam points in the Klondike, and that seemed to me to be an odd way to begin a lecture. This was breaking right into it.

Elspeth Chisholm (EC): What are steam points?

TE: Well, this was a way of revolutionizing the whole [mining] industry by permitting winter mining […]. Anyway, it became apparent that what he was doing was picking up his notes from a manuscript he was just working on, bringing it into class, and there you had it. But there was a curious feeling about the whole thing that he'd taken what seemed to be a very simple proposition and he began to develop a much larger theme […]. Here is what seemed to be a simple technological change, and then he talked about all the ramifications. Before you knew it, in spite of yourself, you're interested, and that took me then back to see what this guy was really talking about because he was obviously using a different way of looking at things. It wasn't the narrative style. [...] [It was] the style I would call focused interaction where you take a central theme like the staple and the media, and it is not a determining force, it's simply a focus. It's a focus for [the] study of [the] interaction of a whole range of variables—political, social, economic. And out of that interaction then you begin to sense an emerging pattern. And this to me was a fascinating breakthrough. And within six months I'd shifted my whole thesis preoccupation, from money and banking to Canadian economic history. But he caught me just like that. [...] The impression when you went to his lecture was, "this is pretty dry stuff," until you began to sense that here was an exploratory, enormously creative mind at work, and you could take it or leave it. If you wanted to work with him, fine. If you wanted to leave him alone, fine. But there's no sense of ever building an Innis school. He never had a collection of disciples. Each went his own way and he got a pat on the head if he said something bright, and he got something very much different if he was stupid. And very often, I got some rough treatment as [I was] floundering over a long period because this was a completely new dimension—it was a whole [new] search for patterns of change over the long period.

EC: Patterns of change?

TE: Well, [...] there's the staple, you've got your cod, your fur, your wheat, the rest of it. You have a series of shifts there. And it can be told in a nice narrative style, as a lot of historians have done. But when you shift the thing around and begin to use the staple simply as a focus to examine a whole set of interactions.

EC: Take the fur trade?

TE: And then, well, alright, you've got two very different systems—the French and the English [...]. You have very different patterns emerging from an interaction of politics, economics, the social structure, religion, based on that study of the same staple—the poor beaver.

EC: Did he concentrate on the beaver?

TE: Well, you can have the whole history of the fur trade in the history of the poor little emblem that we [Canadians] use [...] as a symbol still. [...] Well anyway, it was this technique of what I prefer to call focused interaction that opened up a whole new way of looking at things. You find yourself searching for patterns. You know, one of the things that students have to get when they're trying to read [Innis's] *The Fur Trade* and *The Cod Fisheries*, the first impression is [that] this is deadly stuff—endless pages of heavy going. And yet, if you catch on to the fact that it's something like a detective story, what he is doing, and he's putting it right there for you to see, [he] is sifting, constantly sifting, reworking the material, looking for that insight, looking for the pattern that emerges. And then suddenly you get the purple passages, and you go through chapter after chapter. Watch the process by which he's playing and see his materials. And then suddenly, bang, there's something, and you kick yourself because he brought together two unlikely things, juxtaposing, and a very important insight has been made. And if he's read that way, *The Fur Trade* really is damn interesting reading, and so is the country's [history], and his whole communications work has to be read that way. In other words, you read him very much like a detective story, and there's a sense of participating in a search for the underlying patterns, the things that escape us when we stick [...] [to the] narrative style.

And you have to remember he started off as an economic geographer. [...] But there's also a very hard rock quality about Innis's writing, and it goes back to the heavy stress he put in all his early work on the enormous importance of the physical environment and the physical characteristics of the staple. In other words, the staple was the message and later on the medium was the message. All the way through, the physical factors that he paid a tremendous amount of attention to [...] [are] interacting with the technology, and then you've got this taking place in a larger cultural context. But when you're dealing with a large number of variables you've got to find a focus, and his focus was the staple. [...] You can *feel* the conscious mind working with this—there is a pattern, where is the pattern, pattern, pattern, find the pattern. And through a laborious, enormously I think painful operation, again watch for those insights—they just bounce out at us. When the veterans [of the Second World War] were here and I had classes of five hundred, I used to take out the purple passages in *The Cod Fisheries* and *The Fur Trade* and put them in mimeographs and shoot them out. Well, the trouble was [that] they got the message but didn't know how we arrived at it. And so the whole teaching technique was "this is the insight, now this is how we got there." And they were pretty mature students at that time, and that worked very well.

EC: Would you mind illustrating with what you call a purple passage?

TE: Oh no, I haven't got it handy now. But all you have to do is look every now and then, look for the break away from the quantitative, the more empirical aspects, [and] you'll find the paragraphs.

EC: Is it a judgment?

TE: No, I don't think he was judging. He was simply saying there was some meaning to this admixture [...]. What is the meaning? What clues? What [insight] does it provide us on the whole momentum of change, the pattern of change that's emerging? This [is a] beautiful example of insight that comes from a kind of intuitive process. And there isn't much attention to chronology or narrative, only in a very broad sense. He was breaking with that pattern, completely.

EC: Do you write this way now? Did it affect you to this extent?

TE: Only to a minor degree. I would say yes and that I put a vastly heavier emphasis on the comparative method, on juxtaposing situations, for example, working with what I call North American patterns.

EC: You had said he had no school and I wonder ...

TE: That's right, but he had a tremendous impact on people who found themselves picking up and using Innisian concepts without being aware of the fact. In fact, I had developed his center-margin [approach] [...] It's simply centers interacting with margins and it can be held at many levels—the teacher and the classroom, center-margin. Or within a country. The center of the St. Lawrence interacting with the margins. Or [the] U.S. power center interacting with newly developing countries. And it's not so much what's going on in the center or the margins, it's the interaction between the two, and the form it takes, and the pattern that comes out of that interaction. The pattern may be one of growth [...] within a conventional structure, or one may be development where there's autonomous, exciting change. [...]

You know the European [professor-student] pattern: you've got the big shot and twenty little disciples parroting his solemn prose. [...] He [Innis] was completely impatient with that. [He was an] inner-directed enormously individualistic man who went his own way, and if you wanted to pick up some gems, fine, if you didn't, that's too bad. But none of this grand patriarch dominating a whole collection of younger scholars. He was a powerful man but he was interested in the research. And if you wanted help and if you came to him with a theme, he would really work with you. But if you didn't, you went your own way, it was up to you. You either interacted with him or, if you're a passive margin, you didn't come. So, in that sense, you won't find a school of Innisians. On the other hand, you'll find an awful lot of people who are talking Innis and don't know it. McLuhan at least knows he's talking Innis a lot of the time [...]. He was smart enough to sense that Innis breakthrough very early in the day. I recall when they first met here. It was very interesting seeing the two: one an intellectual Catholic [McLuhan] and the other a hard rock Baptist [...] [although he became] more of an agnostic. But to see these two minds at first clashing, working on completely different wavelengths, and then suddenly each sensing that the other was saying something. And the tragedy is they were just getting to know each other when Innis died. It was a very interesting period. But you will have learned from the trip [with Innis] so let it go with that. Don't argue, don't disagree, [or] agree—that's your business. [...] You are on a real trip, almost psychedelic in a way. And you can share the excitement, because a lot of these are very clearly Innisian concepts that are bubbling up through, exploring it, probing it.

EC: Can you say anything about the switch from the staple to the medium?

TE: Yes, I tried to develop this shortly after he died because it was very interesting. You see, he'd been raised earlier on the work of J.M. Clark [...] [and] Veblen had been a tremendous influence. In fact, Veblen had a lot to do with this larger cultural context on which he developed his themes. [With] J.M. Clark and others, [...] they'd taken him into looking at not only the larger context of change but [also] the dynamics of change over the long period, not the short period sort of stuff. [...] He found that the staple was an admirable device—it was a unifying theme, the sort that [N.B.] Ashby had sought way back in the 1890s. [...]

You find really the beginnings of Canadian economic history in that terribly long footnote in the very first page of his Hudson's Bay railway. You might have a look at that sometime because in a way you have almost a sketch of a good deal of his later research.[1] Anyway, I think he found—and this is still a matter of argument—that the staples theme was extraordinarily useful in the country in its initial phase of growth just when the structure was becoming set before any new patterns had emerged or showed signs of emerging. As Canada moved into the 20th century, and he moved himself into [research on] mining, pulp and paper, and then new industrialism vs. the old, he found the staple less and less an effective

---

1 It is unclear what Easterbrook is referring to as Innis published a paper on this railway in 1930 (*Geographical Review* XX, no. 1) but it does not contain a footnote that fits Easterbrook's description.

means of getting at this larger context of change. It left out too many factors in a more complex economy. When he got into pulp and paper, he sensed that there was a kind of interaction on a much larger scale that he hadn't sensed before. Because once you get into newsprint [...] [you] see it [...] as a shaping force over a much broader range of human experience because that medium [...] affects our whole sensory patterns. We're much more involved, it's the most pervasive technology of all and he made the discovery in working with pulp and paper of a whole new set of interactions in a very much larger scale. The same technique again, [involving] the physical characteristics of the medium. So let us go back: stone, papyrus, paper—you can skip through the whole series of shifts. And then the larger context in which these changes took place, the impact they made, their shaping influence, and how they were, in turn, shaped by the environmental changes of politics, economics, and so on. It was then, again, exactly the same kind of technique as the staple.

EC: He talked a bit about radio, but he didn't take the same trouble [...] going to the electronics industry.

TE: Well you see, he died, what, in '52? Just when radio had made its impact but hadn't been really assimilated. He said [...] the First World War was a war of radio and the book, a nice way of synthesizing or condensing an enormous range of human experience. He had begun to grasp the radio and what it meant. Television really hadn't come into a point where he could develop it.

EC: No, not television, but radio had.

TE: Well, you'll find in his writings references to radio, but he didn't really incorporate it in his treatment.

EC: The point is the pulp and paper industry—perhaps because it was important to Canada's economy more so—absorbed him and obsessed him in this way that you said in a relationship much more than any other components of the radio that the electronics industry did.

TE: Well, he hadn't really moved from mechanization to electronics. Although he was in process, in discussions. I saw a lot of him in the summer before he died. [...] There was a good deal of discussion along these lines—it was already melling, gelling in his mind, but he hadn't gotten around to incorporating [it into] in his larger theme.

That was an extraordinary summer with Innis because he was a man who the doctors had written off, his time was up, and yet I saw him week after week, right up to nearly the end. Never any acceptance—a flat rejection of all the medical evidence. It was extraordinary. It wasn't a matter of heroics—it was the fact that he was so enormously engrossed in his explorations that it was quite inconceivable that the end was near. And he was working intensively on a paper—he was President of the American Economic Association—to be read in December. I went down and participated in that. [...] [He had] every expectation of being there in December and presenting that thing. You can see a mind flatly rejecting reality as it stood because it was inconceivable. Here, his whole life, he was beginning to pull things together in a larger framework and he was cut off. Anne Bezanson, who was a great friend of his, made the remark that perhaps there was some virtue in leaving an edifice unfinished.

EC: What was it she said?

TE: She said there may be some virtue in leaving a structure unfinished for further exploration, amplification, and development that would probably involve more people because it is unfinished. On that note, when I did return from Harvard, that was a question that preoccupied me because I came back in 1937 and spent a year here [completing my PhD]. And [by then] he was off on communications [and] I found [that] instead of talking about staples he was way back in paper and papyrus and tracing through empires, talking about time and space.

It really took some time [for me] to see [...] [that] it was the same technique of focused interaction all over again, only applied on a massive scale. In fact, [his project was] so massive it frightened most of us away from it because this was a canvas that covered all the centuries. You went from reading Byzantium one day and Europe in the 20th century the next, this constant juxtaposing, setting up the pyramids, Wall Street, with a bit of T.S. Eliot. It was almost Joycean in many ways of looking at it. A complete break with narrative. [...] Well once he got into this larger theme this took him into much wider speculations, and one of those, of course, was the creative aspect of the oral tradition. And yet, curiously, he was a very difficult man to communicate with. You really never dialogued with Innis. You spoke, he spoke. He was so enormously absorbed, immersed in what he was doing, he was never shaken out of it to really dialogue with you on something that you might be interested in. It was a kind of one-way flow. You took it or left it. But you know, he'd hand me manuscripts before publication. I'd make my marvelous notes and [would] find that the manuscript would come out intact without me—I had nothing to say, you see. On the other hand, I felt sometimes I did. But [...] [there was] was such an enormous power drive in his research: "move ahead and move out of my way, I'm obsessed," and he was obsessed.

EC: Didn't he listen to you?

TE: Well, it was never apparent. He sifted it through the mind and it came out something very different from what you thought.

EC: He read them but did not reply to you in your terms?

TE: That's right [...] and part of the problem at that time was that I hadn't quite realized the extent of his breakthrough, and I don't think even at the end he had himself. He really was dealing with a very different way of looking at things [...]. I think if I'd had come to grips with it earlier and saw the change in technique, then it'd [have] been much easier for me to communicate [with him]. I was still working [at] that time out of the conventional narrative style and the orthodox. I'd been trained that way, I'd read [that way] all my life, [...] beginning, middle, end, that sort of thing. And then, suddenly, I was trying to converse with a man who was working with a different set of symbols and even words.

EC: And yet George Ferguson told me in the simplest terms of communication and how ...

TE: Oh, that was different [...]. George was a great friend of Innis's, and so was Pete McQueen at Manitoba. [...] They were real cronies, on a social level. Of course, they were the same age group (I was a much younger guy and never felt part of it [...]). But obviously they could exchange stories [...]. Some of them Pete wouldn't tell.

But he [Innis] was an immensely social man with a very small group of close associates. [...] So, this was a kind of social communication—the kind I'm referring to is intellectual communication. And I don't think anybody on an intellectual basis ever achieved close communication with Innis. Because the younger ones who were interested hadn't got the message at that time. It would be much more interesting now if he were here and we could more or less say, "okay, let's go back over the techniques that I found useful" and then I go back to you and found you had them already. Because he didn't know he knew he had them. You see, this center-margin thing bumps right out of *The Cod Fisheries*, but there's not a word about it in *The Cod Fisheries*, or a scattered reference maybe at one point. But then I went back to *The Cod Fisheries* and someone said, "that sounds like I was reading

The Cod Fisheries, it sounds a bit like it" and I thought "you're crazy" so I went back to *The Cod Fisheries*. But the damn thing is there, but not explicit. And I'm not sure he was aware he was using it. In fact, I don't think he really realized that he was achieving such a sharp break from conventional narrative style. And when he gave [the Beit] lectures at Oxford, I'm sure nobody had followed. And then when he read "Minerva's Owl" at the Royal Society, I don't think a person in the room had a clue, and that's a tough piece to read anyway. It's enormously condensed. He never paid any attention to rewrite [...] and you could take it or leave it. It was hard rock mining, if you wanted to dig for nuggets, they were there, but it was up to you. I doubt if he ever *really* reworked a manuscript because he was exploring—he was on the trail, he was punching his way through the thickets in a new land. And [he was engaged in] the sheer excitement of the chase. [...] [He] was a seven day a week, fifteen, eighteen hour-a-day man. He never stopped. And you would hand in a couple of articles you'd done, and he'd hand you a book, you see. [...][Innis had an] enormous, prodigious energy. Physically, you know, he was quite a strong man. My favorite story there is that [Vincent] Bladen had a farm [...] at one time, and we went out on a picnic on one occasion, and one of our chores in return for a beautiful meal was to take up some very large tree roots in the soil. And they're very big things, and you know how those roots spread. Well, I recall that three of us—the other two were bigger than I, I won't mention their names (I'll be nice to them)—spent a couple of hours struggling to take down one. Innis alone in that time took out three, made some remark about my prairie background, then climbed up a tree to an immense height and began to lop off dead limbs, and at the end of the day was obviously fresher than the rest of us. He was an extraordinarily strong person in that way.

EC: Had to be, really.

TE: He had to be, because he never spared himself. If you were working all out, that still wasn't as hard as he was working, and you knew it. Honestly, it wasn't a contempt for his audience, it was when he went in to speak and lecture, he was so engrossed in the material. Just go in and get it, and if you caught on you were with it and this was good. If you didn't, it was dreadful, because time after time there'd be a long and elaborate lecture on some empirical piece that didn't seem to add up to anything. Then he went back to the drawing board and began to say, "where does this fit in?" But it meant you had to work with him.

EC: Well, was he literally and openly angry with the students who didn't get it?

TE: No, no.

EC: You said if you didn't get it was dreadful?

TE: Well, dreadful to you. It was dull, it was boring [...]. [There] was a story told (I wasn't present) where there was a big snowstorm in January, and I think there was a very large class. [...] I think there may have been [only] three or four students in the assembly hall. [...] He had no patience there. If they couldn't come, that's too bad. But that was an attitude in his writing. You see, *The Cod Fisheries* was really finished by the combinations of Bart Brebner and two or three others. It was a matric really that they worked on for months and months. Once you got the message and put it down in some form or other, and then he was pushing on. You [would] never find him talking about the same thing over any extended period because he was on [to] his [next] exploration.

EC: I wish I could understand—I don't. [...] I don't understand the method. I find it very difficult, a very hard study.

TE: Well you see, to begin with, he was dealing with long periods of change, over centuries. This was not the short-term way of your pyrometer and your neat little set of variables that interact in a nice little mechanistic fashion. This was a long sweep over the centuries and the search for the basic elements. Well that meant you were dealing with a tremendous array of variables. It's like a wilderness without a center (someone identified atheism as a wilderness with a center, [...] Chesterton). Without some kind of focus or principle, you're lost.

I found this very useful in [economic] development work, for example. To work out what is the focus, what am I looking for, what is a basic element that I can tie-in [with] the other elements of politics, economics, and so on. It's becoming more and more of a standard technique, but there's no new mystery about it. It isn't a staple seen in itself, if it's used the way he used it. Most of those who are writing on it are working in the conventional narrative story—this is what happened with fur, this is what happened with timber, this is what happened with wheat. And there's this nice linear sequence. That's storytelling, which is good, we need it. But then, what do you get out of the story, what's the message? And the message is the pattern that has emerged from this interaction, and when you get an interaction you must have a central focus.

EC: I just don't quite understand why this is *new* because I always thought approaching things with a theme or a thesis or an interpretation or a pattern was old—something that lies behind every narrative, for that matter. You can't write a short story unless you know what your focus is, what you're trying to say.

TE: Well, the focus isn't what you're trying to say. It's some central element around which you can arrange your material to arrive at something. [...] It's the way it was applied over the very long period. All you have to do is read a conventional story of the fur trade—there are half a dozen of them—and then compare it to them. When you have a narrative, you have a story, you've got the facts. And that's the way we train our students. So you know the facts, you put them down, and there's your answer. But what is happening up here? There's been no center-margin or direction. [...] It is the way he could apply it over such a large span of human experience and the sense of pattern that emerged from it. It's something I've seen in no other writer. It's curious, right toward the end he was turning to philosophy. In the last few weeks, he was reading heavily in that area.

EC: Who?

TE: Oh, Kant. Of course, in the early work he had known Hegel and Leibniz [...]. But I don't know why. [...] A lot of the message [that Innis pursued] never caught on. In other words, an awful lot of the best work of Innis is still not developed. [...] [Innis went] against the grain of the standard narrative style of economic history. Now that the later attempts of the quantitative boys with computers are trying to break in another way, but that's faded—they have no unifying theme now in U.S. economic history, or Canadian for that matter. But it will come out of reworking the Innisian theme in a larger dimension. One of the interesting things right now is the reawakening of interest in his work. Graduate students particularly are picking it up and working at it in a way that wasn't true five years ago. It's quite an extraordinary development and we've got some very keen economic historians who are well-versed in the Innisian tradition who are beginning to develop whole sectors of it. [Abraham] Rotstein is one. [Mel] Watkins, although he's got involved in politics, is another. [...] There's still a good deal more to be developed.

Index

Addison, Joseph 86, 87
Adrianople 57
advertising XXIn37, XXIII, XLV, XLVI,
	XLVII, 16, 39, 40, 71, 72, 73, 75, 86, 87,
	89, 89n170, 90, 91, 92, 93n177, 94, 101
	see also communications
	see also newspapers
	see also press
Africa 57
Akkadians 21
almanacs 83
alphabet 17, 22, 22n62, 23, 29, 52, 75, 79
	American Economic Association (AEA)
		XII, XXXI, XXXVn82, XLVII,
		XLVIII, 46, 95, 97, 98, 102, 145
	See also Innis, Harold Adams
American Revolution 71
Apollo 30
Arabs 57, 62
	see also Islam
architecture 20, 53, 57
	see also cathedrals

Aristotle 28n75, 67
Armenians 22
art XLIII, 55n121, 57, 58
arts 9, 62
Ashby, N.B. 143
Asia 15, 37, 55, 56, 58
Assyria/Assyrians 17, 18, 19, 21, 53
astronomy 29, 71, 79
Athens 23
	see also Greece/Greeks
Australia 99

Babe, Robert E. XV, XX–XXI,
	XXXIV–XXXV
Babylon 53
Babylonia 20, 21, 22, 29
Baghdad 66
balance XIX, XX, XXII, XXIVn45, XXXV,
	XXXVIII, XLVII, LIII, LVn117, 6,
	7, 11, 16, 21, 30, 32, 35, 44, 53, 55, 62,
	68, 72, 82
	see also equilibrium/disequilibrium

see also space-time
see also survival
Balkans 56, 58
Beaverbrook, Lord (Max Aitken) 91
Beit lecture (Oxford University) see
  Minerva's Owl
Bezanson, Anne 145
bias XVII, XX, XXI, XXIn37, XXIVn45,
  XXIX–XXX, XXIXn62, XXXIII, XXXV,
  XXXVII–XXXVIII, XXXIX, XLII–XLV,
  XLIIn96, LI, LII–LV, 4, 9, 11–3, 15, 22,
  29, 53, 63, 75, 77, 89n170
  abstraction, as XXIX
  active force, as XXIX–XXX
  definition XXXVIII, 5, 11
  economics, in XXXII, XLVII, XLIII–
    XLIV, XLVII, XLVIII–XLIX, LIV,
    47, 95, 100, 101, 102
  heuristic tool, as LII
  strategic role XXIX–XXX
  university XLVIn101
  values XLVIII, LII–LIII
  see also advertising
  see also balance
  see also dichotomies
  see also economics
  see also equilibrium/disequilibrium
  see also ideal-types
  see also paper
  see also radio
  see also space
  see also space-time
  see also survival
  see also time
The Bias of Communication, reviews
  of XXIIIn43, XLVIn101, 4, 25
biology 79
Black Death (bubonic plague) 62
Bladen, Vincent XLVIIIn105, 147
Boccaccio, Giovani 68
Bok, Edward W. XXXIV
books 58, 69, 70, 71, 73, 81, 84, 86, 92, 144
  best sellers 73
  Book of the Month Club 73

  dime novels 72
  novels 71, 72
  sellers of 81
  textbooks 73, 86
  see also common law
  see also England
  see also literature
  see also printing/printers
bourses 71
Brady, Alexander XIIIn8
Brebner, John Bartlet 148
British Broadcasting Corporation
  (BBC) 75–6
  see also radio
Broek, Jan O.M. 17n47
Bryce, Lord (James Bryce) 99
Bulgaria/Bulgarian 57, 59
bureaucracy XXIX–XXX, XXXVIIIn90,
  XXXIX, XLIII, 12, 12n37, 13, 18, 22, 28,
  34, 42, 45n109, 49, 54, 55, 57, 60, 62, 65,
  69, 101
  mediating institution, as LIII
  monopoly of knowledge,
    and XXXVIIIn90
  personality type 14
  see also Byzantium
  see also economics
  see also political/politics/politicians
  see also Roman law
  see also Rome
  see also uncertainty
businesses/corporations XXVn47,
  XXXVIII, 6, 12, 40, 43, 46, 92
  bigness, from communications 102
  common law, and 97
  continuity, neglect of 43
  oligopoly 92
  see also economics
  see also markets
  see also monopoly
Byzantium XLIII, 6, 12, 35, 52, 56, 59, 145
  bureaucracy 53, 57, 60, 61, 62, 65
  church 55, 56–62, 64
  culture 56

INDEX | 153

decline 62
executive XLIII, 55, 60
military 53, 56, 57, 58, 62
ideal-type empire XLIII, 53, 56
space-time capacities 6
see also art
see also church
see also Constantinople
see also emperor
see also empires/imperialism
see also Justinian's Institutes
see also promotion
see also religion/religious
see also Rome
see also space-time

cables 92
calendars 21n62
Canada 91, 94, 95
    American imperialism, response to 45
    common law, decline in 45
    intellectual capacities in 26
    nationalism 45
    oral tradition 77
    provinces, divine right of 44
    social science 26, 95
    see also Canadian Broadcasting Corporation
    see also economic history
    see also fur trade
    see also North America
    see also Northwest Company
    see also United States-Canada relations
Canadian Broadcasting Corporation (CBC) 75–6
    see also radio
capacity XX–XXI, XXIn37, XXII, XXIII, XXXVIII
    cultural XXXIII, XLIIn96, XLIV, LV
    intellectual XVII, XXVn46, XXXIII, XL
    unused XX–XXI, XLV, XLVn99, XLVI
    see also capital
    see also economics
    see also overhead costs

see also thought
capital 96
    fixed costs XX, XXXIV, XXXVII
    see also capacity
    see also overhead costs
capitalism XXI, XXVn46, XLV, 99
Carey, James XV, XXII
    McLuhan, critique of XXII
Carpenter, Edmund XV, XVn15, XVI, XLIIIn97
Carthage 34
Cassel, Gustav 97
Castle, Vernon and Irene XXXIV, 102
cathedrals 67
Caxton, William 69, 30–1
censorship 69, 71, 84 85
center-margin relations XXII, XXXIX, LV, 12, 17, 22, 24, 26, 76–7, 91, 95, 142, 146–7, 149
    see also core-periphery relations
    see also empires/imperialism
centralization-decentralization XLI, 5, 17, 21, 29, 34, 42, 50, 65, 69, 75
    law, and 43, 76n153
Charlemagne 61, 65, 67
Charles I 82
Charles II 80
Chaucer, Geoffrey 68, 69
Childe, Gordon 5
China 66, 78
    bureaucracy 66, 69
    written tradition 69
Christianity/Christians XLIV, 20n58, 35, 51, 54, 55, 56, 57, 60, 61, 68
    Bible XXIII, 68
    Christian teaching 67
    democracy 61
    Dominicans 67
    Franciscans 67
    Iconoclastic controversy 60
    Jesus Christ, views of 60
    Mary, position of 60
    social justice 57
    see also church

see also ecclesiastical
see also monasticism/monasteries
see also religion/religious
Christianity and Classical Culture see Cochrane, Charles
church 5, 6, 9, 11, 12, 68
  Anglican 70
  Lutheran 70
  monopoly of knowledge 67
  Roman Catholic XXIII, 70, 82
  space-time capacities 6
  state, and 51, 55, 67
  see also Church of England
  see also common law
  see also dichotomies
  see also ecclesiastical
  see also religion/religious
Church of England 49, 82
Churchill, Winston 74
Cicero 50
city see urban/urbanization
city-state XXIII, XLI, XLIn93, XLII, 18, 28, 29, 32, 46, 50, 61, 62, 64
  see also Athens
  see also Constantinople
  see also Greece/Greeks
civilization XVI–XVII, XXIVn45, XXV, XXVn46, XXVIIIn56, XXXIV, XXXVII–XXXVIII, XLIV, LIII, LV, 3, 4, 11, 15, 22–3, 29, 31, 32, 55, 56, 57, 58, 67, 68, 69n132, 79
  culture, and XXXVII
  Innis on XVI–XVII, XXV, XXVn46, XXXIV, XXXVIII, XLII, 76n151
  river civilizations 21, 22, 29
  survival of XXXIV, XXXVIII, XLII, XLIV, XLVIII, LIV–LV, 4, 17, 31
  see also empires/imperialism
  see also values
Clark, John Maurice 3, 13, 143
Clark, Samuel Delbert XXXVIn86
class 90
  commercial 83
  lower 84, 92
  middle 81, 84
  relations 66
  struggle XXV
  see also income levels
  see also labor
  see also public
classicism/classical studies XXXIV, 31, 35
clay XXIVn45, 17, 20, 21
Cochrane, Charles XXXIIn74, XXXIV, XLI, 9, 34n91, 35, 39, 46
  false doctrine XLI, 35
The Cod Fisheries XXXII, 141, 146–7, 148
coffeehouse 85
Cold War XXVn47, LIV
  impact on Innis XXVn47
  witch hunts 44, 44n108
comics 92, 93
  appeal to different income levels 93
commerce XXIII, XLV, 49, 61, 66, 71, 92, 101, 101n202
common law XXXVII, 5, 9, 32n87, 33, 41–5, 49, 68, 71, 76, 83, 88, 89, 96–7, 100
  characteristics 48
  church, and 76n153
  continuity, and neglect of 43
  courts 85, 88, 99
  democracy, and 43, 76n153
  economics, and 43, 47, 96–7
  freedom, and 43
  freedom of speech/expression 44, 68, 76n153
  language, influences on 76n153
  lawyers 88, 97
  misunderstandings 99–100
  nationalism, and 76n153
  oral tradition 43
  paper industry, and 76n153
  precedent 42, 49, 83, 100
  science 43
  state, power of 76n153
  trade 68, 76n153
  values 33, 45
  writing, implications for 76n153
  see also businesses/corporations

see also Canada
see also England
see also freedom
see also law
see also oral tradition
see also Macmillan, Lord
see also Roman and common law dichotomy
see also social science/social scientists
see also thought
communications XXXIII, XXXIV, XXXVII, XXXVIIIn90, XXXIX, XLV, LII, 4, 5, 8, 14–5, 20, 21, 42, 46, 52, 72, 73, 74, 76, 77, 78, 79, 93, 96, 100
   advertising during booms, influence on 94
   advertising during depressions, influence on 94
   changes in XLVIII, 93
   change, rate of 100
   commands 4, 38
   commerce, and 101n201
   cyclical and secular change, impact on 94–5
   media XXI, XXII, XXIII–XXIV, XXIVn45, XL, 3–4, 5, 6, 12, 24, 35, 66
   nationalism, rise of 68
   oligopolies 92
   orders 52
   problems LII, 15, 39, 46, 96, 100
   revolutionary change, and 101
   speed up of 92, 93, 100
   time, implications for 95
   understanding, and XXIV, XXV, XXVn46, LII
   urban centers, influence on 94
   velocities and preferences, role shaping XXXIII, XXXIV, 94
   values 24
   see also bias
   see also businesses/corporations
   see also conversation/discussion
   see also economics
   see also industrialization/manufacturing

   see also Innis, Harold Adams
   see also monopoly
   see also power/control
   see also sanction
   see also thought
   see also time
   see also transportation
   see also understanding/misunderstanding
communism 15, 75
   see also Cold War
The Communist Manifesto XXV
Comor, Edward XX–XXI, XXXIV–XXXV
competition 5, 9, 12, 13, 17, 22, 50, 54, 72, 88, 102
   cultural 50
   see also monopoly
Concordat of 1516 70
Confucius 66
Constantine 35, 55, 56
Constantinople 32, 35, 53, 55n121, 56, 57, 58, 59, 61, 66, 67
   fall of 62
   see also Byzantium
consumers/consumption XXXIII, XXXIV, XLV, XLVI, XLVII, 61, 94, 102
   see also advertising
   see also marketing
   see also markets
conversation/discussion XIX, XXXIX, 13, 23, 28, 29, 32, 36, 68, 77, 78, 80, 82, 85
   see also oral tradition
   see also understanding/misunderstanding
Coper, Rudolf XIn1
Cordoba 67n130
core-periphery relations XXII, XLIV, 17, 76
   see also center-margin relations
   see also empires/imperialism
course (Economics 4b/*Innis 4b*)
   assignments XLn92, 32n87, 39n100, 108
   Calendar description XII
   content XXXVI–XLIX
   establishment of XII, XXXV
   themes XXXVII

readings XL, XLn92, XLIX–L, 4–10,
14–5, 16, 26–7, 34n91, 38–9, 93n177,
103–7
see also Easterbrook, William Thomas
see also Innis, Harold Adams
creativity 5, 14, 15, 17, 18, 29, 77
see also freedom
see also individualism
see also knowledge
see also thought
Creighton, Donald XII, XXXVIn86, LI
Crete 57
Crimean War 72
see also newspapers
Cromwell, Oliver 80, 84
Crusades 58, 61
culture XXII, XXXVII, XXXVIII, XL,
XLVII, LIII, LIV, LV, 4, 6n14, 10, 12, 16,
37, 39n99, 46, 47, 53, 57, 58, 59, 62, 68,
75–6, 77, 78, 93n177, 96
survival of 6, 75–6
see also center-margin relations
see also values
cybernetics 11n34
see also Wiener, Norbert
Czitrom, Daniel XIV

Dante 68
Death of a Salesman 14
debt *see* economics
Defoe, Daniel 87
democracy XLVI, 17, 18, 19, 55, 61, 76n153,
80, 80n157, 80n158, 83, 84, 88
see also common law
see also Greece/Greeks
see also states/nation-states
Denmark/Danes 65
department stores 92, 93, 101
Deutsch, Karl XXIIIn43, 4, 5, 6, 19–20,
28n74, 79
dialectics XIV, XVIII, XXI, XXIIIn43,
XXXV, XXXVII, XXXIX, XLIV, LV
see also power-knowledge dialectics
dichotomies LII, 5, 11

empire and church XXXVII, 5, 11
force and sanction 11
pricing and technology 94
technology and business 3
see also dialectics
see also common law
see also competition
see also empires/imperialism
see also force
see also monopoly
see also oral and written traditions
dichotomy
order and freedom
see also price system
see also rigidity/flexibility
see also Roman and common law
dichotomy
see also sanction
see also space-time
see also Veblen, Thorstein
Diocletian 55

Easterbrook, William Thomas
change, study of 3
course (Economics 4b/*Innis 4b*),
approach to teaching XIII–XIV, LI,
LVI, 2, 2n6, 6, 32n87, 102
course readings (Economics 4b/*Innis
4b*) XL, XLn92, XLIX–L, 4–10, 14–
5, 16, 26–7, 34n91, 38–9, 93n177
Innis, relationship with XI–XII,
XVIIIn28, XXVI–XXXI, XXXIn67,
XXXVI, XXXVIn89, XXXVII, XLIII,
LI, 140, 144, 145–7
McLuhan, relationship with XVIII,
XVIIIn28, XXXIn67, LI, LIn112,
93n177
seminar series XV–XVI, XVn17
summer meetings with Innis XII–XIII,
XXVIII–XXXI, 144–5
see also *Explorations, Studies in Culture
and Communication*
see also Harold Innis Memorial Fund
Eastern Europe 59, 66

ecclesiastical XLIII, XLIV, 62, 65, 68, 69, 82
    see also Christianity/Christians
    see also church
    see also hierarchy
    see also religion/religious
economic history XXXV, XXXVII, XXXIX, 31, 37, 96, 97, 101, 149
    Canada XXXIII, XXXVI, XLVn99, 37, 47, 94, 101, 143, 149
    United States 47, 149
economics XLVIII, XLIX, LI, 46–7, 78, 79, 95, 96–7, 99–100, 102
    bureaucratization of 45, 97n190
    change 26, 93, 100
    classical 97
    common law countries 47, 96–7
    communication among economists 47
    communications, and XLII, XLVIII, XLIX, 102
    debt XLV, XLVn100
    econometrics 97
    fiscal policy 97
    free technology 94, 94n180
    interest theory and time 95
    liquidity preference 94
    mediating institution, as XLII, XLVII, LIV
    misunderstandings with lawyers 100
    nationalism XLII–XLIII, 47
    neo-classical 97
    Roman law countries 47, 96–7
    time, meaning of for economists 95
    United States XLII–XLIII
    universal approach XXXV, XXXVn82, XLVIII, 96
    values 100
    velocity and preferences XXXIII, XXXIV, 92, 101
    see also bias
    see also capacity
    see also core-periphery relations
    see also dichotomies
    see also economic history
    see also equilibrium/disequilibrium
    see also exchange
    see also fixed capital/costs
    see also income levels
    see also industrialization/manufacturing
    see also Keynes, John Maynard/Keynesianism
    see also law
    see also markets
    see also mercantilism
    see also overhead costs
    see also philosophy
    see also price system
    see also prices
    see also profits
    see also social science/social scientists
    see also tariffs
    see also taxation
    see also trade
    see also understanding/misunderstanding
    see also wealth
Edict of Milan 55
education XXn33, XXIV, 76n151, 29, 31, 62, 65, 67, 68, 70, 79, 81, 91
    mediating institution, as XXII, 76n151
    strategic role of XXn33
    see also Innis, Harold Adams
    see also Postman, Neil
    see also university
Egypt 17, 19, 20n58, 21, 26n70, 29, 32, 53, 56, 65
    monarchy 29
    see also empires/imperialism
    see also rivers/bodies of water
Einstein, Albert 25n68
Elamites 21
El Greco 55n121
Elizabeth I 80, 81, 82, 83
Eliot, T.S. 145
emperor 51, 55, 56, 57, 58, 59–60, 61, 65, 67
    divine power 56, 58, 60
    see also Byzantium
    see also Charlemagne
    see also Diocletian
    see also empires/imperialism

see also religion/religious
see also Rome
empires/imperialism XXIVn45, XXXII, XXXVIII, XLI, 3, 4, 9, 12–3, 17, 18, 22, 28, 32–3, 37, 52, 53, 54, 55, 56–62, 145
   American XLIII, LIV, 44, 53
   British 11
   Byzantine XLIII, 6, 12, 35, 52–5, 56–62, 65
   Chinese 66
   Egyptian 19
   French 11, 42, 65, 68, 72
   Holy Roman 65
   Ottoman 59
   Persian 21, 30, 53, 57, 62
   Roman XXIII, 34–5, 42, 47, 52, 53, 57, 65
   Seleucid 32
   see also Byzantium
   see also Canada
   see also Egypt
   see also England
   see also France
   see also law
   see also Persia/Persians
   see also Rome
   see also space-time
   see also survival
   see also United States
   see also Venice/Venetians
The Engineers and the Price System see Veblen, Thorstein
England 23, 42, 44, 48, 59, 68, 70, 71, 74, 79, 91, 92, 95, 140
   British colonies 71
   civil war 81
   common law 49
   constitution 30, 89
   Crown 44, 81, 82, 85, 89
   freedom of speech/opinion 70, 80–4, 80n158, 88, 89
   Lancaster, House of 81
   Levellers 83
   nationalism 68

   Orders in Council 81, 84
   printing/printers 69–72, 80–2, 83, 84, 86
   Privy Council 81
   Revolution (1688) 85, 88
   South Sea Bubble 87
   Star Chamber 80, 81, 82
   state dominance over church 70
   Stuarts 80, 82, 83, 84
   Tudors 80, 81
   York, House of 81
   see also Church of England
   see also common law
   see also House of Commons
   see also House of Lords
   see also journalism/journalists
   see also law
   see also literature
   see also monarchy/monarchs
   see also Parliament
   see also press
Enlightenment XXIV, 88
entrepreneurial values XXVIIIn56
entrepreneurs 14
equilibrium/disequilibrium XXXVIII, XLI, XLIII, XLV–XLVI, LIII, LIV, LVn117, 4, 6, 7, 11–2, 16, 18, 20n58, 21, 46, 46n110, 74, 75, 92, 96, 97
   see also balance
   see also stability/instability
   see also survival
Eskimos (Inuit) 20n58
exchange XXIII, 15, 46, 66, 70, 71
Explorations, Studies in Culture and Communication XVIn17, XLIIIn97

false doctrine *see* Cochrane, Charles
fashion XXXIII
Ferguson, George V. 146
feudalism 58, 59, 69
   decline of 81
Fielding, Henry 87
finance 70, 71, 94
fixed capital/costs XLV, XLVn99, 3, 73
   see also capacity

see also capital
see also economics
see also overhead costs
Flanders 66
force XXXVII, 10, 20n59, 21, 22n62, 30, 35, 50, 52, 53, 56, 57, 60, 71, 72, 74
   see also invasions
Ford Foundation XVIn17
France 23, 59, 66, 68, 69, 70, 72, 140
   absolutism 70
   church-state relations 65, 70, 72
   monarch's use of Roman law 67
   paper exports 69, 72
   see also French Revolution
   see also Roman law
Franco-Prussian War 72
   see also newspapers
Franks 61
freedom XXXVII, XLIX, 4, 12, 13, 14, 18, 29, 30, 32, 33, 35, 46, 48, 80–4, 99, 99n197, 102
   of speech/expression 44, 61, 70, 80–4, 80n158
   see also common law
   see also conversation/discussion
   see also creativity
   see also England
   see also individualism
   see also liberalism
   see also order and freedom
   see also press
   see also thought
freedom of the press *see* press
French Revolution 49, 72
fur trade XLII, 3, 22, 23, 28n73, 37, 39n100, 46, 140–1, 149
The Fur Trade in Canada 141

Geneva 72
Genoa/Genoese 59
Genovese, Frank XIIIn7, XIIIn8
geography/topography XLVIIIn104, 17, 23, 29, 71, 79, 92, 141
   law, impact on 42

George III 89
German Historical School 96–7
Germany 70, 74, 75
Gower, Sir Earnest XLn92
Graham, Gerald 25n68
Great Britain *see* England
Greece/Greeks XIX, XX, XXIII, XXIV, XXXIV–XXXV, XXXIX, XLII, 13, 16, 17, 18, 20n58, 23, 24, 28–30, 32–3, 34, 39, 42, 46, 50, 54, 55, 56, 58, 59, 62
   arts 32
   balance in 30, 30n83
   contradictions 30
   culture XL
   democracy XLIII, 30, 55
   economy 30
   education 32
   Greek tradition, the XL–XLI, XLIII, 13, 29–30
   ideal-type culture XL–XLI, XLIn93, 22, 28, 29, 30
   idealism 32
   intelligence 29, 32
   law 29, 41, 42, 50
   rationalism 32
   religion 29, 30
   science 32
   values 29, 32–3, 50
   see also Athens
   see also city-state
   see also Hellenism
   see also oral tradition
   see also philosophy
guilds 61
   copyists 69
   manuscripts 69

Hammurabi 21
Harold Innis Memorial Fund XXXVI
Harvard Business School 41
Havelock, Eric XVn15, XVII–XVIII, XVIIIn27, XX, XXIII, LI, 9, 39, 46
Hebrews 22
   see also Jews

see also Semites
Hegel, Georg 149
Helleiner, Karl 31
Hellenism 58, 62
Henry VIII 70, 81
heresy 60, 68, 82
   see also church
   see also ecclesiastical
   see also writing
Heyer, Paul XVI
hierarchy XXIVn45, 43, 52, 53, 60, 62, 65
   see also ecclesiastical
   see also order
   see also promotion
   see also theocracy
hieroglyphics 19
Hittites 21
Hobbes, Thomas 71
Holland 12, 70, 71, 79, 83
   free press in 69
Hollywood 15
Hood, William C. 37
Hope, Bob 76
horse 20n59, 52
horse and chariot XXIII
House of Commons 85, 87–8, 89
   see also England
   see also Parliament
House of Lords 85, 87
   see also England
   see also Parliament
humanities XXIV, LII, 78
Hungary/Hungarians 62
Huns 56
hydro-electricity XX, XXXII, XLVI

ideal-types XXIX–XXX, XXIXn62, XXIXn64, XL–XLI, XLII, XLIII, LII, 22, 28, 33, 48, 53
   see also bias
   see also bureaucracy
   see also Byzantium
   see also empires/imperialism
   see also Greece/Greeks
   see also oral tradition

   see also values
   see also written tradition
income levels 92, 93
India 66, 78
   bureaucracy 69
   oral tradition 69
individualism XXIII, XLIn93, XLII, XLIII, 13, 14, 15, 18, 29, 30, 33, 35, 46, 48, 50, 54, 55, 56, 62, 81, 99, 100, 142
   aggressive 46
   origins 50
   overdone produces tyrants XLIn93, 30
   see also bureaucracy
   see also creativity
   see also entrepreneurs
   see also freedom
   see also knowledge thought
   see also values
industrialization/manufacturing 3, 4, 5, 52, 68, 69, 69n132, 70, 73, 75, 90, 96, 101–2
   newspapers 72, 90, 92, 93, 101–2
   Industrial Revolution as turning point for communications 72
Innis, Donald XXVIn49, XXVIIIn58, LI
Innis, Mary Quayle XXXIn66, XXXVI, LI
Innis, Harold Adams, approach and methodology XIV, XVII–XVIII, XIX–XXIII, XXIn37, XXIV–XXVI, XXIVn45, XXXII–XXXIII, XXXIn74, XXXIV–XXXV, XXXVII–XXXIX, XL, XLII, XLIV, XLVI, LI–LIII, LIV, LV, 2–6, 7, 11–13, 14, 15, 17, 19–20, 23–4, 32n87, 35, 36, 38, 44, 45, 46, 47, 47n111, 51n117, 77, 91, 94–6, 140–2, 144, 145–7, 148–9
   change, theory of 5, 6, 11, 13, 20, 23, 93, 142
   cultural historian, as XXXIX, 4, 13, 25
   dialectical materialism XXII, XXIIn45, XXIVn45, XXXV, LI, LIII
   Easterbrook, relationship with XI–XII, XVIIIn28, XXVI–XXXIII, XXXIn67, XXXVI, XXXVIn89, XLIII, LI, 140, 144–7

INDEX

economic geographer, as 141
final paper ("The Decline in the Efficiency of Instruments Essential in Equilibrium") XXXIII, XXXV, XLV, XLVII, XLVIII, 46, 79, 91, 95–102, 110
focused interaction approach 140, 141, 145, 148–9
friends XII, XXVI, XXXIIn74, 145, 146
illness and death XII–XIII, XXX–XXXI, XXXIn66, XLI, 1, 31, 36, 143, 144–5, 149
intuitionist 11, 32n87, 142
juxtapositions, use of XIIIn8, XVIIIn29, XX, XXIX–XXX, LII, 11, 94, 141, 142, 145
mass media, disdain for XLVIIn103, 15
McLuhan, relationship with XVIIIn28, XXVIn49, 93n177, 143
media, understanding of XV, XVII, XIX–XXIII, XXIVn45, XXIX, XXXVII, XL, XLIII, XLV, LII–LIII, LV, 4, 53, 140
media ecology XIV–XVII
pedagogy XVII, XVIIIn29, XXIV, XXVn47, XXVII–XXX, XLII, 142–3, 147–8
pessimism 13, 45, 77
political economy XVII–XVIII, XXII, XXIII–XXIV, XXIVn45, LI, LIn112, LIIn115, LV, 47
prescience LIII–LIV
print capitalism, on XIX, XXI
prose style XXIV–XXV, XXVn47
senses 16, 23, 144
skepticism 45
specialization, opposition to XXXV, XLII, LII, LIII, LV, 31, 38, 78, 95–6
staples research XX, 3, 4, 5, 37, 78, 140–1, 143
staples to communications research transition XXXIII–XXXIV, XLII, 3, 3n8, 4, 25, 37–8, 46, 143–4

values and strategies XXn33, XXIX, XXX, XXXIX, XLIn93, XLII, XLIX, LII, LIII, LIV–LV, LIVn116, 13, 14, 24, 25, 31, 48, 76n151, 77, 78, 142, 145–6, 147
  as teacher XIII, XIIIn7, XIIIn8, XXVII, 139–40, 141, 142–3, 147–8
technological/media determinism XXIVn45, XLVIII, XLVIIIn104, 19–20, 23, 28n73, 78, 140
technological historian, as 5, 94
threats received XXVn47
university XXXn65, 7
  see also balance
  see also bias
  see also center-margin relations
  see also civilization
  see also classicism/classical studies
  see also *The Cod Fisheries*
  see also core-periphery relations
  see also course (Economics 4b/*Innis 4b*)
  see also dialectics
  see also dichotomies
  see also Easterbrook, William Thomas
  see also fur trade
  see also *The Fur Trade in* Canada
  see also geography/topography
  see also Greece/Greeks
  see also ideal-types
  see also knowledge
  see also marketing
  see also *Minerva's Owl*
  see also newspapers
  see also philosophy
  see also social science
  see also thought
  see also wisdom
innovation 5, 32, 93
  see also creativity
  see also Innis, Harold Adams
  see also technological/media determinism
  see also technology/techniques
Inquisition 68
insurance 66

institutions XIV, XXIV, XXVIIn55, XXXVII, XXXVIII, XXXIX, XLII, XLVIIIn104, LIV, 3, 5, 11, 19, 23–4, 25, 37, 94, 100
   media, as XX, XXII–XXIII, XXIV, XXIVn45, XXXVIn89, XL, XLI, LII, 100
   values, and XXXVIII, XL, 11
invasions 18, 19, 20–1, 30, 53, 54, 59, 61, 61n125, 65, 66, 69
   see also force
iron 20n59, 21
Isauria/Isaurians 59
Islam 57, 59, 65, 66, 67
Italy 57, 58, 66, 67, 69, 75

James I 82
Japan 15
Jews 67
   see also Hebrews
   see also Semites
Johnson, Samuel 87
journalism/journalists 83, 87, 88, 89n170
   branch of commerce 92
Joyce, James XXX, 145
judges 42, 99, 100
Justinian 57
   see also Justinian's Institutes
Justinian's Institutes 48, 50, 57, 59
   see also Byzantium
   see also Roman law

Kant, Immanuel XXXIIn74, 149
Kassites 21, 35
Keynes, John Maynard/Keyesianism XLIII–XLIV, 62–3
Kiev 58
king/queen see monarchy/monarchs
king-priest relationship 17, 19, 21, 53
Knight, Frank XXVIn49, XXXVIIIn90, LI, 13, 25n68
knowledge 5
   dead XXX, XXXIX, LIII, 15, 71
   living XXX, LIII

mechanization of XIII, XV, XIX, XXI, XXV, XXVn46, XXVn47, XXX, XXXIII, XXXIX, XLVIII, LIII, LIV, 15, 72, 73, 74, 76n153, 77, 144
monopoly of XV, XVII, XXIII, XXXIV, XXXVIII, XXXIX, XL–XLI, XLII, XLIV, LIV, 12, 16–7, 21, 26n70, 29, 65, 67, 68, 70, 75, 78, 96
   see also advertising
   see also bias
   see also bureaucracy
   see also church
   see also creativity
   see also fashion
   see also thought
   see also truth
   see also understanding/misunderstanding
Kroeber, Alfred 31, 39
Kuznets, Simon 97

labor 5, 96
   see also class
Ladies Home Journal XXXIV
language/words XVII–XVIII, XIX, XXV, XXVn46, XLn92, XL, XLIIn96, 4, 8, 15, 16–7, 20, 21, 22, 28, 29, 33, 37, 54, 73, 81, 96, 99
   Arabic 67
   English 42
   Greek 57, 61, 67
   mediating institution, as XIV, XL, LIII
   Latin XLIV, 42, 57, 61, 67, 68
   law 41, 42–3
   Russian 74
   see also common law
   see also mathematics
   see also music
   see also Roman law
   see also statistics
   see also vernacular
law XLIIn96, XLIV, 9, 17, 21, 29, 30, 32n87, 33, 34, 35, 39–40, 41–5, 49–51, 56, 57, 59, 60, 62, 66, 68, 73, 96–9, 99–101, 99n197

bureaucracy 67
canon 41, 67
case 49, 100
code 49
commercial 47
constitutions, unwritten 48, 49, 71
constitutions, written, 44, 48, 49, 71
copyright 71, 84
customary 29, 41, 42, 43, 68
English language and 42
factor in history 48
human rights 50
ideal-types 33
imperialism, and 41, 44
jury system 68
libel 71, 82, 85, 89, 92
licensing 83, 84, 85
mediating institution, as XIV, XLI, XLIV, LIII
natural 29, 50
patents 83, 84
principles 42, 43
property rights 68
revolutionary change, obstacle to 101
secular 41, 58, 59
sedition 81, 82, 85, 88, 89
state, authority/role of 50
treason 81, 84, 85, 88
treaties 44, 47
true 50
unwritten 33, 34, 48
written (codified) 33, 34, 41, 42, 44, 47, 48, 66
see also centralization-decentralization
see also common law
see also economics
see also England
see also geography/topography
see also Greece/Greeks
see also judges
see also Justinian's Institutes
see also language/words
see also lawyers
see also Parliament
see also Roman and common law dichotomy
see also Roman law
see also Rome
see also states/nation-states
see also United States
lawyers 41, 43, 67, 88–9, 97
  common law countries 43
  misunderstandings with economists 100
  see also law
Leibniz, Gottfried 149
liberalism LIVn116, 13, 18, 76n151
libraries 19n55, 32, 62, 67n130
Lilburne, John 83
literacy 54, 68, 75, 87, 91, 93
  see also education
  see also reading/readers
literature 54, 62, 67, 58, 69, 71, 87
  drama 69
  Roman Catholic 83
  revolutionary 75
  sensational 73
  see also books
Locke, John 71, 86, 88
The Lonely Crowd see Riesman, David

Macedonia 32, 34, 53, 59
Machiavelli, Niccolo 69
Macmillan, Lord (Hugh Pattison Macmillan) 48, 49
Maine, Henry Sumner 31
magazines 15, 88
Magna Carta 42, 81
Magyars 65
Malthus, Thomas 97
manufacturing *see* industrialization/manufacturing
marketing XV, XXXII
  women, to XXXIV, 98, 102
  see also advertising
  see also consumers/consumption
markets XXXIII, XXXVIII, 6, 12, 73, 92, 93, 95, 102
  mass 93, 93n177 101

see also advertising
see also businesses/corporations
see also consumers/consumption
see also economics
see also marketing
see also monopoly
see also trade
Marshall, Alfred 37, 95, 97
Martel, Charles 57
Marx, Groucho 76
Marx, Karl XXV, 96
mass production *see* industrialization/manufacturing
Massey Report *see Royal Commission on National Development in the Arts, Letters and Sciences*
mathematics 98, 99
  medium facilitating understanding 99
McLuhan, Marshall XV, XVn13, XVI, XVIn17, XVII–XXI, XXIn37, XXVIIn56, XLIIIn97, LI, LIn112, LIIIn115, 16, 30n80, 143
  technological/media determinism XXII
  see also Easterbrook, William Thomas
  see also Innis, Harold Adams
  see also *The Mechanical Bride*
McQueen, Robert "Pete" 146
The Mechanical Bride 16, 93n177
  see also Easterbrook, William Thomas
  see also Innis, Harold Adams
  see also McLuhan, Marshall
Mediterranean *see* rivers/bodies of water
media ecology XIn1, XVI, XVIIn24, XVIII, XXI, XXIV–XXV, XXVI, LII, LV, LVn117
  see also *Explorations, Studies in Culture and Communication*
  see also Toronto School of Communication
mercantilism 23, 58, 69
military *see* force
  see also invasions
Mill, John Stuart 97

Minerva's Owl XXIII, XXVIII, XXXII, 147
  see also Innis, Harold Adams
Milton, John 83
monarchy/monarchs 19, 21, 67
  absolutism 53, 60, 84
  court patronage 68
  divine right of kings 19, 34, 44, 51, 55, 80, 82
monasticism/monasteries XX, XXIII, XLIV, 58, 62, 65, 66, 67, 68, 70
Mongols 66
monopoly XXXVII, 4, 5, 9, 17, 18, 20, 22, 49, 50, 53, 54, 58, 66, 68, 70, 71, 79, 81, 83, 84, 85, 90, 97, 101
  of communication XLI, 19, 20, 22, 28, 32, 49, 69
  cultural 50
  of language XXV
  of space 53, 76
  of time 53
  see also businesses/corporations
  see also competition
  see also power/control
monopoly of knowledge *see* knowledge
music 99

nation XXXVII, 3, 6, 37, 58, 64, 89, 95, 98, 99
  mediating institution, as XIV, XLIV, LIII, 47
  see also nationalism
  see also states/nation-states
National Film Board 76n151
nationalism XLII–XLIII, XLIV, XLV, XLVI, LIII, LIV, 45, 57, 61, 64, 68, 70, 75, 76, 81, 98-9
  economic nationalism XXXIII, 47, 95
  mediating institution, as XIV, XX, LIII
  monopoly of knowledge 75
  printing 76n153
  rise of 68
  see also Canada
  see also common law

see also economics
see also monarchy/monarchs
see also understanding/misunderstanding
see also United States
see also vernacular
natural science *see* science
Nazism 74
Nef, John XXVIn49, 98n192
Netherlands *see* Holland
news 70, 73, 85
   speed up of transmission 92
   see also advertising
   see also England
   see also newspapers
   see also press
   see also public
news appeal 91
news ballads 83
news sheets 71, 83
newsbooks 84
newsletters 85
newspapers XXXIII–XXXIV, XLV, XLVI–XLVII, 4, 12n39, 71, 72–4, 75, 79, 85, 86, 87, 88, 89n170, 90, 93, 94, 101–2
   economic development 3, 94
   circulation 72, 86, 91–2, 93
   editorials 92
   England vs. United States 92
   fines 88
   government vs. opposition 87
   liquidity preference 94
   pictorials 92
   preferments 87
   publishers 85, 88, 89, 90–1
   radio, competition with 92, 93
   sensationalism 73, 86, 90, 91
   spatial-temporal implications XLVII
   subscriptions 87
   subsidies 80, 86, 87
   tabloids 92
   turnover 91, 93
   war news 71, 72, 90
   see also advertising
   see also England

see also industrialization/manufacturing
see also journalism/journalists
see also markets
see also power/control
see also press
see also price system
see also prices
see also stability/instability
see also taxation
see also United States
newsprint 90–1, 144
Nineteen Eighty-Four XL, 16–7, 33n88
Norsemen 65
North America XLIV, 11, 17, 37, 44, 72, 80
   economists in 95
   see also Canada
   see also United States
Northcliffe, Lord (Alfred Harmsworth) 91
Northwest Company XLII, 46

Ong, Walter XVn15
oral tradition XIX, XX, XXIn37, XXXIX, 13, 14, 16, 18, 19, 20n58, 22, 23, 29, 30, 35, 42, 43, 47, 57, 66, 68, 69, 76n152, 76–7, 145
   ideal-type XXIXn62
   see also common law
   see also conversation/discussion
   see also orality
   see also oral and written traditions dichotomy
   see also Roman law
oral and written traditions dichotomy XXXVII, 5, 11, 17, 23, 28, 29, 32, 32n87, 34, 62, 67, 99
   see also oral tradition
   see also printing/printers
   see also written tradition
orality XIX–XX, XLIII, XLV, 9, 62
   see also oral tradition
   see also oral and written traditions dichotomy
   see also printing/printers

order XLI, 4, 13, 16, 23, 30, 32, 34n91, 35, 86
  and law 48
  see also bureaucracy
  see also order and freedom
  see also power/control
  see also sanction
  see also stability/instability
order and freedom XIV, XIX, XXIX–XX, XXXIIn74, XXXVII, XXXIX, XL, XLI, XLIn93, XLII, XLVIII, LIV, 13, 14, 22, 30, 32, 32n87, 33, 34n91, 46, 100
  see also freedom
  see also knowledge
  see also order
  see also values
Oriental authority 55
Oriental Club 31, 31n86
Oriental despotism 57
Orwell, George *see Nineteen Eighty-Four*
Ostrogoths 56
overhead costs XXXIV, XLV, XLVn99, 3, 90
  see also capacity
  see also capital
  see also economics
  see also fixed capital/costs
Overton, Richard 83

painting 53, 55n121
Palestine 22, 54
pamphlets 70, 83, 84, 86
Papacy/popes 56, 57, 58, 61, 65, 67, 70
paper XXIVn45, XLIV, 5, 54, 63, 65, 66, 67, 68, 69, 70, 78, 79, 86, 144, 145
  bias of 75
  manufacturing 66–7, 72
  mass production of 90
  see also common law
  see also printing/printers
papyrus XXIVn45, XLIII, 17, 18, 19, 22, 29, 34, 35, 62, 65, 78, 144, 145
parchment XXIVn45, XLIII, XLIV, 35, 54, 62, 63, 65, 68, 70, 78
Pareto, Vilfredo 96

Paris 65
Parker, Ian XXXVI, XXXVIn89, LIII
Parliament 43, 44, 68, 71, 82, 83, 84–5, 85n162, 86, 87–9
  legal supremacy 71
  see also England
  see also House of Commons
  see also House of Lords
  see also law
  see also newspapers
  see also power/control
Parsons, Talcott 97
Persia/Persians 18, 54
  see also empires/imperialism
philosophy XXXIIn74, XXXIV–XXXV, 30, 41, 47n111, 54, 62, 149
  and economics 49
  see also Greece/Greeks
  see also Smith, Adam
  see also thought
Phoenicians 22, 29
Plato XIX, XXn33, XXVn46, XLIn93, 23, 28
poetry XIX, 22, 23, 29
Poitiers 57
Polanyi, Karl 7
political economy *see* Innis, Harold Adams
political/politics/politicians XXXVIII, XXXIX, XLI, XLIII, XLV, XLVI, LIV–LV, 6, 12, 17, 18, 19, 20n58, 21, 23, 26, 26n70, 28, 29, 30, 32, 32n87, 35, 41, 42, 43, 44, 45, 46, 49, 51, 52, 53, 54, 55, 56, 59–60, 62–3, 65, 68, 69, 70, 71, 72, 80, 82, 85, 88, 92, 98, 140
  bureaucratization 45
  Roman law countries 43
  tolerance 71
  see also common law
  see also democracy
  see also newspapers
  see also power/control
  see also press
  see also Roman law
postal service 52, 92

Postman, Neil XIn1, XVI, XVIIn24,
    XXn33, XXIV–XXV, XXVn46, XXVn47
power/control XXXIV, XXXVIII, XLI,
    XLIV, LIII, LV, 11, 12, 16, 29, 35, 46, 56,
    60, 61, 62, 72, 73, 80, 83, 85, 86, 88, 98,
    99, 101
  communications/mass media, and
      XXXVII, 3–4, 5, 15, 21, 72, 80, 84, 85,
      87, 90, 91
  executive 43, 44
  see also bureaucracy
  see also businesses/corporations
  see also center-margin relations
  see also centralization-decentralization
  see also commands
  see also core-periphery relations
  see also empire/imperialism
  see also force
  see also knowledge
  see also monopoly
  see also political/politics/politicians
  see also public
  see also religion/religious
  see also sanction
  see also space-time
  see also states/nation-states
  see also United States
  see also wealth
power-knowledge dialectics XIX, XXVn46,
    XXXVII, LV
press XXXIII, XLIV, XLVI, 3, 80n157, 73,
    74, 79, 80n157, 85, 89n170, 94, 101
  competition 88
  free press 69, 74, 80, 88, 90
  freedom of the XLVI, 54, 70, 76n153,
      79, 80, 83, 84, 88, 89, 90, 92
  political press 74, 87, 92
  see also common law
  see also democracy
  see also England
  see also freedom
  see also journalism/journalists
  see also newspapers

price system XXIII, XXXIII, XXXIV,
    XLVII, XLVIII, 79, 91, 93, 94, 101
  engineer, dichotomy with 94
  mediating institution, as XXIII
prices XXXVII, XLVI, 3, 61, 72, 86, 90, 91
  fixed pricing (one price system) XLVI,
      XLVII, 91, 92, 93, 95
priests/priesthood 19, 21, 29, 67
  see also Egypt
  see also king-priest relationship
  see also knowledge
printing/printers XXXIII, XLIV, XLV, 3,
    54, 63, 65n128, 69–70, 71, 76n153, 79,
    80–2, 83, 84, 86, 90
  block-printing 66, 69
  industrialization of XXVn46, XXXII, 90
  Germany 69
  Low countries 69
  religious wars 74
  see also England
  see also Italy
  see also nationalism
profits 61
  see also prices
  see also wealth
progress XXVn46, LIV, 37, 49, 75
  definition XLIIn96, 98
  measured using statistics 98
  see also stability/instability
  see also time
Promethean paradox XXVn46
promotion 52, 53
  see also hierarchy
propaganda 39, 40
  Nazi 74
prose XIX, 23, 71
public XLV, 15–6
  interests 71
  manipulation of LIV, 38, 73–5, 91
  mass 54, 73, 74, 76, 83, 84, 89, 91, 92, 93
  reading 71, 72
public opinion XXXVII, XXXIX, LIV, 3, 15,
    29, 83, 84, 85, 87, 88, 100, 101

168 | INDEX

public policy XLVII
publishing XXV, 72
   see also newspapers
pulp and paper XXXII, 3, 37, 101, 144
pyramids 4n10, 19, 145

Rabelais, Francois 69
radio XXI, XXIn37, XXIII, XXVn46, XLV, 3, 5, 15, 28, 74, 144
   bias of XLV, 75
   competition with newspapers 92, 93
   oral tradition 76n152
   written tradition 76n152
   see also British Broadcasting Corporation
   see also Canadian Broadcasting Corporation
rational/rationalism/irrationalism *see* thought
reading/readers 65
   see also books
   see also education
   see also literacy
   see also literature
   see also newspapers
   see also pamphlets
   see also press
Reformation 70
religion/religious XLIII, 12–3, 18, 19, 20, 26n70, 30, 34, 49, 50, 51, 53–62, 68, 71, 75, 82, 84
   Buddhism 66, 69
   Calvinism 14, 70
   emperor worship 34
   Episcopalianism 71
   mediating institution, as XXII, 19, 51
   Mithraism 54
   mystery 30, 54
   mysticism 54, 60
   Oriental 54
   Protestantism 82
   Puritanism 60, 82, 84
   reason, vs. 50, 71, 79
   sects 70, 81
   toleration 70, 80, 83, 84

wars 74
   see also Byzantium
   see also Christianity/Christians
   see also church
   see also ecclesiastical
   see also Greece/Greeks
   see also monarchy/monarchs
   see also monasticism/monasteries
   see also priests/priesthood
   see also theocracy
   see also time
Renaissance 59, 62, 70
reporters *see* journalism/journalists
Ricardo, David 97
Riesman, David 14
rigidity/flexibility XXXVII, XLVn99, 34, 36, 45n109, 53, 61, 71, 73, 76n153, 101
   law, of 30, 32, 34, 43, 48, 49, 68
   oral tradition 17
   written tradition 17, 34
   see also bureaucracy
rivers/bodies of water 17, 19, 22, 29, 65
Robinson, Henry 83
Roman and common law dichotomy 32n87, 33, 34n91, 41–3, 47–49, 96–101
Roman civil law 5n15, 32n87, 33–4, 48, 59
   see also law
   see also Roman law
Roman law XXXVII, 5n15, 9, 32n87, 33, 41–5, 57, 59, 60, 62, 76, 98, 101
   bureaucratization 101
   characteristics 48
   codification 34, 41, 50–1
   commerce, and 67
   economics, and 47, 96–7, 98, 101
   emperors use of vs. Papacy 67
   France 41, 42
   misunderstandings 99–100
   North America 44
   oral tradition 47
   spatial/territorial control 44
   trade 67
   urban centers 67
   see also law

see also Justinian's Institutes
see also Macmillan, Lord
see also Roman and common law dichotomy
see also Roman law
see also law
see also Roman civil law
see also Rome
see also social science/social scientists
see also written tradition
Rome 39, 48, 54, 55, 56–7, 61, 62
  army 55
  bureaucracy 55, 56–7
  democracy 55
  Eastern empire 35, 55, 57, 58, 59, 61, 66
  emperor worship 34
  executive 55
  legal developments in 34, 50–1
  Pax Romana 34
  religion 34
  Western empire 34–5, 54, 55, 56, 58, 59, 61, 66
  written tradition 34
  see also Byzantium
  see also emperor
  see also empires/imperialism
Roosevelt, Franklin Delano 74, 100
Rostow, Walt 97
Rothermere, Lord (Harold Harmsworth) 91
Rotstein, Abraham 149
Royal Commission on National Development in the Arts, Letters and Sciences LIII
Russell, Bertrand 25n68
Russia/Soviet Union 15, 58, 59, 74, 99

sanction XXVIIn53, XXXVII, XXXIX, 4, 11, 12–3, 15–6, 40, 44, 60, 93n177
  definition XXVIIn55, XXXIX
  and force 11
  see also institutions
  see also order
  see also power/control
  see also space-time
  see also stability/instability

see also time
see also United States
Schumpeter, Joseph XLIV, 62, 96
science LII, 5, 17, 29, 71, 72, 78, 79
Scotland 49
  see also Smith, Adam
sculpture 20, 57
semantics *see* language/words
Semites 20–1
  see also Hebrews
  see also Jews
Serbia/Serbs 59
Seven Years War 86
Shakespeare, William 70
Sicily 57
silk 61
Simons, Henry C. 13
Slavs 57, 59
Smith, Adam 49
  Roman law influences 97
Smollett, Tobias 87
social media LIV
social science/social scientists LII, LIII, 43, 78, 95
  biases of 47
  and common law 43, 97
  economic historians 26
  reflective thought 47
  and Roman law 43, 98, 101
  time, meaning of 95
  universal approach XXXII–XXXIII, XXXV, LII, 5, 97
  see also communications
  see also economics
  see also education
  see also knowledge
  see also mathematics
Socrates XXVn46, 22–3
  Socratic dialogue XIX, XXIV
space XXIn37, XXII, XXIVn45, XXXVII, XLIII, 16, 18, 21, 23, 54, 66, 69, 95, 100, 101
  borders 13, 17, 34, 54, 98, 99
  bureaucracy XXIX

states/nation-states XXXVIII, 6, 12
territory 12
see also bias
see also force
see also geography/topography
see also invasions
see also markets
see also space-time
space-time (time-space) XXXIV, XXXVIII,
  XXXIX, XL, XLIII, XLIV, XLVII,
  LII–LIV, 4, 5, 6, 9, 11, 12, 15, 16, 19,
  24, 26n70, 32, 33, 35, 52, 62, 65, 66, 91,
  100, 145
see also bias
see also space
see also time
Spain 17, 57, 59, 67
Spengler, Oswald 31
Spry, Irene LI
stability/instability XVI–XVII, XXXIII,
  XXXVIII, XXXIX, XLIn93, XLIII, 4, 12,
  13, 16, 18, 19, 30, 32, 46, 49, 55, 59, 61–2,
  73, 77, 80, 85, 91, 92, 101
see also civilization
see also equilibrium/disequilibrium
see also order
see also survival
see also time
see also uncertainty
Stamp Act (1765) 71
Stamp tax (1712) 86
staples *see* Innis, Harold Adams
states/nation-states XXI, XXXV, XXXVII,
  XXXVIII, XLII, XLIV, XLVI, LIII, LV,
  3, 4, 6, 12, 22, 23, 26, 37, 47, 53, 54, 56,
  59–60, 61, 65, 67, 68, 73, 74, 75, 83, 86,
  95, 98, 99, 101
  divine right of 44
  mediating institutions, as 23
  nationalism 68
  regulations 61, 81, 83, 84, 85, 86, 99
  secular 21, 35, 41, 60, 65
  see also church
  see also common law
  see also law
  see also nation
  see also power/control
  see also space
  see also statistics
statistics XLIIn96, 97, 98–9
  focus on national problems 98
  vs. mathematics 98–9
  mechanized knowledge XXI
  mediating language, as a 98–9
  vs. music 99
  Russia 99
  see also Australia
  see also economics
  see also understanding/misunderstanding
steam power 72, 90
Steele, Richard 87
stereotyping 90
stone XXIVn45, 17, 18, 19, 20–1, 21n61, 23,
  29, 144
Strate, Lance XIn1, XXVI, LVn117
suicide/suicidal 13, 75
  cultural XLVIII, 77
  see also civilization
  see also survival
Sumerians 20–1, 26n70, 53
survival XIn1, XXXIV, XXXVII, XXXVIII,
  XXXIX–XL, XLII, XLIV, XLVn99,
  XLVI, XLVIn101, XLVIII, LIII, LIV–
  LV, 4, 5, 6, 10, 11–3, 15–6, 17, 20, 31, 33,
  37, 46, 52, 53, 61, 77, 93n177
  see also balance
  see also bias
  see also bureaucracy
  see also civilization
  see also space-time
  see also stability/instability
  see also suicide/suicidal
  see also time
  see also values
  see also wisdom
Swift, Jonathan 86, 87
Switzerland, free press in 69
Syria 56

tariffs 72, 90–1
taxation 71, 80, 85, 86, 87, 90, 92, 97
technological/media determinism XVII–XXIV, XXIn37, XXIIIn43, XXIVn37, XXIVn45, XL,
XLVIIIn104, LV
   see also Innis, Harold Adams
   see also technology/techniques
technology/techniques XVII–XX, XXXIII, XXXVII; XXXVIII, XL, XLIIn96, 4, 5, 9, 11, 15, 17, 20, 23, 38, 40, 69n132, 71, 73, 75, 78, 80, 85, 90, 92, 93, 94, 95
   see also Innis, Harold Adams
   see also progress
   see also technological/media determinism
   see also time
telegraph XXXIII, 90, 92, 93, 101
telephone 101
television (TV) 15, 28, 38, 144
Teutonic 42, 65
theocracy 18, 19, 21
thought, creative XXIX
   freedom of XXXIX, LIVn116, 13, 17, 78
   intellectual abstractions XXIII, XXIX, 43, 78
   rational/rationalism/irrationalism XXXIII, XLVII, XLVIII, 29, 32, 35, 62, 81, 91
   reflective/unreflective XIX, XXI, XXIX, XXXV, XLI, XLII, XLV, XLVII, XLVIII–XLIX, 26, 47, 76n151, 91, 102
   see also common law
   see also creativity
   see also knowledge
   see also Nineteen Eighty-Four
   see also understanding/misunderstanding
time XXI, XXIn37, XXIVn45, XXX, XXXIII, XXXIV, XLVII–XLVIII, 12, 16, 20, 21n62, 24, 26, 54, 65, 95
   the afterlife 54, 59, 62
   bureaucracy XXIX, XLIII
   duration/continuity XVI–XVII, XLIII, 6, 12, 15, 18, 32, 35, 41, 43, 44, 49, 52, 54, 55, 59, 60, 66, 98, 99, 100

eternity/immortality 12, 53, 59, 62
foresight/forethinker 73, 99
interval, as an 95
long-run XXIX, XLIV, 3, 6, 12, 41, 49, 62–3, 95
neglect/annihilation of XXXVIII, LIV
short-run XLVII, 3, 6, 12, 41, 62–3, 95
speed 92, 93, 94, 95
technology's implications 95
   see also bias
   see also bureaucracy
   see also business/corporations
   see also common law
   see also newspapers
   see also progress
   see also sanction
   see also space/time
   see also suicide/suicidal
   see also survival
   see also United States
time-space *see* space-time
The Times (of London) 72, 90
Toronto School of Communication XV, XVn15
Toynbee, Arnold 4, 13, 31, 39, 76, 76n151
trade XXIVn45, XXXIII, XLIV, 22, 29, 33n91, 34, 46, 47, 52, 56, 58, 59, 61, 64, 67, 68, 69, 71, 75, 76n153, 101
   see also common law
   see also core-periphery relations
   see also fur trade
translations 67, 68
transportation XXXIV, 3, 21, 52, 65, 72, 92, 93
   speed up 92
truth XIX, XXIV, XXXV, 23, 29, 85
Turkey/Turks 20n58, 58, 59
Twain, Mark 89, 89n171
Two Ways of Thinking see Macmillan, Lord

uncertainty XLIII, 4, 20, 45n109, 49, 54, 61–2
   bureaucratization 49
   see also stability/instability

understanding/misunderstanding XXXV, XXXVIII, XLI–XLII, XLV, XLIX, LII, LVn117, 4, 37–8, 70, 73–4, 98, 99, 100
see also conversation/discussion
see also lawyers
see also mathematics
see also music
see also statistics
see also thought
see also World War I
see also World War II
United Kingdom see England
United Nations XXXV, 37
United States XXXIX, XLIII, 12, 15, 23, 30, 48, 72, 73–4, 92, 93, 95
American colonies 71, 79
Bill of Rights 71, 90
centralization of power 44
constitution 30, 44, 71, 101
common law, decline of 44
divine right of 44
misunderstandings with Europeans 98
nationalism XLII–XLIII, LIV, 98
neglect of continuity 44
penny press 90
Roman law, rise of 44
sanction LIV, 44
stamp tax 86
Supreme Court 44
written law in 44, 48
see also American Revolution
see also Cold War
see also economic history
see also economics
see also empires/imperialism
see also newspapers
see also North America
see also press
see also statistics
see also United States-Canada relations
United States-Canada relations 76–7
university XLIV, XLVIn101, 29, 37, 41, 97
business and government pressures XXVn47

institutionalized research 14
mediating institution, as XLVI
see also education
see also social science/social scientists
University of Paris 67
urban/urbanization XLIV, 61, 66, 68, 90, 94
Usher, Abbott P. 5, 66

values XIV, XVIII, XIX, XXVIIIn56, XXXV, XXXVII, XXXVIII, XXXIX, XLIn93, XLVIII, LII, LIII, LV, 10, 11, 13, 15, 18, 23, 24, 33, 34n91, 35, 46, 76, 77, 96
active force, as 24
commodity/commercial 76–7
and media 24, 76
see also bias
see also civilization
see also common law
see also dichotomies
see also liberalism
see also Values Discussion Group
Values Discussion Group XXVII, XXVIIn56
Veblen, Thorstein XXXIIIn76, 3, 4n9, 13, 94, 95, 143
Venice/Venetians 58, 59
vernacular XLIV, 54, 62, 67, 68, 69, 70, 71, 73, 79, 81
see also common law
see also language/words
see also nationalism
see also printing/printers
see also publishing
Vikings 20n58
Visigoths 35, 56

Wall Street 145
Walpole, Robert 87
Walter, John 90
war see Crimean War
see also England
see also force

   see also Franco-Prussian War
   see also invasions
   see also newspapers
   see also religion/religious
   see also Seven Years War
   see also World War I
   see also World War II
water *see* rivers/bodies of water
Watkins, Mel XXXVI, LIII
Watson, Alexander John XV
wealth XX, 58, 61
Weber, Max XXIXn62, XLIII
   see also ideal-types
Wentworth, Peter 82
Western Europe 67, 73, 77
   misunderstandings with Americans 98
Wiener, Norbert 5, 38, 39
Wilde, Oscar 98
William and Mary 85
Willits, Joseph XLVIIIn105
wisdom XXVn46, XLIII, XLIX, LV, 55, 102
   see also knowledge
   see also thought
   see also survival

women *see* marketing
Woolworth *see* department stores
World War I 73–4, 144
World War II 74
Wright, Chester XXVIn49, XLVIIIn105, 95
written tradition XIX, XX, 12, 22, 23, 34, 49, 62, 67, 69, 71, 76n152
   ideal-type XXIXn62
   see also oral tradition
   see also oral and written traditions dichotomy
   see also printing/printers
   see also writing
writing XXIII, XXV, XXX, XLIII, XLIV, 12, 18, 19, 20, 21, 22, 23n66, 28, 29, 30, 52, 54, 57, 66, 69, 79
   brush 66
   heretical 67
   political 87
   speculative 72
   see also common law
   see also heresy
   see also oral and written traditions dichotomy
   see also written tradition

Lance Strate
General Editor

This series is devoted to scholarship relating to media ecology, a field of inquiry defined as the study of media as environments. Within this field, the term "medium" can be defined broadly to refer to any human technology or technique, code or symbol system, invention or innovation, system or environment. Media ecology scholarship typically focuses on how technology, media, and symbolic form relate to communication, consciousness, and culture, past, present and future. This series is looking to publish research that furthers the formal development of media ecology as a field; that brings a media ecology approach to bear on specific topics of interest, including research and theoretical or philosophical investigations concerning the nature and effects of media or a specific medium; that includes studies of new and emerging technologies and the contemporary media environment as well as historical studies of media, technology, and modes and codes of communication; scholarship regarding technique and the technological society; scholarship on specific types of media and culture (e.g., oral and literate cultures, image, etc.), or of specific aspects of culture such as religion, politics, education, journalism, etc.; critical analyses of art and popular culture; and studies of how physical and symbolic environments function as media.

For additional information about this series or for the submission of manuscripts, please contact:
    Lance Strate, Series Editor | *strate@fordham.edu*

To order other books in this series, please contact our Customer Service Department:
    peterlang@presswarehouse.com (within the U.S.)
    orders@peterlang.com (outside the U.S.)

Or browse online by series:
    www.peterlang.com

www.ingramcontent.com/pod-product-compliance
Lightning Source LLC
Chambersburg PA
CBHW061712300426
44115CB00014B/2657